Bloom's Modern Critical Views

Modern Critical Views

W.E.B. Du BOIS

Edited and with an introduction by
Harold Bloom
Sterling Professor of the Humanities
Yale University

CHELSEA HOUSE PUBLISHERS
Philadelphia

Bloom's Modern Critical Views: W.E.B. Du Bois

Chelsea House
An imprint of Infobase Publishing
132 West 31st Street
New York NY 10001

Library of Congress Cataloging-in-Publication Data

W.E.B. Du Bois / Harold Bloom, editor.
    p. cm. — (Modern critical views)
    Includes bibliographical references and index.
     ISBN 0-7910-5915-4 (alk. paper)
    1. Du Bois, W.E.B. (William Edward Burghardt), 1868–1963—
Political and social views. 2. Du Bois, W.E.B. (William Edward Burghardt),
1868–1963—Criticism and interpretations. 3. Afro-Americans—Intellectual life.
4. Afro-Americans—Politics and government. 5. United States—Race relations.
6. Politics and literature—United States—History—20th century. 7. Afro-American
aesthetics. 8. Black nationalism—United States. I. Bloom, Harold. II. Series.
    E185.97.D73 W163 2001
    05.896'073'092—dc21   [B] 00-050945

Contributing Editor: Jaynce Marson
Produced by: Robert Gerson Publisher's Services, Santa Barbara, CA

Printed in the United States of America

Lake 10 9 8 7 6 5 4 3

This book is printed on acid-free paper.

Contents

Editor's Note

My Introduction muses on Ralph Waldo Emerson's influence on W.E.B. Du Bois, and on the influence of both Emerson and Du Bois on Ralph Ellison's 1952 masterwork *Invisible Man*.

In this volume's first essay, Du Bois himself recalls the educational atmosphere in which he found himself as one of the few African-American students at Harvard University in the last years of the 19th century.

Introduction

Nearly a century ago, in 1903, W.E.B. Du Bois, in his *The Souls of Black Folk*, composed one of the central passages of African American literary consciousness:

> After the Egyptian and Indian, the Greek and Roman, the Teuton and Mongolian, the Negro is a sort of seventh son, born with a veil, and gifted with second sight in this American world,—a world which yields him no true self-consciousness, but only lets him see himself through the revelation of the other world. It is a peculiar sensation, this double consciousness, this sense of always looking at one's self through the eyes of others, of measuring one's soul by the tape of a world that looks on in amused contempt and pity. One ever feels his two-ness, an American, a Negro; two souls, two thoughts, two unreconciled strivings; two warring ideals in one dark body, whose dogged strength alone keeps it from being torn

Whether Du Bois was aware that he was revising Emerson, I do not know, but there seems an ironic modification of Emerson embedded in Du Bois's double consciousness. For Emerson, the double consciousness was universal, and was also primarily a positive goad to self-trust:

> 'Man is the dwarf of himself. Once he was permeated and dissolved by spirit. He filled nature with his overflowing currents. Out from him sprang the sun and moon; from man, the sun; from woman, the moon. The laws of his mind, the periods of his actions externized themselves into day and night, into the year and the seasons. But, having made for himself this huge shell, his waters retired; he no longer fills the veins and

1

veinlets; he is shrunk to a drop. He sees, that the structure still
fits him, but fits him colossally. Say, rather, once it fitted him,
now it corresponds to him from far and on high.

He adores timidly his work. Now is man the follower of the
sun, and woman the follower of the moon. Yet sometimes he
starts in his slumber, and wonders at himself and his house, and
muses strangely at the resemblance betwixt him and it. He
perceives that if his law is still paramount, if still he have
elemental power, if his word is sterling yet in nature, it is not
conscious power, it is not inferior but superior to his will. It is
Instinct.' Thus my Orphic poet sang.

At present, man applies to nature but half his force. He
works on the world with his understanding alone. He lives in it,
and masters it by a penny-wisdom; and he that works most in it,
is but a half-man, and whilst his arms are strong and his digestion
good, his mind is imbruted, and he is a selfish savage. His relation
to nature, his power over it, is through the understanding; as by
manure; the economic use of fire, wind, water, and the mariner's
needle; steam, coal, chemical agriculture; the repairs of the
human body by the dentist and the surgeon. This is such a
resumption of power, as if a banished king should buy his
territories inch by inch, instead of vaulting at once into his
throne. Meantime, in the thick darkness, there are not wanting
gleams of a better light,—occasional examples of the action of
man upon nature with his entire force,—with reason as well as
understanding. Such examples are, the traditions of miracles in
the earliest antiquity of all nations; the history of Jesus Christ;
the achievements of a principle, as in religious and political
revolutions, and in the abolition of the Slave-trade; the miracles
of enthusiasms, as those reported by Swedenborg, Hohenlohe,
and the Shakers; many obscure and yet contested facts, now
arranged under the name of Animal Magnetism; prayer;
eloquence; self-healing; and the wisdom of children. These are
examples of Reason's momentary grasp of the sceptre; the
exertions of a power which exists not in time or space, but an
instantaneous in-streaming causing power. The difference
between the actual and the ideal force of man is happily figured by
the schoolmen, in saying, that the knowledge of man is an evening
knowledge, *vespertina cognitio*, but that of God is a morning
knowledge, *matutina cognitio*.

Du Bois has his own version of the split between the mere Understanding and the illuminating Reason, but his terms are necessarily social, and not metaphysical. What Emerson measured as an asset, Du Bois shrewdly weighed as a dialectical burden, a challenge to African American intellectuals and artists, a challenge profoundly painful but pragmatically provocative. The legacy of Du Bois is endless, and all but constitutes a poetics of pain.

His long life (Du Bois died in Ghana, at the age of ninety-five, on August 27, 1963) allowed a seventy-year campaign in black activism, still unmatched in epic grandeur, and sometimes Quixotic in its later gestures. Quite aside from his enormous and ongoing influence upon later and current African American intellectuals, Du Bois remains perpetually readable. A bitter ironist, Du Bois ranks high in any hierarchy of American polemical writing. His anger, inevitable and incessant, is disciplined by his need to persuade as well as exhort. Granted his extraordinary endurance and persistence, he remains an exemplary figure, one who would not give up.

A way of assessing the continued relevance of Du Bois is to consider the relation of his "double consciousness" to Ralph Ellison's *Invisible Man* (1952), still the most eminent work of African American literature nearly a half-century after its initial publication. William Lyne, a scholar of Du Bois's effect upon black writers, tries to separate out the strands of *Invisible Man*'s fusion of literary High Modernism (Henry James, T. S. Eliot, James Joyce) and a "Blues consciousness," the jazz element in Ellison's work. Lynne's attempt is admirable, yet attempts to take apart what the novelist has accomplished: a permanent, dialectical interplay of James Joyce and Louis Armstrong.

Ellison fiercely scorned his mindless critics, black and white, who insisted that his adherence to the aesthetic criteria of High Modernism represented a betrayal of the folk ethos. Berndt Ostendorf, the distinguished German scholar of African American culture, is brilliantly exact in describing Ellison's highly deliberate revision of Emerson and of Du Bois:

> What Ralph Waldo Emerson and W.E.B. Du Bois called *double consciousness* Ellison prefers to call a *double vision*. This revision of Emerson's and Du Bois's concept provides a key example, in fact, of Ellison's turning an apparent liability into an asset.

Invisible man's "double vision" is compared by Ostendorf to the great critic Kenneth Burke's idea of "perspectives by incongruity." Burke saw *Invisible Man* as reconstituting its epoch, which from an African American perspective might well be termed "the epoch of W.E.B. Du Bois."

W.E.B. DU BOIS

Harvard in the Last Decades of the 19th Century

Harvard University in 1888 was a great institution of learning. It was 236 years old and on its governing board were Alexander Agassiz, Phillip Brooks, Henry Cabot Lodge and Charles Francis Adams; and a John Quincy Adams, but not the ex-President. Charles William Eliot, a gentleman by training and a scholar by broad study and travel, was president. Among its teachers *emeriti* were Oliver Wendell Holmes and James Russell Lowell. Among the active teachers were Francis Child, Charles Eliot Norton, Charles Dunbar, Justin Winsor and John Trowbridge; William Goodwin, Frank Taussig, Nathaniel Shaler, George Palmer, William James, Francis Peabody, Josiah Royce, Barrett Wendell, Edward Channing, and Albert Bushnell Hart. A young instructor who arrived in 1890 was George Santayana. Seldom, if ever, has any American university had such a galaxy of great men and fine teachers as Harvard in the decade between 1885 and 1895.

To make my own attitude toward Harvard of that day clear, it must be remembered that I went to Harvard as a Negro, not simply by birth, but recognizing myself as a member of a segregated caste whose situation I accepted but was determined to work from within that caste to find my way out.

About the Harvard of which most white students conceived I knew little. Of fraternities I had not even heard of Phi Beta Kappa, and of such

From *The Autobiography of W.E.B. Du Bois: A Soliloquy on Viewing My Life from the Last Decade of Its First Century.* © 1968 by International Publishers Co., Inc.

important social organizations as the Hasty Pudding Club, I knew nothing. I was in Harvard for education and not for high marks, except as marks would insure my staying. I did not pick out "snap" courses. I was there to enlarge my grasp of the meaning of the universe. We had for instance no chemical laboratory at Fisk. Our mathematical courses were limited; above all I wanted to study philosophy! I wanted to get hold of the basis of knowledge, and explore foundations and beginnings. I chose, therefore, Palmer's course in ethics, but he being on Sabbatical for the year, William James replaced him, and I became a devoted follower of James at the time he was developing his pragmatic philosophy.

Fortunately I did not fall into the mistake of regarding Harvard as the beginning rather than the continuing of my college training. I did not find better teachers at Harvard, but teachers better known, who had had wider facilities for gaining knowledge and had a broader atmosphere for approaching truth.

I hoped to pursue philosophy as my life career, with teaching for support. With this program I studied at Harvard from the Fall of 1888 to 1890, as undergraduate. I took a varied course in chemistry, geology, social science and philosophy. My salvation here was the type of teacher I met rather than the content of the courses. William James guided me out of the sterilities of scholastic philosophy to realist pragmatism; from Peabody's social reform with a religious tinge, I turned to Albert Bushnell Hart to study history with documentary research; and from Taussig with his reactionary British economics of the Ricardo school, I approached what was later to become sociology. Meantime Karl Marx was mentioned but only incidentally and as one whose doubtful theories had long since been refuted. Socialism as dream of philanthropy or as will-o-wisp of hotheads was dismissed as unimportant.

When I arrived at Harvard, the question of board and lodging was of first importance. Naturally, I could not afford a room in the college yard in the old and venerable buildings which housed most of the well-to-do students under the magnificent elms. Neither did I think of looking for lodgings among white families, where numbers of the ordinary students lived. I tried to find a colored home, and finally at 20 Flagg Street, I came upon the neat home of a colored woman from Nova Scotia, a descendant of those black Jamaican Maroons whom Britain deported after solemnly promising them peace if they would surrender. For a very reasonable sum, I rented the second story front room and for four years this was my home. I wrote of this abode at the time: "My room is, for a college man's abode, very ordinary indeed. It is quite pleasantly situated—second floor, front, with a bay window and one other window. The door is on the southwest corner. As you enter you will perceive the bed in the opposite corner, small and decorated with floral designs calculated to puzzle a botanist. It is a good comfortable bed, however, and my landlady keeps it neat. On the left hand is a bureau with a mirror of doubtful accuracy. In front of the bay window is a stand with three shelves of books, and on the left of the bureau is an improvised bookcase made of unpainted boards and uprights, containing most of my library of which I am growing quite proud. Over the heat register, near the door, is a mantle with a plaster of Paris pug-dog and a calendar, and the usual array of odds and ends. A sofa, commode, trunk, table and chairs complete the floor furniture. On the wall are a few quite ordinary pictures. In this commonplace den I am quite content."

Later I became a boarder at Memorial Hall, which was the great dining hall of the University, and after that a member of the Foxcraft Club, where many students of moderate means boarded.

Following the attitudes which I had adopted in the South, I sought no friendships among my white fellow students, nor even acquaintanceships. Of course I wanted friends, but I could not seek them. My class was large, with some 300 students. I doubt if I knew a dozen of them. I did not seek them, and naturally they did not seek me. I made no attempt to contribute to the college periodicals, since the editors were not interested in my major interests. Only one organization did I try to enter, and I ought to have known better than to make this attempt. But I did have a good singing voice and loved music, so I entered the competition for the Glee Club. I ought to have known that Harvard could not afford to have a Negro on its Glee Club traveling about the country. Quite naturally I was rejected.

I was happy at Harvard, but for unusual reasons. One of these circumstances was my acceptance of racial segregation. Had I gone from Great Barrington high school directly to Harvard, I would have sought companionship with my white fellows and been disappointed and embittered by a discovery of social limitations to which I had not been used. But I came by way of Fisk and the South and there I had accepted color caste and embraced eagerly the companionship of those of my own color. This was, of course, no final solution. Eventually with them and in mass assault, led by culture, we Negroes were going to break down the boundaries of race; but at present we were banded together in a great crusade and happily so. Indeed, I suspect that the prospect of ultimate full human intercourse without reservations and annoying distinctions, made me all too willing to consort now with my own and to disdain and forget as far as was possible that outer, whiter world.

In general, I asked nothing of Harvard but the tutelage of teachers and the freedom of the laboratory and library. I was quite voluntarily and willingly outside its social life. I sought only such contacts with white teachers as lay directly in the line of my work. I joined certain clubs like the Philosophical Club; I was a member of the Foxcraft dining club because it was cheap. James and one or two other teachers had me at their homes at meal and reception. I found friends, and most interesting and inspiring friends, among the colored folk of Boston and surrounding places. Naturally social intercourse with whites could not be entirely forgotten, so that now and then I joined its currents and rose or fell with them. I escorted colored girls to various gatherings, and as pretty ones as I could find to the vesper exercises, and later to the class day and commencement social functions. Naturally we attracted attention and the *Crimson* noted my girl friends; on the other part came sometimes the shadow of insult, as when at one reception a white woman seemed determined to mistake me for a waiter.

In general, I was encased in a completely colored world, self-sufficient and provincial, and ignoring just as far as possible the white world which conditioned it. This was self-protective coloration, with perhaps an inferiority complex, but with belief in the ability and future of black folk.

My friends and companions were taken mainly from the colored students of Harvard and neighboring institutions, and the colored folk of Boston and surrounding towns. With them I led a happy and inspiring life. There were among them many educated and well-to-do folk; many young people studying or planning to study; many charming young women. We met and ate, danced and argued and planned a new world.

Toward whites I was not arrogant; I was simply not obsequious, and to a white Harvard student of my day, a Negro student who did not seek recognition was trying to be more than a Negro. The same Harvard man had much the same attitude toward Jews and Irishmen.

I was, however, exceptional among Negroes in my ideas on voluntary race segregation; they for the most part saw salvation only in integration at the earliest moment and on almost any terms in white culture; I was firm in my criticism of white folk and in my dream of a Negro self-sufficient culture even in America.

This cutting off of myself from my white fellows, or being cut off, did not mean unhappiness or resentment. I was in my early manhood, unusually full of high spirits and humor. I thoroughly enjoyed life. I was conscious of understanding and power, and conceited enough still to imagine, as in high school, that they who did not know me were the losers, not I. On the other hand, I do not think that my white classmates found me personally objectionable. I was clean, not well-dressed but decently clothed. Manners I regarded as more or less superfluous, and deliberately cultivated a certain brusquerie. Personal adornment I regarded as pleasant but not important. I was in Harvard, but not of it, and realized all the irony of my singing "Fair Harvard." I sang it because I liked the music, and not from any pride in the Pilgrims.

With my colored friends I carried on a lively social intercourse, but necessarily one which involved little expenditure of money. I called at their homes and ate at their tables. We danced at private parties. We went on excursions down the Bay. Once, with a group of colored students gathered from surrounding institutions, we gave Aristophanes' *The Birds* in a Boston colored church. The rendition was good, but not outstanding; not quite appreciated by the colored audience, but well worth doing. Even though it worked me near to death, I was proud of it.

Thus this group of professional men, students, white collar workers and upper servants, whose common bond was color of skin in themselves or in their fathers, together with a common history and current experience of discrimination, formed a unit which like many tens of thousands of like units across the nation had or were getting to have a common culture pattern which made them an interlocking mass; so that increasingly a colored person in Boston was more neighbor to a colored person in Chicago than to the white person across the street.

Mrs. Ruffin of Charles Street, Boston, and her daughter Birdie were often hostesses to this colored group. She was a widow of the first colored judge appointed in Massachusetts, an aristocratic lady, with olive skin and high piled masses of white hair. Once a Boston white lady said to Mrs. Ruffin ingratiatingly: "I have always been interested in your race." Mrs. Ruffin flared: "Which race?" She began a national organization of colored women and published the *Courant*, a type of small colored weekly paper which was spreading over the nation. In this I published many of my Harvard daily themes.

Naturally in this close group there grew up among the young people friendships ending in marriages. I myself, out-growing the youthful attractions of Fisk, began serious dreams of love and marriage. There, however, were still my study plans to hold me back and there were curious other reasons. For instance, it happened that two of the girls whom I particularly liked had what was to me then the insuperable handicap of looking like whites; while they had enough black ancestry to make them "Negroes" in America. Yet these girls were intelligent and companionable. One went to Vassar College which then refused entrance to Negroes. Years later when I went there to lecture I remember disagreeing violently with a teacher who thought the girl ought not to have "deceived" the college by graduating before it knew her Negro descent! Another favorite of mine was Deenie Pindell. She was a fine forthright woman, blonde, blue-eyed and fragile. In the end I had no chance to choose her, for she married Monroe Trotter.

Trotter was the son of a well-to-do colored father and entered Harvard in my first year in the Graduate School. He was thick-set, yellow, with close-cut dark hair. He was stubborn and straight-laced and an influential member of his class. He organized the first Total Abstinence club in the Yard. I came to know him and joined the company when he and other colored students took a trip to Amherst to see George Forbes and William H. Lewis graduate in the class with Calvin Coolidge.

Lewis afterward entered the Harvard Law School and became the celebrated center of the Harvard football team. He married the beautiful Bessie Baker who had been with us on that Amherst trip. Forbes, a brilliant, cynical dark man, later joined with Trotter in publishing the *Guardian*, the first Negro paper to attack Booker T. Washington with open opposition. Washington's friends retorted by sending Trotter to jail when he dared to heckle Washington in a public Boston meeting on his political views. I was not present nor privy to this occurrence, but the unfairness of the jail sentence helped lead me eventually to form the Niagara Movement, which later became a founding part of the NAACP.

Thus I lived near to life, love and tragedy; and when I met Maud Cuney, I became doubly interested. She was a tall imperious brunette, with gold-bronze skin, brilliant eyes and coils of black hair; daughter of the Collector of Customs at Galveston, Texas. She came to study music and was a skilled performer. When the New England Conservatory of Music tried to "jim-crow" her in the dormitory, we students rushed to her defense and we won. I fell deeply in love with her, and we were engaged.

Thus it is clear how in the general social intercourse on the campus I consciously missed nothing. Some white students made themselves known to me and a few, a very few, became life-long friends. Most of my classmates, I knew neither by sight nor name. Among them many made their mark in life: Norman Hapgood, Robert Herrick, Herbert Croly, George Dorsey, Homer Folks, Augustus Hand, James Brown Scott and others. I knew none of these intimately. For the most part I do not doubt that I was voted a somewhat selfish and self-centered "grind" with a chip on my shoulder and a sharp tongue.

Something of a certain inferiority complex was possibly a cause of this. I was desperately afraid of intruding where I was not wanted; appearing without invitation; of showing a desire for the company of those who had no desire for me. I should in fact have been pleased if most of my fellow students had wanted to associate with me; if I had been popular and envied. But the absence of this made me neither unhappy nor morose. I had my "island within" and it was a fair country.

Only once or twice did I come to the surface of college life. First I found by careful calculation that I needed the cash of one of the Boylston prizes in oratory to piece out my year's expenses. I got it through winning a second oratorial prize. The occasion was noteworthy by the fact that another black student, Clement Morgan, got first prize at the same contest.

With the new increase at Harvard of students who grew up outside of New England, there arose at this time a certain resentment at the way New England students were dominating and conducting college affairs. The class marshal on commencement day was always a Saltonstall, a Cabot, a Lowell, or some such New England family. The crew and most of the other heads of athletic teams were selected from similarly limited social groups. The class poet, class orator and other commencement officials invariably were selected because of family and not for merit. It so happened that when the officials of the class of 1890 were being selected in early spring, a plot ripened. Personally, I knew nothing of it, and was not greatly interested. But in Boston and in the Harvard Yard the result of the elections was of tremendous significance; for this conspiratorial clique selected Clement Morgan as class orator. New England and indeed the whole country reverberated.

Morgan was a black man. He was working in a barber shop in St. Louis at the time when he ought to have been in school. With the encouragement and help of a colored teacher whom he later married, he came to Boston and entered the Latin School. This meant that when he finally entered Harvard, he entered as freshman in the orthodox way and was well acquainted with his classmates. He was fairly well received, considering his color. He was a pleasant unassuming person and one of the best speakers of clearly enunciated English on the campus. In his junior year, he had earned the first Boylston prize for oratory, in the same contest where I won second prize. It was, then, logical for him to become class orator and yet this was against all the traditions of America. There were editorials in the leading newspapers, and the South especially raged and sneered at the audience of "black washerwomen" who would replace Boston society at the next Harvard commencement.

At the same time, the action was contagious and that year and the next in several leading Northern colleges colored students became the class orators. Ex-President Hayes, as I shall relate later, sneered at this fact. While, as I have said, I had nothing to do with this plot, and was not even present at the election which chose Morgan, I was greatly pleased at this breaking of the color line. Morgan and I became fast friends and spent a summer giving readings along the North Shore to help our college costs.

Harvard of this day was a great opportunity for a young man and a young American Negro and I realized it. I formed habits of work rather different from those of most of the other students. I burned no midnight oil. I did my studying in the daytime and had my day parceled out almost to the

minute. I spent a great deal of time in the library and did my assignments
with thoroughness and with prevision of the kind of work I wanted to do
later. From the beginning my relations with most of the teachers at Harvard
were pleasant. They were on the whole glad to receive a serious student, to
whom extra-curricular activities were not of paramount importance and one
who in a general way knew what he wanted.

Harvard had in the social sciences no such leadership of thought and
breadth of learning as in philosophy, literature and physical science. She was
then groping and is still groping toward a scientific treatment of human action.
She was facing at the end of the century a tremendous economic era. In the
United States, finance was succeeding in monopolizing transportation, and
raw materials like sugar, coal and oil. The power of the trust and combine was
so great that the Sherman Act was passed in 1890. On the other hand, the tariff
at the demand of manufacturers continued to rise in height from the McKinley
to the indefensible Wilson tariff making that domination easier. The
understanding between the industrial North and the New South was being
perfected and in 1890 the series of disfranchising laws began to be enacted by
the Southern states destined in the next 16 years to make voting by Southern
Negroes practically impossible. A financial crisis shook the land in 1893 and
popular discontent showed itself in the Populist movement and Coxey's Army.
The whole question of the burden of taxation began to be discussed.

These things we discussed with some clearness and factual
understanding at Harvard. The tendency was toward English free trade and
against the American tariff policy. We reverenced Ricardo and wasted long
hours on the "Wages-fund." I remember Frank Taussig's course supporting
dying Ricardean economics. Wages came from what employers had left for
labor after they had subtracted their own reward. Suppose that this profit was
too small to attract the employer, what would the poor worker do but starve?
The trusts and monopolies were viewed frankly as dangerous enemies of
democracies, but at the same time as inevitable methods of industry. We were
strong for the gold standard and fearful of silver. The attitude of Harvard
toward labor was on the whole contemptuous and condemnatory. Strikes like
the railway strikes of 1886 and the terrible Homestead strike of 1892, as well
as Coxey's Army of 1894, were pictured as ignorant lawlessness, lurching
against conditions largely inevitable.

Karl Marx was mentioned, only to point out how thoroughly his
theses had been disproven; of his theory itself almost nothing was said.
Henry George was given but tolerant notice. The anarchists of Spain, the
nihilists of Russia, the British miners—all these were viewed not as part of
the political development and the tremendous economic organization but
as sporadic evils. This was natural. Harvard was the child of its era. The

intellectual freedom and flowering of the late 18th and early 19th centuries were yielding to the deadening economic pressure which would make Harvard rich and reactionary. This defender of wealth and capital, already half ashamed of Charles Sumner and Wendell Phillips, was willing finally to replace an Eliot with a manufacturer and a nervous warmonger. The social community that mobbed Garrison, easily electrocuted Sacco and Vanzetti.

It was not until I was long out of college that I realized the fundamental influence man's efforts to earn a living had upon all his other efforts. The politics which we studied in college were conventional, especially when it came to describing and elucidating the current scene in Europe. The Queen's Jubilee in June 1887, while I was still at Fisk, set the pattern of our thinking. The little old woman at Windsor became a magnificent symbol of Empire. Here was England with her flag draped around the world, ruling more black folk than white and leading the colored peoples of the earth to Christian baptism, and as we assumed, to civilization and eventual self-rule.

In 1885, Stanley, the traveling American reporter, became a hero and symbol of white world leadership in Africa. The wild, fierce fight of the Mahdi and the driving of the English out of the Sudan for 13 years did not reveal its inner truth to me. I heard only of the martyrdom of the drunken Bible-reader and freebooter, Chinese Gordon.

The Congo Free State was established and the Berlin Conference of 1885 was reported to be an act of civilization against the slave trade and liquor. French, English and Germans pushed on in Africa, but I did not question the interpretation which pictured this as the advance of civilization and the benevolent tutelage of barbarians. I read of the confirmation of the Triple Alliance in 1891. Later I saw the celebration of the renewed Triple Alliance on the Tempelhofer Feld, with the new young Emperor William II, who, fresh from his dismissal of Bismarck, led the splendid pageantry; and finally the year I left Germany, Nicholas II became Tsar of all the Russias. In all this I had not yet linked the political development of Europe with the race problem in America.

I was repeatedly a guest in the home of William James; he was my friend and guide to clear thinking; I was a member of the Philosophical Club and talked with Josiah Royce and George Palmer; I remember vividly once standing beside Mrs. Royce at a small reception. We ceased conversation for a moment and both glanced across the room. Professor Royce was opposite talking excitedly. He was an extraordinary sight: a little body; indifferently clothed; a big red-thatched head and blazing blue eyes. Mrs. Royce put my thoughts into words: "Funny-looking man, isn't he?" I nearly fainted; yet I knew how she worshipped him.

I sat in an upper room and read Kant's *Critique* with Santayana; Shaler invited a Southerner, who objected to sitting beside me, out of his class; he said he wasn't doing very well, anyway. I became one of Hart's favorite pupils and was afterwards guided by him through my graduate course and started on my work in Germany. Most of my courses of study went well. It was in English that I came nearest my Waterloo at Harvard. I had unwittingly arrived at Harvard in the midst of a violent controversy about poor English among students. A number of fastidious Englishmen like Barrett Wendell had come to Harvard about this time; moreover New England itself was getting sensitive over Western slang and Southern drawls and general ignorance of grammar. Freshmen at this time could elect nearly all their courses except English; that was compulsory, with theses, daily themes and tough examinations.

On the other hand, I was at the point in my intellectual development when the content rather than the form of my writing was to me of prime importance. Words and ideas surged in my mind and spilled out with disregard of exact accuracy in grammar, taste in word or restraint in style. I knew the Negro problem and this was more important to me than literary form. I knew grammar fairly well, and I had a pretty wide vocabulary; but I was bitter, angry and intemperate in my first thesis. Naturally my English instructors had no idea of nor interest in the way in which Southern attacks on the Negro were scratching me on the raw flesh. Ben Tillman was raging in the Senate like a beast and literary clubs, especially rich and well-dressed women, engaged his services eagerly and listened avidly. Senator Morgan of Alabama had just published a scathing attack on "niggers" in a leading magazine, when my first Harvard thesis was due. I let go at him with no holds barred. My long and blazing effort came back marked "E"—not passed!

It was the first time in my scholastic career that I had encountered such a failure. I was aghast, but I was not a fool. I did not doubt but what my instructors were fair in judging my English technically even if they did not understand the Negro problem. I went to work at my English and by the end of that term had raised it to a "C." I realized that while style is subordinate to content, and that no real literature can be composed simply of meticulous and fastidious phrases, nevertheless that solid content with literary style carries a message further than poor grammar and muddled syntax. I elected the best course on the campus for English composition, English 12.

I have before me a theme which I wrote October 3, 1890, for Barrett Wendell, then the great pundit of Harvard English. I wrote: "Spurred by my circumstances, I have always been given to systematically planning my future, not indeed without many mistakes and frequent alterations, but always with what I now conceive to have been a strangely early and deep appreciation of the fact that to live is a serious thing. I determined while in high school to go to college—partly because other men did, partly because I foresaw that such discipline would best fit me for life. . . . I believe, foolishly perhaps, but sincerely, that I have something to say to the world, and I have taken English 12 in order to say it well." Barrett Wendell liked that last sentence. Out of 50 essays, he picked this out to read to the class.

Commencement was approaching, when one day I found myself at midnight on one of the swaggering streetcars that used to roll out from Boston on its way to Cambridge. It was in the Spring of 1890, and quite accidentally I was sitting by a classmate who would graduate with me in June. As I dimly remember, he was a nice looking young man, almost dapper; well dressed, charming in manner. Probably he was rich or at least well-to-do, and doubtless belonged to an exclusive fraternity, although that did not interest me. Indeed I have even forgotten his name. But one thing I shall never forget and that was his rather regretful admission (which slipped out as we gossiped) that he had no idea as to what his life work would be, because, as he added, "There's nothing in which I am particularly interested!"

I was more than astonished; I was almost outraged to meet any human being of the mature age of 22 who did not have his life all planned before him—at least in general outline; and who was not supremely, if not desperately, interested in what he planned to do.

Since then, my wonder has left my classmate, and been turned in and backward upon myself: how long had I been so sure of my life-work and how had I come so confidently to survey and plan it? I now realize that most college seniors are by no means certain of what they want to do or can do with life; but stand rather upon a hesitating threshold, awaiting will, chance or opportunity. Because I had not mingled intimately or understandingly with my white Harvard classmates, I did not at the time realize this, but thought my unusual attitude was general.

In June 1890, I received my bachelor's degree from Harvard *cum laude* in philosophy. I was one of the five graduating students selected to speak at commencement. My subject was "Jefferson Davis." I chose it with deliberate intent of facing Harvard and the nation with a discussion of slavery as illustrated in the person of the president of the Confederate States of America. Naturally, my effort made a sensation. I said, among other things: "I wish to consider not the man, but the type of civilization which his life represented: its foundation is the idea of the strong man—Individualism coupled with the rule of might—and it is this idea that has made the logic of even modern history, the cool logic of the Club. It made a naturally brave and generous man, Jefferson Davis: now advancing civilization by murdering Indians, now hero of a national disgrace, called by courtesy the Mexican War; and finally as the crowning absurdity, the peculiar champion of a people fighting to be free in order that another people should not be free. Whenever this idea has for a moment escaped from the individual realm, it has found an even more secure foot-hold in the policy and philosophy of the State. The strong man and his mighty Right Arm has become the Strong Nation with its armies. Under whatever guise, however a Jefferson Davis may appear as man, as race, or as a nation, his life can only logically mean this: the advance of a part of the world at the expense of the whole; the overwhelming sense of the I, and the consequent forgetting of the Thou. It has thus happened that advance in civilization has always been handicapped by shortsighted national selfishness. The vital principle of division of labor has been stifled not only in industry, but also in civilization; so as to render it well nigh impossible for a new race to introduce a new idea into the world except by means of the cudgel. To say that a nation is in the way of civilization is a contradiction in terms and a system of human culture whose principle is the rise of one race on the ruins of another is a farce and a lie. Yet this is the type of civilization which Jefferson Davis represented; it represents a field for stalwart manhood and heroic character, and at the same time for moral obtuseness and refined brutality. These striking contradictions of character always arise when a people seemingly become convinced that the object of the world is not civilization, but Teutonic civilization."

A Harvard professor wrote to *Kate Field's Washington*, then a leading periodical: "Du Bois, the colored orator of the commencement stage, made a ten-strike. It is agreed upon by all the people I have seen that he was the star of the occasion. His paper was on 'Jefferson Davis,' and you would have been surprised to hear a colored man deal with him so generously. Such phrases as a 'great man,' a 'keen thinker,' a 'strong leader,' and others akin occurred in the address. One of the trustees of the University told me yesterday that the paper was considered masterly in every way. Du Bois is from Great Barrington, Massachusetts, and doubtless has some white blood in his veins. He, too, has been in my classes the past year. If he did not head the class, he came pretty near the head, for he is an excellent scholar in every way, and altogether the best black man that has come to Cambridge."

Bishop Potter of New York wrote in the *Boston Herald*: "When at the last commencement of Harvard University, I saw a young colored man appear . . . and heard his brilliant and eloquent address, I said to myself: 'Here is what an historic race can do if they have a clear field, a high purpose, and a resolute will.'"

The New York *Nation* commented editorially: "When the name of William Edward Du Bois was called and a slender, intellectual-looking mulatto ascended on the platform and made his bow to the President of the University, the Governor of Massachusetts, the Bishop of New York, and a hundred other notables, the applause burst out heartily as if in recognition of the strange significance of his appearance there. His theme . . . heightened this significance. Du Bois handled his difficult and hazardous subject with absolute good taste, great moderation, and almost contemptuous fairness."

Already I had now received more education than most young white men, having been almost continuously in school from the age of six to the age of 22. But I did not yet feel prepared. I felt that to cope with the new and extraordinary situations then developing in the United States and the world, I needed to go further and that as a matter of fact I had just well begun my training in knowledge of social conditions.

I revelled in the keen analysis of William James, Josiah Royce and young George Santayana. But it was James with his pragmatism and Albert Bushnell Hart with his research method, that turned me back from the lovely but sterile land of philosophic speculation, to the social sciences as the field for gathering and interpreting that body of fact which would apply to my program for the Negro. As undergraduate, I had talked frankly with William James about teaching philosophy, my major subject. He discouraged me, not by any means because of my record in his classes. He used to give me A's and even A-plus, but as he said candidly, there is "not much chance for anyone earning a living as a philosopher." He was repeating just what Chase of Fisk had said a few years previously.

I knew by this time that practically my sole chance of earning a living combined with study was to teach, and after my work with Hart in United States history, I conceived the idea of applying philosophy to an historical interpretation of race relations.

In other words, I was trying to take my first steps toward sociology as the science of human action. It goes without saying that no such field of study was then recognized at Harvard or came to be recognized for 20 years after. But I began with some research in Negro history and finally at the suggestion of Hart, I chose the suppression of the African slave trade to America as my doctor's thesis. Then came the question as to whether I could continue study in the graduate school. I had no resources in wealth or friends. I applied for a fellowship in the graduate school of Harvard and was appointed Henry Bromfield Rogers fellow for a year and later the appointment was renewed; so that from 1890 to 1892 I was a fellow at Harvard University, studying in history and political science and what would have been sociology if Harvard has yet recognized such a field.

My grandfather Du Bois died while I was at Harvard, and although the settlement of the estate was held up for lack of exact data concerning my father's death, eventually $400 was paid me during my senior year. I finished the first draft of my thesis and delivered an outline of it at the seminaries of

American history and political economy December 7, 1891. I received my master's degree in the Spring. I was thereupon elected to the American Historical Society and asked to speak in Washington at their meeting in December 1892. *The New York Independent* noted this among the "three best papers presented," and continued:

"The article upon the 'enforcement of the Slave Laws' was written and read by a black man. It was thrilling when one could, for a moment, turn his thoughts from listening to think that scarcely thirty years have elapsed since the war that freed his race, and here was an audience of white men listening to a black man—listening, moreover, to a careful, cool, philosophical history of the laws which had not prevented the enslavement of his race. The voice, the diction, the manner of the speaker were faultless. As one looked at him, one could not help saying 'Let us not worry about the future of our country in the matter of race distinctions.'"

I began with a bibliography of Nat Turner and ended with this history of the suppression of the African Slave Trade to America; neither needed to be done again at least in my day. Thus in my quest for basic knowledge with which to help guide the American Negro I came to the study of sociology, by way of philosophy and history rather than by physics and biology. After hesitating between history and economics, I chose history. On the other hand, psychology, hovering then on the threshold of experiment under Hugo Munsterberg, soon took a new orientation which I could understand from the beginning. I worked on my thesis, "The Suppression of the African Slave Trade to the United States of America," and hoped to get my doctor's degree in another two years.

Already I had made up my mind that what I needed was further training in Europe. The German universities were at the top of their reputation. Any American scholar who wanted preferment went to Germany for study. The faculties of Johns Hopkins, and the new University of Chicago, were beginning to be filled with German Ph.D's, and even Harvard had imported Munsterberg for the new experimental psychology, and Kuno Frank had long taught there. British universities did not recognize American degrees and French universities made no special effort to encourage American graduates. I wanted then to study in Germany. I was determined that any failure on my part to become a recognized American scholar must not be based on any lack of modern training.

I was confident. So far I had met no failure. I willed and lo! I was walking beneath the elms of Harvard—the name of allurement, the college of my youngest, wildest visions. I needed money; scholarships and prizes fell into my lap—not all I wanted or strove for, but all I needed to keep in school. Commencement came and standing before governor, president, and grave gowned men, I told them certain truths, waving my arms and breathing fast. They applauded with what may have seemed to many as uncalled-for fervor, but I walked home on pink clouds of glory! I asked for a fellowship and got it. I announced my plan of studying in Germany, but Harvard had no more fellowships for me. A friend, however, told me of the Slater Fund and how the board was looking for colored men worth educating.

No thought of modest hesitation occurred to me. I rushed at the chance. It was one of those tricks of fortune which always seem partly due to chance: In 1882, the Slater Fund for the education of Negroes had been established and the board in 1890 was headed by ex-President R. B. Hayes. Ex-President Hayes went down to Johns Hopkins University which admitted no Negro students and told a "darkey" joke in a frank talk about the plans of the fund. The *Boston Herald* of November 2, 1890, quoted him as saying: "If there is any young colored man in the South whom we find to have a talent for art or literature or any special aptitude for study, we are willing to give him money from the education funds to send him to Europe or give him advanced education." He added that so far they had been able to find only "orators." This seemed to me a nasty fling at my black classmate, Morgan, who had been Harvard class orator a few months earlier.

The Hayes statement was brought to my attention at a card party one evening; it not only made me good and angry but inspired me to write ex-President Hayes and ask for a scholarship. I received a pleasant reply saying that the newspaper quotation was incorrect; that his board had some such program in the past but had no present plans for such scholarships. I wrote him referring him to my teachers and to others who knew me, and intimating that his change of plan did not seem to me fair or honest. He wrote again in apologetic mood and said that he was sorry the plan had been given up; that he recognized that I was a candidate who might otherwise have been given attention. I then sat down and wrote Mr. Hayes this letter:

May 25, 1891

Your favor of the 2nd. is at hand. I thank you for your kind wishes. You will pardon me if I add a few words of explanation as to my application. The outcome of the matter is as I expected it would be. The announcement that any agency of the American people was willing to give a Negro a thoroughly liberal education and that it had been looking in vain for men to educate was to say the least rather startling. When the newspaper clipping was handed me in a company of friends, my first impulse was to make in some public way a categorical statement denying that such an offer had ever been made known to colored students. I saw this would be injudicious and fruitless, and I therefore determined on the plan of applying myself. I did so and have been refused along with a number of cases beside mine.

As to my case I personally care little. I am perfectly capable of fighting alone for an education if the trustees do not see fit to help me. On the other hand the injury you have—unwittingly I trust—done the race I represent, and am not ashamed of, is almost irreparable. You went before a number of keenly observant men who looked upon you as an authority in the matter, and told them in substance that the Negroes of the United States either couldn't or wouldn't embrace a most liberal opportunity for advancement. That statement went all over the country. When now finally you receive three or four applications for the fulfillment of that offer, the offer is suddenly withdrawn, while the impression still remains.

If the offer was an experiment, you ought to have had at least one case before withdrawing it; if you had given aid before (and I mean here toward liberal education—not toward training plowmen) then your statement at Johns Hopkins was partial. From the above facts I think you owe an apology to the Negro people. We are ready to furnish competent men for every European scholarship furnished us off paper. But we can't educate ourselves on nothing and we can't have the moral courage to try, if in the midst of our work our friends turn public sentiment against us by making statements which injure us and which they cannot stand by.

That you have been looking for men to liberally educate in the past may be so, but it is certainly strange so few have heard it. It was never mentioned during my three years stay at Fisk University. President J. C. Price of Livingstone [then a leading Negro spokesman] has told me that he never heard of it, and students from various other Southern schools have expressed great surprise at the offer. The fact is that when I was wanting to come to Harvard, while yet in the South, I wrote to Dr. Haygood [Atticus G. Haywood, a leader of Southern white liberals] for a loan merely, and he never even answered my letter. I find men willing to help me thro' cheap theological schools, I find men willing to help me use my hands before I have got my brains in working order, I have an abundance of good wishes on hand, but I never found a man willing to help me get a Harvard Ph.D.

Hayes was stirred. He promised to take up the matter the next year with the board. Thereupon, the next year I proceeded to write the board:

"At the close of the last academic year at Harvard, I received the degree of Master of Arts, and was reappointed to my fellowship for the year 1891–92. I have spent most of the year in the preparation of my doctor's thesis on the Suppression of the Slave Trade in America. I prepared a preliminary paper on this subject and read it before the American Historical Association at its annual meeting at Washington during the Christmas holidays. . . . Properly to finish my education, careful training in a European university for at least a year is, in my mind and the minds of my professors, absolutely indispensable." I thereupon asked respectfully for "aid to study at least a year abroad under the direction of the graduate department of Harvard or other reputable auspices" and if this was not practicable, "that the board loan me a sufficient sum for this purpose." I did not of course believe that this would get me an appointment, but I did think that possibly through the influence of people who thus came to know about my work, I might somehow borrow or beg enough to get to Europe.

I rained recommendations upon Mr. Hayes. The Slater Fund Board surrendered, and I was given a fellowship of $750 to study a year abroad; with the promise that it might possibly be renewed for a second year. To salve their souls, however, this grant was made as half gift and a half repayable loan with five per cent interest. I remember rushing down to New York and talking with ex-President Hayes in the old Astor House, and emerging walking on air. I saw an especially delectable shirt in a shop window. I went in and asked about it. It cost three dollars, which was about four times as much as I had ever paid for a shirt in my life; but I bought it.

ARLENE A. ELDER

Swamp versus Plantation: Symbolic Structure in W.E.B. Du Bois' The Quest of the Silver Fleece

Although in the past commentators on the writing of W.E.B. Du Bois have concentrated upon his historical and sociological works, some recent critics are intrigued by his fictional presentation of the black adventure in America. Most of this new critical interest centers upon his trilogy, *The Black Flame* (1957–1961), a historically based saga of the Mansart family. Du Bois' first novel, *The Quest of the Silver Fleece* (1911), is, nonetheless, equally interesting in its artistic presentation of the economic, political, and social forces shaping black life. It is a crowded and complex work, shifting its action from the rural South to Washington, D.C. and back again, and achieves its unity of plot and statement through a carefully constructed framework of contrasting symbols. *The Quest of the Silver Fleece* is structured upon the clash of two opposing world views, that of the Swamp and that of the Plantation. The Swamp represents all that is free, wild, joyful, and loving, the Plantation, all that is self-serving and exploitative.

Du Bois successfully avoids the obvious trap of simplistically equating the Swamp with black life and the Plantation with white. While his main concern in the book is to demonstrate the physical and mental serfdom which trapped blacks even after Emancipation and to suggest effective courses of action to overcome this kind of slavery, he recognizes that some

From *Phylon* 34, no. 4 (1973). © 1973 by Atlanta University.

whites, too, were oppressed by economic and political conditions and that some blacks knowingly profited from the subservience of their people. Therefore, he presents self-sacrificial whites, like Miss Smith, the Northern schoolteacher who devotes her life to educating Southern blacks, and Afro-Americans like Caroline Wynn, who have capitulated to the world's injustice and wish only to manipulate it to their own advantage. Plantation and Swamp morality, then, have more to do with the tone of the soul than with the color of the skin.

Nor does Du Bois paint the Swamp mentality as all good and the Plantation view as all evil. Primitivism, which is the weaker side of Swamp life, he shows as insufficient to advance a people in an industrial economy. Primitivism consists of limiting qualities, historically generated in blacks, such as the subservience, ignorance, and acceptance of degradation found in the swamp witch, Elspeth, which must be eliminated before blacks can compete with whites. Moreover, for all its inhumane aspects, the Plantation viewpoint does encourage ambition and a thirst for knowledge, which Du Bois considers essential for any group's success. Racial, class, and even human advancement, then, rest for Du Bois in the development of the best qualities of both philosophies.

The actual swamp in the book is an area a short distance from the white-dominated town and farms. It is both ugly and beautiful, a source of nightmares as well as dreams, of despair as well as hope, a spot where black exploitation has traditionally festered as well as the place where black self-determination could ultimately flourish.

Its first description suggests the danger, despair, and loss of vision which it represents: "Night fell. The red waters of the swamp grew sinister and sullen. The tall pines lost their slimness and stood in wide blurred blotches all across the way, and a great shadowy bird arose, wheeled and melted, murmuring, into the black-green sky." Deep in the darkness of the swamp is the hut of Elspeth, "an old woman—short, broad, black and wrinkled, with fangs and pendulous lips and red, wicked eyes." It is in this hut that local white men gather at night to drink and carry on the ante-bellum tradition of sexually exploiting black women.

Zora, the wild, ignorant "elf-girl," was born in the swamp and knows it intimately. Hating Elspeth, her mother, and the sordid life at the hut, she lives in a private world of fantasy, conjuring up creatures symbolic of both the beauty and ugliness she sees around her. "And over yonder behind the swamps," she imagines, "is great fields full of dreams." Zora's dreams, spawned by the contrasts she observes, hang "like big flowers, dripping dew and sugar and blood." The inhabitants of her dream-land reflect both the hope and despair of her life:

"And there's little fairies there that hop about and sing, and devils—great ugly devils that grabs at you and roasts and eats you if they gits you! . . . Some devils is big and white, like ha'nts; some is long and shiny, like creepy, slippery snakes; and some is little and broad and black. . . ."

Many of the blacks of the region bedevil themselves and participate in the creation of their own hell by rejecting the education Miss Smith offers and forgetting any dreams they once had of escaping the oppressive conditions of tenant farming. Because they cannot read the contracts they are required to sign, they ignorantly bind themselves for life to the wealthy white Cresswells. At first, they even reject the chance for self-determination which Zora offers them with her plan for a black-run farming commune. They cling, instead, to the old gospel of happiness-in-the-hereafter fed to them by the self-serving Preacher Jones. Ignorance, fear, jealousy of each other, despair, and hopeless acquiescence in their own debasement are the self-defeating qualities which the hag, Elspeth, and the terrible "gray and death-like wilderness" of the swamp represent.

There is, however, a beautiful, joyous, vibrant aspect to the swamp which is reflected in the souls of some of the black and white characters. Zora, "black, and lith, and tall, and willowy," with her music, her poetry, and her dreams is Du Bois' most striking representative of good Swamp qualities. Despite the area's general gloom, at times the "golden sun" pours "floods of glory through the slim black trees," and "the mystic sombre pools [catch] . . . and [toss] . . . back the glow in darker duller crimson." The intensity of this description is reflected in Zora, her "heavy hair" bursting from its fastenings and lying "in stiffened, straggling masses, bending reluctantly to the breeze, like curled smoke." She recognizes in herself the pent-up aspirations of her people and dreams eventually not of her childhood devils and dripping blood but of the escape from Elspeth which Miss Smith and the world beyond the swamp offer to her.

Her plans for escape are dependent upon the Silver Fleece, the special crop of cotton which she and Bles grow on her island deep in the swamp. From its sale, she intends to finance her education. Du Bois extends the symbol of the Fleece to include all the cotton grown in the South and uses it to reveal the close relationship Southern blacks feel with the soil and the difference between this kinship and the Plantation mentality's emphasis upon property and profits.

"I don't like to work," Zora once confided to Bles. "You see, mammy's pappy was a king's son, and kings don't work. I don't work; mostly I dreams. But I can work, and I will—for the wonder things—and for you." As a matter of fact, she works until her hands are raw and bleeding, clearing the island to plant the magic cotton seeds. She even comes close to losing her life in a flood, building dikes to protect her young crop. The tender, young cotton sprouts become her new "dream-children, and she tended them jealously; they were her Hope, and she worshiped them."

It is thematic that it is Elspeth who provides the seed, "wonder seed sowed with the three spells of Obi in the old land ten thousand moons ago," and sows it herself in a ritual during the dark of the moon. Its product is magnificent, but neither its inherent value nor Elspeth's magic is sufficient to guarantee Zora's success in an exploitative society.

Although Zora's relationship to the Silver Fleece is intensely personal, her love of the land and complete involvement in the creative process of growth is representative of the attitude of her people. Bles rapturously describes the sprouting cotton to Mary Taylor, his Northern-born teacher: ". . . we chop out the weak stalks, and the strong ones grow tall and dark, till I think it must be like the ocean—all green and billowy; then come little flecks there and there and the sea is all filled with flowers—flowers like little bells, blue and purple and white." Other blacks, "huge bronze earth-spirits," who harvest the crops do so joyously, although they know that most of the profits from their labor will fatten the pockets of the Cresswells: "The cry of the Naked was sweeping the world, and yonder in the night black men were answering the call. They knew not what or why they answered, but obeyed the irresistible call with hearts light and song upon their lips—the Song of Service."

Du Bois recognizes worldwide economic forces at work in the production and sale of Southern crops. The blacks, most directly responsible for the cotton, however, know next to nothing about supply and demand or fair profits and wages. This ignorance, the author suggests, is one of the major reasons for black entrapment. Even when coupled with child-like joy in the harvest and pride in the land, black ignorance can only result in black powerlessness. Nevertheless, Du Bois appreciates the richness of the workers' natural, creative relationship with the land and describes it lyrically: "All the dark earth heaved in mighty travail with the bursting bolls of the cotton while black attendant earth spirits swarmed above, sweating and crooning to its birth pains."

The Plantation viewpoint is most clearly distinguished from that of the Swamp by its purely economic attitude toward the cotton crop: ". . . the poetry of Toil was in the souls of the laborers. . . . Yet ever and alway [sic] there were tense silent white-faced men moving in that swarm who felt no poetry and heard no song. . . ." To the white Southern landowners and their counterparts, the Northern speculators, the cotton sings only of profits.

Plantation mentality, North or South, is paternalistic, exploitative, self-deceptive, and, ultimately, cruel.

Recognizing Zora's crop as the most valuable ever produced on their land, Harry Cresswell, nevertheless, denigrates it as "extra cotton," worthy only to be turned into lint, and through dishonest financial manipulation manages to cheat her of the entire crop and even to place her twenty-five dollars in his debt. Zora's loss is common. The blacks all find themselves deeper in debt after each year's toil. They are kept at their labor by false promises of freedom, cheated by contracts "binding the tenant hand and foot to the landlord," and threatened with being sold out and put in the chain-gang if they resist.

Nor is this exploitation aimed solely at blacks. Southern poor whites, employees in the mills which Northern capitalization brought with it, are as over-worked, cheated, and trapped as the black tenant farmers. In the third part of the novel, when it appears that the oppressed of both races might combine and, through their superior numbers, overwhelm the wealthy landlords, John Taylor, the Northern speculator, remarks, "even if they do ally themselves, our way is easy: separate the leaders, the talented, the pushers of both races from their masses, and through them rule the rest by money." Although the blacks, because of racial bigotry and their historical position as serfs in the South, are the primary victims of men of Plantation mentality, any member of a powerless minority is in danger.

Furthermore, the Plantation morality is no respecter of social rank. Not only poor whites, but Southern "aristocrats," as well, are in danger of becoming victims if they are ignorant of the economic complexities affecting them. The prospect of a poor cotton crop and the persuasive arguments of John Taylor convince Colonel Cresswell to forget his "southern honor" and to entangle his fellow cotton planters in a business deal from which he stands to make two million dollars in five years. When Taylor announces his plan to form an "All-Cotton combine" and corner the year's market, the Colonel asks, "And the other planters?":

> "They come in for high-priced cotton until we get our grip."
> "And then?"
> "They keep their mouths shut or we squeeze 'em and buy the
> land. We propose to own the cotton belt of the South."

At this revelation, Colonel Cresswell automatically starts from his seat and indignantly sputters something about betraying "southern gentlemen" to Northern interests. But the chance for tremendous profits quickly outweighs the sense of honor by which he likes to believe he lives, and he agrees to the scheme.

Taylor, as well as the Cresswells, is obviously a Plantation type. The only difference that Du Bois recognizes between Northern and Southern manifestations of the attitude is the degree of self-deception Southerners have traditionally allowed themselves. In most matters involving other whites, Colonel Creswell is much more honest than John Taylor. "But there was one part of the world which his code of honor did not cover," and this was the part inhabited by blacks. Despite the fact that he, himself, has a mulatto granddaughter, he still looks upon blacks as inherited property. As long as they remain "faithful niggers" like Johnson and Preacher Jones, the Colonel ignores them, cheating them periodically in the comfortable, time-honored way, content to be oblivious to their existence. When blacks try to break out of the rigid class-race structure of Plantation economics, however, as Zora does with her Silver Fleece, or when she attempts to buy the swamp for her farm commune, he is willing to perjure himself and others to maintain the status quo. "The uninitiated," Du Bois explains,

> . . . cannot easily picture himself the mental attitude of a former slave-holder toward property in the hands of a Negro. Such property belonged of right to the master, if the master needed it; and since ridiculous laws safeguarded the property, it was perfectly permissible to circumvent such laws. No Negro starved on the Cresswell place, neither did any accumulate property. Colonel Cresswell saw to both matters.

It is this fractured concept of honor which John Taylor most dislikes about his Southern father-in-law and business partner, and it is his refusal to cooperate in cheating Zora of the swamp which leads to the destruction of their relationship. No less self-serving than Cresswell, Taylor, nevertheless, is a genuine admirer of talent and ambition, whether they belong to a white or a black. "The weak and the ignorant of all races he despised and had no patience with them." The able, he respects. And it is only the able, Du Bois insists, who can hope to undermine Southern paternalism and overcome Northern indifference.

Throughout the first part of the novel, the story of Jason and the Golden Fleece appears as a mythic referent for Du Bois' Plantation-Swamp dichotomy. The story is first alluded to by Mary Taylor, who, responding to Bles's lyrical description of the growth of the cotton, murmurs, "The Golden Fleece—it's the Silver Fleece!" Pleased by the opportunity to "uplift" one of her charges, she tells the boy of Jason and the Argonauts and is startled and puzzled by his response:

"All yon is Jason's." He pointed with one sweep of his long arm to the quivering mass of green-gold foliage that swept from swamp to horizon. "All yon golden fleece is Jason's now," he repeated.

"I thought it was—Cresswell's," she said.

"That's what I mean." . . .

"I am glad to hear you say that," she said methodically, "for Jason was a brave adventurer—"

"I thought he was a thief."

"Oh, well—those were other times."

"The Cresswells are thieves now."

To Mary Taylor, the Jason myth embodies the values of ambition, daring, and heroism; to Bles, the "stealing" of the Fleece represents an immorality basic to an outlook which values property and power over people. The cotton means only gold to those Northerners and Southerners who maintain and enforce the Plantation system, rather than the bounty and beauty of the earth, as it does to Bles and his people.

The Jason story is also employed, however, to reveal the shortcomings of Swamp mentality. When Bles tells Zora of Jason and Medea, she asks,

"Do you s'pose mammy's the witch?"

"No; she wouldn't give her own flesh and blood to help the thieving Jason."

She looked at him searchingly.

"Yes, she would, too."

By maintaining her cabin for the pleasures of the local whites, Elspeth has sold Zora and others into a moral slavery. Her nonresistance increases her own helplessness and is reflective of the general condition of her people.

Weakness and ignorance, the dark sides of Swamp life, are qualities which both Zora and Bles realize that they and their race must outgrow. Both travel North in the second part of the novel in quest of personal development. What they find there is a political version of the Plantation morality which they hoped to leave behind in the South.

In his picture of Northern blacks, Du Bois suggests that the victims of exploitation frequently adopt the very techniques which were used against them. The members of Washington's black middle class seem to Bles "at times like black white people—strangers in way and thought." Caroline Wynn, a confidante of white politicians and an influential force in black social circles, is cynical about the promises of the democratic system and is willing to compromise with the whites in power to mislead the black electorate if it means her own security and advancement.

"I use the world," she explains; "I did not make it; I did not choose it." Sophisticated in the intricacies of political manipulation, she undertakes to mold Bles into a charismatic, but controllable, racial leader. Her goal is not the elimination of the injustices of a racist society, but a secure foothold for herself within that society. She schemes to have Bles appointed Register of the Treasury and envisions herself, not as Mrs. Bles Alwyn, but as the wife of the new Register of the Treasury.

Bles's refusal to defend the Republican Party, after it has capitulated to Southern pressure and abandoned a racially important education bill, seals his political and personal fate. The enraged Republicans drop him as quickly as they dropped the piece of legislation and fill the position of Register with Samuel Stillings, a "shrewd" black man who has jealously plotted against Bles all along. Just as rapidly, Caroline Wynn agrees to become Mrs. Stillings.

While Du Bois clearly rejects the opportunism which determines Carrie Wynn's choices, he understands her, just as he understands Colonel Cresswell. Her youthful ambition to be recognized as an artist was quickly thwarted by the racial realities of Washington, D.C.: "she found nearly all careers closed to her." Even her job as a teacher is precariously dependent upon political circumstances. Her early disappointment, moreover, is daily reinforced by the insults of the jim crow city in which she must live. Her decision that idealism and honesty are commodities too dear and self-deceptive for Afro-Americans, Du Bois realizes, stems from years of social and economic injustice.

Within the tensions of Caroline's and Bles's relationship, then, Du Bois subtly reinforces the structural symbolism of the earlier part of the book. As a spokesman for the simple, hopeful members of his race, Bles insists upon absolute honesty in his dealings with both races in Washington. As a spokesman for those blacks who, because of disillusionment and a desire for wealth and power, have accepted the tactics of the Plantation, Carrie Wynn considers deception the only useful tool for the Afro-American. "Honesty," she tells Bles, is "a luxury few of us Negroes can afford." Limited by her desire for social acceptance and material advancement, she rejects Bles as an anomaly: "that good Miss Smith has gone and grafted a New England conscience on a tropical heart, and—dear me!—but it's a gorgeous misfit." This suggestion, that in order to succeed, blacks must continue the tradition of deception foisted upon them in slavery days, is every bit as destructive of racial progress as the particular kind of debasement practiced in Elspeth's cabin. Caroline Wynn wishes Bles to deceive other blacks about the intentions of the Republicans, thereby personally securing the Party's patronage. Elspeth receives free rent from the Cresswells for her services.

The third segment of the novel returns Du Bois' protagonists to the South. Like Bles, Zora has encountered the power politics of Northern life and, through her betrayal by Mrs. Vanderpoole, has learned that self-reliance is the only solution for her people. Moreover, she has spent her time in the North well, educating herself through literature and observation to the complexities of the world at large. She returns to the swamp not as the defeated "elf child" who left it, but as a woman, worldly-wise, and dedicated to leading her people out of their morass of powerlessness.

What Zora learned in the North was the necessity of maintaining in her people the best values of the Swamp—their honesty, joy, and reverence of the land—while infusing them with cleverness and ambition, the best aspects of the Plantation. As she demonstrates in her handling of Colonel Cresswell when he attempts to cheat her out of the land she has purchased from him, she has become cognizant of the political changes which accompanied the industrialization of the South and understands the regional psychology well enough to predict local reactions to her efforts. She informs Bles that she intends to take Cresswell to court and believes that she stands a good chance of winning because the men in power in the town are no longer the landowners, but the rising lower class of whites who share, to some degree, her class concerns. Moreover, after studying the laws governing her land purchase, she intends to conduct the case against the Colonel herself: "as a black woman fighting a hopeless battle with landlords, I'll gain the one thing lacking . . . the sympathy of the court and the bystanders." When Bles replies incredulously, "Pshaw! From these Southerners?" she explains:

> "Yes, from them. They are very human, these men, especially the laborers. Their prejudices are cruel enough, but there are joints in their armor. They are used to seeing us either scared or blindly angry, and they understand how to handle us then, but at other times it is hard for them to do anything but meet us in a human way."

Like Caroline Wynn, Zora realizes the necessity of knowing the people with whom she must deal, recognizing their weaknesses and strengths, and turning them to her own use. Unlike her Northern counterpart, however, Zora intends to deceive no one, and her only selfishness is her ambition for her people. Furthermore, by the close of the book, she has moved beyond strictly racial concerns and sees her struggle as one in behalf of the oppressed class of both races.

It is fitting, in terms of Du Bois' dichotomies, that Zora, not Bles, develops into the far-seeing political leader. Bles's defeat in Washington is predictable and demonstrates the powerlessness of ignorant idealism in the face of entrenched corruption. His defeat is an honorable one, of course, but does nothing toward advancing social justice. Zora's success, on the other hand, depends largely upon her perception of political realities. She is not tricked by traitorous blacks or manipulative whites because she sees her situation clearly and does not rely on either of these groups for help. The worst quality of the Swamp is the powerlessness and ignorance which fester in it; Bles, despite his training at Miss Smith's, demonstrates these traits in Washington. Zora moves from her sure knowledge of white values and laws and with the strength of black farmers committed to working with and for each other.

Even the love story between the two main characters can be understood in terms of Du Bois' symbols. Bles's attitude toward Zora "had always been one of guidance, guardianship, and instruction. He had been judging her and weighing her from on high, looking down upon her with thoughts of uplift and development." This is, obviously, the same attitude as that of the most benevolent Southern whites towards blacks, one of superiority and paternalism. Bles rejects Zora because he discovers that life in Elspeth's cabin has left her "impure." He is concerned only with not appearing a fool in others' eyes and reveals himself finally insensitive to the realities of the master-slave relationship. Unlike Zora, he has been affected by the conventional standards of Mary Taylor; significantly, it is she who tells him of Zora's past. It is only when he suffers, himself, and realizes the insufficiency of his past training and returns to the swamp that he is enlightened enough to appreciate Zora's true worth.

Zora, even after she becomes a student in Miss Smith's school, resists Mary Taylor's instruction. Mary Taylor forfeits any claim she might have to moral superiority over her ignorant charges by despising the black students and eagerly becoming Mrs. Harry Cresswell in order to escape from her dark-skinned pupils to "the lighter touches of life . . . new books and periodicals and talk of great philanthropies and reforms." Echoing the sentiments of Booker T. Washington, Du Bois' antagonist, and of most of the whites in the novel, she "believed it wrong to encourage the ambitions of these children to any great extent; she believed they should be servants and farmers, content to work under present conditions until those conditions could be changed; and she believed that the local white aristocracy, helped by Northern philanthropy, should take charge of such gradual changes." Zora becomes and remains a protegé of Miss Smith, who is frequently exasperated and outraged by her young, white colleague.

In *The Souls of Black Folk* (1903), the work for which he is most widely known, Du Bois comments on the valuable contribution which the culture of Afro-Americans could make to American society: "all in all, we black men seem the sole oasis of simple faith and reverence in a dusty desert of dollars and smartness." "Smartness," nevertheless, is a quality he deems essential for his people and, despite his reservations about the effectiveness of the Freedman's Bureau, credits it with "best of all . . . inaugurat[ing] the crusade of the New England schoolma'am." Because of the nation's unwillingness to commit itself morally and financially to the development of the newly freed blacks, the Bureau eventually failed, and in 1903, Du Bois could look around him and see that "in well-nigh the whole rural South the black farmers are peons, bound by law and custom to an economic slavery, from which the only escape is death or the penitentiary."

The Quest of the Silver Fleece is the fictional working out of this problem in American racial history. Its understandings are long-held concerns of Du Bois; its symbolic structure is his attempt at an artistically effective framework for presenting his convictions about social, political, and economic tensions, North and South, black and white.

DARWIN T. TURNER

W.E.B. Du Bois and the Theory of a Black Aesthetic

During the past decade many black artists and critics began to insist that work by Afro-Americans must be created and evaluated according to a Black Aesthetic. That is, the work must be appropriate to Afro-American culture and people, and its excellence must be defined according to black people's concepts of beauty. In *The Crisis of the Negro Intellectual* (1967), Harold Cruse pointed to the need for a Black Aesthetic when he castigated Negro critics for failing to establish an appropriate perspective of the relationship of Negro art to Negro culture. Cruse accused critics of rejecting their own folk culture in order to adopt models and ideas devised and approved by whites. Thus, Cruse charged, most Negro critics ignored what should have been their major responsibility: to encourage and to determine standards for original ideas, methods, materials and styles derived from the unique character of black American culture. In even sharper tones today, such critics as Imamu Amiri Baraka, Larry Neal, Don L. Lee, Hoyt Fuller, and Addison Gayle, Jr.—to name only a few of the most prominent—insist that black artists must seek subjects, themes and styles within the culture of black folk, that they must use these materials for the benefit of black Americans, and that the resulting art must be evaluated according to criteria determined by black people.

Of course it is not new for a nation, race, or ethnic group to devise an individual aesthetic. To the contrary, a cursory view of the history of

From *Studies in the Literary Imagination* 7, no. 2 (Fall 1974). © 1974 by Georgia State University.

European, English, and American literature reveals such a kaleidoscope that one wonders how anyone could argue that only one aesthetic can exist or could deny that any group has a right to define its own aesthetic. An aesthetic, after all, is merely a judgment of what is beautiful according to the tastes of the judge. After determining what kinds of drama were preferred by cultivated Greeks, Aristotle propounded a standard for drama. If William Shakespeare had followed that aesthetic, he might have written excellent imitations of Greek drama, but he would not have created the melodramatic shatterings of unity that dismayed Augustan critics and delighted the Romantics. Dante and Chaucer taught readers to respect the beauty of their native languages. With scant regard for the beliefs of the subjects in question, Rudyard Kipling and James Fenimore Cooper prescribed criteria for determining the beauty in the character of a "good" native. Many people have found beauty in the political theories of Machiavelli or of John Locke, but few would argue that both theories derive from the same aesthetic. When Emerson, Melville and Whitman pronounced the need for an American literature, they were arguing for an American aesthetic for literature. Equally diversified standards of beauty could be revealed in a history of painting, music, philosophy, or any of the humanistic pursuits. The fact is that any group of people which feels its identity as a group shapes and defines its own aesthetic, which it is free to change in a subsequent generation or century.

It should not be surprising, therefore, that black Americans should insist upon a need of a Black Aesthetic; for, if their African ancestry has not always bound them together, they have nevertheless found identity as a group in their exclusion from certain prerogatives of American citizenship. What is surprising then is not the concept of a Black Aesthetic in literature but that, even before the Harlem "Renaissance," it was articulated distinctly by W.E.B. Du Bois, who has been identified disparagingly with the conservative literary practices of The Genteel Tradition and with the efforts of Negroes to become assimilated by separating themselves from the folk culture. Nevertheless, before the New Negro movement had been labeled, years before Langston Hughes insisted upon the right of new artists to express their individual dark-skinned selves without caring whether they pleased white or black audiences, W.E.B. Du Bois proposed a Black Aesthetic or—as I prefer to designate it in relation to Du Bois—a theory of art from the perspective of black Americans.

Du Bois did not clearly define or delimit his theory. Despite his sustained interest in art, Du Bois was a social scientist and a political leader who considered art—especially literature—to be a vehicle for enunciating and effecting social, political, and economic ideas. Therefore, he sketched literary theory rather than constructing it with the total concentration characteristic of one whose major concern is the art itself. Moreover, like other theorists, Du Bois sometimes experienced difficulty with the practical applications of his theories. For instance, although he first urged black writers to present life exactly as they saw it, he later feared that the writers were over-emphasizing lurid aspects. Consequently, to correct what he considered an imbalance, he began to urge more conservative pictures of Negro life. One must admit also that Du Bois, unlike Wordsworth or T. S. Eliot, never created in his fiction, drama, and poetry the great work which would both illustrate and justify his literary theory.

Despite whatever weaknesses he may have revealed in definition or application, there is value in examining Du Bois' theory of black art—not only because it was of extreme importance to his efforts to create a strong and respected black population, but also because he was able to pronounce it from a prominent public platform during the Harlem "Renaissance," a significant moment in the development of literature by Afro-Americans. A more complete study should examine the relationships between Du Bois' theories and his own writing. And certainly a study should analyze the relationships between his theories and the work of black writers of the Renaissance. This paper, however, is restricted to an examination of Du Bois' theory of black art as he shaped it and applied it as editor of *The Crisis* through the height of the Renaissance to the mid-Depression moment at which his insistence on the importance of independent black institutions became one of the wedges to separate him from the National Association for the Advancement of Colored People.

In 1921, the dawning of a literary Renaissance might have been viewed in the historical research of Carter G. Woodson and the cultural history of Benjamin Brawley. Its rays may have been glimpsed in the popularity of the musical *Shuffle Along*, written by Miller, Lyles, Sissle and Blake or in the interest in black people displayed by such white writers as Ridgely Torrence and Eugene O'Neill.

By 1921, however, W.E.B. Du Bois had been working for many years as editor of *The Crisis* to promote literary activity and to foster racial pride through literature. As early as 1912 he had solicited manuscripts from and had published work by such previously unknown writers as Georgia Johnson, Fenton Johnson, and Jessie Fauset. In an editorial in 1920 he had recited his pride in the accomplishments of *The Crisis* and the need for a "renaissance of American Negro literature":

> Since its founding, THE CRISIS has been eager to discover
> ability among Negroes, especially in literature and art. It

remembers with no little pride its covers by Richard Brown, William Scott, William Farrow, and Laura Wheeler; and its cartoons by Lorenzo Harris and Albert Smith; it helped to discover the poetry of Roscoe Jamison, Georgia Johnson, Fenton Johnson, Lucian Watkins, and Otto Bahanan; and the prose of Jessie Fauset and Mary Eflie Lee. Indeed, THE CRISIS has always preferred the strong matter of unknown names, to the platitudes of well-known writers; and by its Education and Children numbers, it has shown faith in the young.

One colored writer, Claude McKay, asserts that we rejected one of his poems and then quoted it from Pearson's; and intimates that colored editors, in general, defer to white editors' opinions. This is of course, arrogant nonsense. But it does call our attention to the need of encouraging Negro writers. We have today all too few, for the reason that there is small market for their ideas among whites, and their energies are being called to other and more lucrative ways of earning a living. Nevertheless, we have literary ability and the race needs it. A renaissance of American Negro literature is due; the material about us in the strange, heart-rending race tangle is rich beyond dream and only we can tell the tale and sing the song from the heart.

By 1921, Du Bois was inculcating pride in Afro-American children through his publication of *The Brownies' Book*, in which—writing as "The Crow"—he taught respect for the blackness of the crow.

In a more characteristic manner, writing with the confidence which Alain Locke later identified with the "New Negro," Du Bois admonished Negroes to accept artistic presentations of the truth of Negro life. In "Criteria for Negro Art," he wrote:

We are so used to seeing the truth distorted to our despite, that whenever we are portrayed on canvas, in story or on the stage, as simple humans with human frailties, we rebel. We want everything said about us to tell of the best and highest and noblest in us. We insist that our Art and Propaganda be one.

This is wrong and the end is harmful. We have a right, in our effort to get just treatment, to insist that we produce something of the best in human character and that it is unfair to judge us by our criminals and prostitutes. This is justifiable propaganda.

On the other hand we face the truth of Art. We have criminals and prostitutes, ignorant and debased elements, just as all folks have. When the artist paints us he has a right to paint us whole and not ignore everything which is not as perfect as we would wish it to be. The black Shakespeare must portray his black Iago as well as his white Othello.

We shrink from this. We fear that evil in us will be called racial, while in others it is viewed as individual. We fear that our shortcomings are not merely human but foreshadowing and threatenings of disaster and failure. The more highly trained we become the less we can laugh at Negro comedy—we will have it all tragedy and the triumph of dark Right over pale Villainy.

The results are not merely negative—they are positively bad. With a vast wealth of human material about us, our own writers and artists fear to paint the truth lest they criticize their own and be in turn criticized for it. They fail to see the Eternal Beauty that shines through all Truth, and try to portray a world of stilted artificial black folk such as never were on land or sea.

Thus, the white artist, looking in on the colored world, if he be wise and discerning, may often see the beauty, tragedy and comedy more truly than we dare.

Admitting that some white writers, such as Thomas Dixon, might see only exaggerated evil in Negroes, Du Bois nevertheless insisted that blacks would survive any honest treatment of Afro-American life:

We stand today secure enough in our accomplishment and self-confidence to lend the whole stern human truth about ourselves to the transforming hand and seeing eye of the Artist, white and black, and Sheldon, Torrence and O'Neill are our great benefactors—forerunners of artists who will yet arise in Ethiopia of the Outstretched Arm.

Within the next two years the Renaissance of the New Negro produced its first literary works: *Shuffle Along* (1921) was enthusiastically received by a Broadway audience; Claude McKay and Jean Toomer created *Harlem Shadows* (1922) and *Cane* (1923); Willis Richardson's *The Chip Woman's Fortune* (1923) became the first serious play by an Afro-American to be staged on Broadway. Even during these early triumphs, however, Du Bois worried about a barrier which might obstruct the creation of honest black art—the prejudice of American audiences, who expected blacks to be "*bizarre and unusual and funny for whites.*"

In the same essay, written for a predominantly white audience rather than the more mixed audience of *The Crisis*, Du Bois' exploration of the possibilities for Negroes in the contemporary theater led him to more optimistic conclusions. If they could escape from the prejudiced expectations of white audiences, they could create strong Negro drama by emphasizing their blackness.

As evidence, Du Bois cited The Ethiopian Art Theatre's successful performances of *Salome, The Chip Woman's Fortune*, and *The Comedy of Errors a la Jazz*. Published statements by the company explained that Director Raymond O'Neill restrained the black performers from attempting to imitate the more inhibited white actors. Instead, he encouraged them "to develop their peculiar racial characteristics—the freshness and vigor of their emotional responses, their spontaneity and intensity of mood, their freedom from intellectual and artistic obsession."

Du Bois was even more pleased by the Ethiopian Players' selection of black subjects. Unintentionally paraphrasing William Dean Howells's earliest praise of Paul Laurence Dunbar, Du Bois insisted that blacks could make a distinctive contribution to American drama by interpreting black subjects. He did not oppose black actors who wished to demonstrate their ability to perform "white" roles for white audiences. Nor did he deny the usefulness of expanding the cultural awareness of black audiences by staging "white" plays for them. Of greatest importance, however, was the opportunity for black actors and writers to examine "their own terrible history of experience."

Black writers, he admitted, would develop slowly. The race needed to gain "something of that leisure and detachment for artistic work which every artist must have." As evidence that serious black dramatists were emerging despite their lack of leisure, he called attention to his own *The Star of Ethiopia*, a pageant commemorating blackness.

Wise men believe, Du Bois concluded, "that the great gift of the Negro to the world is going to be a gift to Art." The Ethiopian Players were significantly promoting awareness of this talent by beginning to peel from drama critics "the scales that blinded them for years to the beauty of Negro folk songs, that make them still deaf to the song of Negro singers and but half-alive to the growing Negro drama and the ringing Negro actor."

Even in less laudatory reviews, Du Bois thrilled to Negro writers who truthfully and seriously probed into problems of Afro-American life. Although he complained that Jean Toomer weakened *Cane* by too little knowledge of Georgia, excessive striving for artistic effect, dearth of feeling, and "much that is difficult or even impossible to understand," Du Bois boasted:

The world of black folk will some day arise and point to Jean
Toomer as a writer who first dared to emancipate the colored
world from the conventions of sex. It is quite impossible for most
Americans to realize how straight-laced and conventional thought
is within the Negro World, despite the very unconventional acts of
the group. Yet this contradiction is true. And Jean Toomer is the
first of our writers to hurl his pen across the very face of our sex
conventionality. . . . [His women are] painted with a frankness that
is going to make his black readers shrink and criticize; and yet they
are done with a certain splendid, careless truth.

In 1925, writing for a predominantly white audience, Du Bois became
the first significant critic to probe issues not fully resolved today, even though
they are fundamental to the establishment of a Black Aesthetic: what is the
difference between art by a Negro and Negro art? Or, what are the unique
characteristics of Negro art?

Although he praised Henry O. Tanner, Charles W. Chesnutt, and
William Stanley Braithwaite as artists, Du Bois denied that they had
contributed significantly to American Negro art. American Negro art, he
explained, was a group expression consisting of biographies written by slaves
and by free blacks who had achieved

. . . poetry portraying Negro life and aspirations, and activities,
of essays on the "Negro Problem" and novels about the "Color
Line" . . . pictures and sculptures meant to portray Negro
features and characteristics, plays to dramatize the tremendous
situation of the Negro in America, and, of course, . . . music.

American Negro art "was built on the sorrow and strain inherent in
American slavery, on the difficulties that sprang from Emancipation, on the
feelings of revenge, despair, aspirations, and hatred which arose as the Negro
struggled and fought his way upward."

Whenever a mass of millions having such common memories and
experiences are granted intellectual freedom and economic wealth, Du Bois
explained, they will establish a school of art which, whether using new
methods of art, will inevitably bring new content—a truth which is different
from anything else in the world: "If this truth . . . is beautifully expressed and
transformed from sordid fact into art it becomes, from its very origin, new,
unusual, splendid."

The uniqueness of Afro-American artistic expression had been revealed
and discovered in "new music, new rhythm, new melody and poignant, even

terrible, expressions of joy, sorrow, and despair." This new music was earning respect. Next to win recognition would be Negro literature, which presented "new phrases, new uses of words, experiences unthought of and unknown to the average white person." Creating "a distinct norm and a new set of human problems," the new writers were impeded only by white readers' inability to understand the work and by black readers' stubborn demands for favorable propaganda. As the new artists matured, they would improve in thought and style. In the process of maturing, they would move from the wild music, laughter, and dancing of slavery into a more deliberate, purposeful, restrained, but true artistic expression.

The conclusion of Du Bois' magnificent effort to define Afro-American art betrays a weakness which gives a curious ambivalence to his criticism. He could identify the substance of that art but not the spirit. Whenever the spirit manifested itself in an exuberance which offended his temperament—his personal preference for decorum—Du Bois, wincing, felt compelled to excuse or denounce the work. Because he did not believe such wildness to be a characteristic inherent in the Afro-American psyche, he identified it, if genuine, as evidence of the manner in which slavery had distorted or repressed the psychological development of blacks. Just as often, he feared that the wildness was not a sincere expression of the artist but an effort to attract popularity from white critics by repeating the clichés about the character of black people. Unable to resolve this dilemma, which he failed to perceive as a dilemma, Du Bois at times seems a genteel anachronism as a critic during an era characterized by wildness of whites, as well as blacks. This was the gay Jazz Age of sheiks and flappers, raccoon coats and skirts that bared the knees, bootleg gin and speakeasies where one Charlestoned in shooting distance of well-known racketeers, "new" morality and trial marriages, free love and lurid front page headlines about the latest love-nest scandal. It was an era of youth, in which many whites, Freuding themselves from their Puritan inhibitions, enviously projected upon blacks the image of the primitive untroubled by the inhibitions of society. In such an era, it is not surprising that even a relatively sedate but young Countee Cullen atavistically boasted that his heart was "pagan-mad" and that the blood of blacks was hotter than that of whites. Not so for New-England-born, Harvard-trained W.E.B. Du Bois, who was fifty-seven-years old before Cullen published his first volume of poems. Quite simply, Du Bois knew that he was not pagan-mad; but he was Negro. Therefore, Negroes were not inherently pagan-mad. Therefore such wildness was not essential to, or desirable in, Negro life and art.

Instead one sought Beauty and Truth. In *The Crisis* of May 1925, Du Bois proclaimed a new editorial policy:

We shall stress Beauty—all Beauty, but especially the beauty of Negro life and character; its music, its dancing, its drawing and painting and the new birth of its literature. The growth which *The Crisis* long since predicted is sprouting and coming to flower. We shall encourage it in every way . . . keeping the while a high standard of merit and never stooping to cheap flattery and misspent kindliness.

At the same time, Du Bois continued his demands that black readers accept realistic portraits:

We are seriously crippling Negro art and literature by refusing to contemplate any but handsome heroes, unblemished heroines and flawless defenders, we insist on being always and everywhere all right and often we ruin our cause by claiming too much and admitting no faults.

As early as 1926, however, Du Bois' statements reveal the ambivalent sentiments or the inherent contradictions which have deceived critics who unsuspectingly have fixed Du Bois at one or another of his positions. In a complimentary review of *The New Negro* (1925), Du Bois wrote:

With one point alone do I differ. . . . Mr. Locke has newly been seized with the idea that Beauty rather than Propaganda should be the object of Negro literature and art. His book proves the falseness of this thesis. This is a book filled and bursting with propaganda, but it is a propaganda for the most part beautiful and painstakingly done. . . .
. . . If Mr. Locke's thesis is insisted upon too much it is going to turn the Negro Renaissance into decadence. It is the fight for Life and Liberty that is giving birth to Negro literature and art today and when, turning from this fight or ignoring it, the young Negro tries to do pretty things or things that catch the passing fancy of the really unimportant critics and publishers about him, he will find that he has killed the soul of Beauty in art.

In the same issue of *The Crisis*, Du Bois, announcing the second annual Krigwa awards competition in literature and art, emphasized both his belief that Negro art must act as propaganda and his willingness to accept reflections of all avenues of Afro-American life:

> We want especially to stress the fact that while we believe in
> Negro art we do not believe in any art simply for art's sake. . . .
> We want Negro writers to produce beautiful things but we stress
> the things rather than the beauty. It is Life and Truth that are
> important and Beauty comes to make their importance visible
> and tolerable. . . .
>
> Write then about things as you know them. . . . In *The Crisis*,
> at least, you do not have to confine your writings to the portrayal
> of beggars, scoundrels and prostitutes; you can write about
> ordinary decent colored people if you want. On the other hand
> do not fear the Truth. . . . If you want to paint Crime and
> Destitution and Evil paint it. . . . Use propaganda if you want.
> Discard it and laugh if you will. But be true, be sincere, be
> thorough, and do a beautiful job.

Undoubtedly, Du Bois remembered the dictum of John Keats that Beauty is Truth and Truth is Beauty. With whatever license is granted to a poet, however, Keats ignored any responsibility for explaining his meaning. More lucidity is generally required of a literary critic.

If one extracts the essence of Du Bois' instruction to black readers, his rebuttal of Locke's doctrine, and his exhortation to prospective contestants, one recognizes a general pronouncement that literature by blacks must be unflinchingly true to Afro-American life even in its pictures of the ugly and the unheroic. It also must be didactic and beautiful. Even viewed superficially, the proposition seems difficult to use as a touchstone for any single work of art.

The critical process is further complicated by Du Bois' failure to clarify his abstractions. Although he occasionally perceived the need, he never successfully defined Beauty in relation to material, thought, or method— perhaps because he presumed his taste to be characteristic of all people. In "Criteria of Negro Art," a speech prepared for the 1926 Chicago Conference of the NAACP, Du Bois made his most detailed effort to resolve the question of the relation of beauty to Afro-American art; yet, in his initial premise, he reflected his assumption that his standards were the standards for all blacks— at least for all cultivated blacks. "Pushed aside as we have been in America," he wrote, "there has come to us not only a certain distaste for the tawdry and flamboyant but a vision of what the world could be if it were really a beautiful world." Du Bois continued:

> After all, who shall describe Beauty? What is it? I remember
> tonight four beautiful things: The Cathedral at Cologne, a forest

in stone, set in light and changing shadow, echoing with sunlight and solemn song; a village of the Veys in West Africa, a little thing of mauve and purple, quiet, lying content and shining in the sun; a black and velvet room where on a throne rests, in old and yellowing marble, the broken curves of the Venus of Milo; a single phrase of music in the Southern South—utter melody, haunting and appealing, suddenly arising out of night and eternity, beneath the moon.

Du Bois' rhetoric is persuasive. His emphasis is upon apparent catholicity of taste. Yet a question obtrudes. Does the beauty of the scene at Cologne depend upon the viewer's reaction to a particular style of architecture and a particular quality of song? Would Du Bois' sense of ultimate beauty in the scene have been marred if the music had not been "solemn song" but jazz?

Even if Du Bois had resolved questions about Beauty, he still would have failed to appreciate the complexity of Pilate's question. Du Bois perceived a difference between a black man's and a white man's awareness of the Truth of Negro life. But he failed to comprehend that black men themselves may differ in their visions of the Truth of Afro-American life. In consequence, whereas he rejected obviously idealized portraits as untrue, he often admitted bewilderment that young authors never wrote about the decent, hard working Negroes in their own families. Moreover, although he graciously urged young writers to describe the sordid if they wished, he soon suspected them of rejecting authentic pictures of low black life in favor of derogatory stereotypes.

I do not intend to demean Du Bois by suggesting that his definitions, criteria, and perceptions are inferior to those of other artists and critics still esteemed by many literary scholars. To the contrary, compared with others of his century—or any century—he fares well. His concept of Beauty certainly is as valid and as meaningful as Edgar Allan Poe's definition of poetry. Du Bois' assumption that his visions of Beauty and Truth were universally accepted is no more arrogant than Matthew Arnold's presumption that, from his preferences in poetry, he had acquired touchstones with which to measure the excellence of the poetry of any country. Instead of wishing to demean Du Bois, I merely suggest that, because he based his critical judgment on abstractions which were concrete to him but not necessarily to all other black contemporaries, the application of his theory to particular works of black writers sometimes resulted in appraisals significantly different from those of younger black artists, who shared their own perceptions of Beauty and Truth.

Significantly, although his interest in Beauty and Truth suggests a concern for "universal" values—a concept too often used to minimize the work of a black writer on a theme of black life, Du Bois' discussions of Beauty and Truth in literature always led him to a position strikingly comparable in spirit, if not always in detail, to that adopted by many current exponents of Black Arts: literature must serve a function for the good of black people, and its worth must be judged by black people.

He concluded his discussion of Beauty in "Criteria of Negro Art":

Thus it is the bounden duty of black America to begin this great work of the creation of Beauty, of the preservation of Beauty, of the realization of Beauty, and we must use in this work all the methods that men have used before. And what have been the tools of the artist in times gone by? First of all, he has used the Truth—not for the sake of truth, not as a scientist seeking truth, but as one upon whom Truth eternally thrusts itself as the highest handmaid of imagination, as the one great vehicle of universal understanding. Again artists have used Goodness— goodness in all its aspects of justice, honor and right—not for sake of an ethical sanction but as the one true method of gaining sympathy and human interest.

The apostle of Beauty thus becomes the apostle of Truth and Right not by choice but by inner and outer compulsion. Free he is but his freedom is ever bounded by Truth and Justice; and slavery only dogs him when he is denied the right to tell the Truth or recognize an ideal of Justice.

Thus all Art is propaganda and ever must be, despite the wailing of the purists. I stand in utter shamelessness and say that whatever art I have for writing has been used always for propaganda for gaining the right of black folk to love and enjoy. I do not care a damn for any art that is not used for propaganda.

And in rhetoric prophetic of a Black Aesthetic, he surged to a climax:

. . . the young and slowly growing black public still wants its prophets almost equally unfree. We are bound by all sorts of customs that have come down as second-hand soul clothes of white patrons. We are ashamed of sex and we lower our eyes when people will talk of it. Our religion holds us in superstition. Our worst side has been so shamelessly emphasized that we are denying we have or ever had a worst side. In all sorts of ways we are hemmed in and our new young artists have got to fight their way to freedom.

The ultimate judge has got to be you and you have got to build yourselves up into that wide judgment, that catholicity of temper which is going to enable the artist to have his widest chance for freedom. We can afford the Truth. White folk today cannot. As it is now we are handing everything over to a white jury. If a colored man wants to publish a book, he has got to get a white publisher and a white newspaper to say it is great; and then you and I say so. We must come to the place where the work of art when it appears is reviewed and acclaimed by our own free and unfettered judgment.

Du Bois argued that young black writers were being diverted from their artistic responsibilities especially by the popularity of Carl Van Vechten's *Nigger Heaven*, which he denounced as "an affront to the hospitality of black folk (who admitted Van Vechten to their circles) and to the intelligence of white." In Du Bois' opinion the book was pernicious, not only because its commercial success persuaded blacks to pander to white stereotypes of their life but also because it destroyed both Beauty and Truth:

It is a caricature. It is worse than untruth because it is a mass of half-truths. . . . [To Van Vechten] the black cabaret is Harlem; around it all his characters gravitate. . . . Such a theory of Harlem is nonsense. The overwhelming majority of black folk there never go to cabarets. . . .

Something they have which is racial, something distinctly Negroid can be found; but it is expressed by subtle, almost delicate nuance, and not by the wildly, [sic] barbaric drunken orgy in whose details Van Vechten revels. . . .

Van Vechten is not the great artist who with remorseless scalpel probes the awful depths of life. To him there are no depths. It is the surface mud he slops about in. . . . Life to him is just one damned orgy after another, with hate, hurt, gin and sadism.

Both Langston Hughes and Carl Van Vechten know Harlem cabarets; but it is Hughes who whispers,
"One said he heard the jazz band sob
When the little dawn was grey."
Van Vechten never heard a sob in a cabaret. All he hears is noise and brawling.

Earlier Du Bois had lamented the limitations of Dubose Heyward's *Porgy* because, by excluding educated Afro-American Charlestonians, it implied that the waterfront world was a total picture of black life in that city. Nevertheless, Du Bois now insisted that Porgy himself had a human and interesting quality absent from Van Vechten's characters.

How does one determine that a writer has created characters who are human as well as interesting? Can any reader truly determine whether an author has delineated degraded characters with compassion or has exploited them?

Du Bois could not find answers to these questions. Perhaps his orientation to scientific research persuaded him that sincerity can be measured. Or perhaps, more concerned with other matters, he did not even consider the questions fully; the theory was clear to him at least. A black should write honestly about the Afro-Americans he knew. So created, a work would sparkle with Truth and Beauty. It would be useful black literature. If, however, the writer seemed excessively absorbed with cabaret life, Du Bois was prepared to impale him with the pen reserved for those who dished up black humanity piping hot to a slobbering white public.

Even if he did not fully examine questions needed to clarify his own criteria of art, Du Bois nevertheless quickly sensed a possible weakness in his efforts to propagandize for the race by encouraging young blacks to write about themselves. What if, for the sake of publication, they all began to imitate Van Vechten?

Earlier in 1926, Du Bois had initiated a symposium on "The Negro in Art." He asked various authors and publishers to consider several questions:

> Are writers under obligations or limitations as to the kinds of characters they portray? Should authors be criticized for painting the best or the worst characters of a group? Can publishers be criticized for failing to publish works about educated Negroes? What can Negroes do if they are continually painted at their worst? Should Negroes be portrayed sincerely and sympathetically? Isn't the literary emphasis upon sordid, foolish and criminal Negroes persuading readers that this is the truth and preventing authors from writing otherwise? Is there danger that young colored writers will follow the popular trend?

The overlapping questions reveal Du Bois' basic concern: is the literary world conspiring to typify Negroes by sordid, foolish, and criminal characters? And if so, what can be done to prevent that?

Some of the responses by whites must have confirmed Du Bois' worst fears. Carl Van Vechten bluntly stated that the squalor and vice of Negro life *would* be overdone "for a very excellent reason." Such squalor and vice offer "a wealth of novel, exotic, picturesque material." He discounted pictures of wealthy, cultured Negroes as uninteresting because they were virtually identical with those of whites, a pronouncement which validates Du Bois' convictions about Van Vechten's superficiality. The only thing for the black writer to do, Van Vechten concluded, was to exploit the vice and squalor before the white authors did.

Henry Mencken chided blacks for failing to see the humor in the derogatory caricatures created by Octavius Cohen. Instead of applying scientific criteria to art, he added, blacks should write works ridiculing whites. Mencken did not explain who would publish the caricatures of whites.

Another white author, John Farrar, shrugged off the stories of Octavius Cohen with the admission that they amused him immensely and seemed not to libel Negroes. In contrast, although he confessed scant knowledge of the South, he thought Walter White's novel *The Fire in the Flint* "a trifle onesided." William Lyons Phelps mildly admonished Negroes to correct false impressions by setting good examples in their lives. Having no answers but more questions, Sinclair Lewis proposed a conference to consider the issues. He also suggested establishing a club for blacks—at a small hotel in Paris.

Sherwood Anderson reminded *The Crisis* that he had lived among Negro laborers, whom he had found to be "about the sweetest people I know," as he had said sometimes in his books. In short, he wrote, Negroes were worrying too much and being too sensitive; they had no more reason to complain about their portraits in literature than whites would have. Julia Peterkin asserted that Irish and Jewish people were not offended by caricatures, so Negroes should not be. She used the occasion to praise the "Black Negro Mammy" and to chastize Negroes for protesting against a proposal in Congress to erect a monument to the Mammy.

Such responses probably did not surprise Du Bois, but they strengthened his conviction that black writers must fight for their race. Even the sympathetic white writers revealed flaws. For example, Paul Green's Pulitzer Prize winning play, *In Abraham's Bosom*, impressed Du Bois as an example of "the defeatist genre of Negro art which is so common. . . . The more honestly and sincerely a white artist looks at the situation of the Negro in America the less he is able to consider it in any way bearable and therefore his stories and plays must end in lynching, suicide or degeneracy." Du Bois added that, even if such a writer learned differently by observing black people's refusal to accept failure, the publisher or producer would prohibit a portrayal of triumphant blacks. Pathetic, inevitable defeat or exotic degeneracy—these would be the dominant images of black life unless black writers corrected the images.

In April, 1927, while announcing the annual competition in literature and art, Du Bois reminded his readers of the impressive black heritage revealed in the fine arts of Ethiopia, Egypt, and the rest of Africa. In contemporary America, he insisted, that heritage must be continued in the art of spoken and written word. It must not be restrained by the white person's desire for silly and lewd entertainment; it must not be blocked by the black person's revulsion from unfavorable images. "The Negro artist must have freedom to wander where he will, portray what he will, interpret whatever he may see according to the great canons of beauty which the world through long experience has laid down." Du Bois was beginning to sound like his future son-in-law Countee Cullen. He would now accept anything black writers wanted to do if only they did it beautifully, but he was no more specific about his concept of Beauty.

When James Weldon Johnson published *God's Trombones* (1927), Du Bois rejoiced at Johnson's preservation of the Negro idiom in art, Johnson's beautiful poetry, and Aaron Douglass' wild, beautiful, unconventional, daring drawings, which were stylized to emphasize Negroid rather than Caucasian features of the black figures.

But works by whites continued to disappoint him even when they were sufficiently good to be recommended to his readers. His praise of *Congaree Sketches* by E. C. L. Adams was dampened by what he felt to be a significant omission:

> even to the lowest black swamp peasant there are the three worlds ever present to his imagination: his own, the world of the risen black man and the world of white folks. No current folk lore can omit any one of these and be true, complete and, therefore . . . artistic.

In the entire collection, Du Bois complained, he found not one allusion to the rising black man characterized by ambition, education, and aspiration to better earthly things.

In 1928, black writers provided Du Bois with examples which he used to illustrate his concept of the difference between praiseworthy black literature and atrocious black literature. He hailed Nella Larsen's *Quicksand* as a "fine, thoughtful and courageous novel," the best by any black writer since Chesnutt. Subtly comprehending the curious cross currents swirling about black Americans, the author, he felt, created an interesting character, fitted her into a close plot, and rejected both an improbable happy ending and the defeatist theme: "Helga Crane sinks at last still master of her whimsical, unsatisfied soul. In the end she will be beaten down even to death but she never will utterly surrender to hypocricy [sic] and convention."

In contrast, Du Bois stated that Claude McKay's *Home to Harlem* was a shameful novel, redeemed only by the fact that the author was "too great a poet to make any complete failure in writing." Du Bois noted virtues in the work: the beautiful, fascinating changes on themes of the beauty of colored skins; McKay's emphasis upon the fact that Negroes are physically and emotionally attracted to other Negroes rather than to whites; and the creation of Jake and Ray, interesting and appealing characters. Despite these commendably perceptive insights into black life, Du Bois argued, *Home to Harlem* pandered to white people's enjoyment of Negroes portrayed in

> that utter licentiousness which conventional civilization holds white folk back from enjoying—if enjoyment it can be called. That which a certain decadent section of the white American world, centered particularly in New York, longs for with fierce and unrestrained passions, it wants to see written out in black and white and saddled on black Harlem. . . . [McKay] has used every art and emphasis to paint drunkenness, fighting, lascivious sexual promiscuity and utter absence of restraint in as bold and as bright colors as he can. . . . Whole chapters . . . are inserted with no connection to the main plot, except that they are on the same dirty subject. As a picture of Harlem life or of Negro life anywhere, it is, of course, nonsense. Untrue, not so much on account of its facts but on account of its emphasis and glaring colors.

Between the levels of *Quicksand* and *Home to Harlem*, Du Bois placed Rudolph Fisher's *The Walls of Jericho*. Fearful that casual readers would draw from it only echoes of Van Vechten and McKay, Du Bois stressed the psychological validity of the two working-class black people who are the focus of the major plot. The book's weaknesses were the excessive sophistication and unreality of the background and such minor characters as Jinx and Bubber, who speak authentically but do not seem as human as the major figures. But, Du Bois continued in bewilderment, Fisher "has not depicted Negroes like his mother, his sister, his wife, his real Harlem friends. He has not even depicted his own soul. The glimpses of better class Negroes are ineffective make-believes." Why, Du Bois asked. Hearing no answer, he concluded with the hope that Fisher's novel was an indication of black novelists' movement upward from Van Vechten and McKay.

Despite his frequent attacks upon white authors' distortions of black life and black people, Du Bois did not contend that white Americans could never portray blacks successfully. Exceptions occurred: Paul Green wrote sincerely even though he belabored the defeatist theme; the E. C. L. Adams book, *Nigger to Nigger*, was a sincere attempt to collect and present the philosophy of black peasants. Nevertheless, such exceptions did not relieve his skepticism:

> I assume that the white stranger cannot write about black people. In nine cases out of ten I am right. In the tenth case, and Du Bose Heywood [sic] is the tenth case, the stranger can write about the colored people whom he knows; but those very people whom he knows are sometimes so strange to me, that I cannot for the life of me make them authentic.

In the waning moments of the Renaissance, Du Bois seemed increasingly reluctant to castigate an Afro-American writer except when that writer rejected his blackness. For example, although he had previously objected to Wallace Thurman for glib, superficial comments on black life and culture, Du Bois, when reviewing *The Blacker the Berry*, merely remonstrated with Thurman for not believing his thesis:

> The story of Emma Lou calls for genius to develop it. It needs deep psychological knowledge and pulsing sympathy. And above all, the author must believe in black folk, and in the beauty of black as a color of human skin. I may be wrong, but it does not seem to me that this is true of Wallace Thurman. He seems to me himself to deride blackness. . . .
>
> It seems that this inner self-despising of the very thing that he is defending, makes the author's defense less complete and sincere.

Du Bois' review of Marc Connelly's *Green Pastures* (1930) was a peroration of what he had tried to teach to readers, writers, and critics during the decade:

> All art is propaganda, and without propaganda there is no true art. But, on the other hand, all propaganda is not art. . . . If a person portrays ideal Negro life, the sole judgment of its

success is whether the picture is a beautiful thing. . . . If he caricatures Negro life, and makes it sordid and despicable, the critic's criterion is . . . solely, is the idea well presented? . . . The difficulty with the Negro on the American stage, is that the white audience . . . demands caricatures, and the Negro, on the other hand, either cringes to the demand because he needs the pay, or bitterly condemns every Negro book or show that does not paint colored folk at their best. Their criticisms should be aimed at the incompleteness of art expression—at the embargo which white wealth lays on full Negro expression—and a full picturing of the Negro soul.

In the early years of the 1930's, while America floundered in an economic depression, it was clear that night had fallen on the heyday of the Harlem Renaissance. If Afro-Americans—intelligentsia, artists, and workers alike—were not cast out, they were at least ignored by a huge republic trying to pull itself erect. As Du Bois re-examined the position of blacks in America during those troubled times, he re-evaluated his own ideas about the appropriate course for his people. For a decade, from a platform within an integrated and pro-integrationist NAACP, he had argued that black writers must do things for black people and must be judged by black people. Now he extended that concept of black independence and black control to the entire spectrum of black existence in America: black people must develop and control strong black institutions for the good of black people. Coming as it did from the pages of the voice of the NAACP, and from a man whom white supremacists had vilified as the chief advocate of integration, the idea probably was even more startling when Du Bois expressed it in the 1930's than when, a quarter of a century later, Stokely Carmichael re-introduced it tersely as "Black Power."

Although Du Bois seemed unable to convert those who immediately attacked his position, he tried repeatedly to explain the logic which guided him to a seemingly inescapable conclusion. Personally, he still believed the best society to be an integrated one—a fact which should be obvious to anyone who remembered that, for more than twenty-five years, he had dedicated himself to effecting the full integration of blacks into American society. Despite his private desires, however, he was compelled to admit a bitter truth:

> . . . that we are segregated, apart, hammered into a separate unity by spiritual intolerance and legal sanction backed by mob law, . . . that this separation is growing in strength and fixation; that it is worse today than a half-century ago and that no

character, address, culture, or desert is going to change it in one
day or for centuries to come.

In such a deplorable circumstance, it is futile to pretend that one is
simply an American: one must recognize that he is a Negro. It is pointless to
argue that there is no such creature as an American Negro when twelve
million human beings are identified and treated as Negroes. It is senseless to
continue to debate whether or not segregation is desirable; segregation is a
fact. In such a circumstance, the only matter for American Negroes to debate
is what they can do to prevent their genocide. The solution, he explained,
was to "carefully plan and guide our segregated life, organize in industry and
politics to protect it and expand it and above all to give it unhampered
spiritual expression in art and literature."

A step which blacks could take immediately was to make their
institutions more serviceable by concentrating on their true purpose. That is,
as one could no longer deny the fact of being Negro, so it was absurd to
pretend that a Negro college was just another American college. It must be
recognized as a Negro institution:

> A Negro university in the United States of America begins with
> Negroes. It uses that variety of English idiom which they
> understand; and above all, it is founded on a knowledge of the
> history of their people in Africa and in the United States, and
> their present condition . . . then it asks how shall these young
> men and women be trained to earn a living and live a life under
> the circumstances in which they find themselves.

Beginning with such a premise, he explained, the Negro university
would expand from the examination of black life, history, social
development, science, and humanities into a study of all life and matter in the
universe. The study must begin with a focus on black people, and it must
continue from the perspective of black people. This is not merely the best
route, it is the only route to universality.

In the antithesis of this theory, Du Bois found reasons for his failure to
bring about the kind of literary Renaissance of which he had dreamed—one
in which honest, artistic literary works about blacks by blacks would be
bought and read by blacks. Such a Renaissance never took root, he now
argued; the so-called "Renaissance" failed

> because it was a transplanted and exotic thing. It was a literature
> written for the benefit of white people and at the behest of white

readers, and starting out privately from the white point of view. It never had a real Negro constituency and it did not grow out of the inmost heart and frank experience of Negroes; on such an artificial basis no real literature can grow.

By the time he published *Dusk of Dawn* seven years later, Du Bois had practiced his theory. After severing connections with the NAACP, Du Bois had returned to Atlanta University to help develop a strong black institution. Although he was less interested in explaining artistic theory than he had been earlier, his brief summation in *Dusk of Dawn* roots him firmly in a Black Aesthetic and identifies him, more clearly than any previous statement, as a progenitor of a Black Arts movement. Creative art, he stated, was essential to the development and transmission of new ideas among blacks:

> The communalism of the African clan can be transferred to the Negro American group. . . . The emotional wealth of the American Negro, the nascent art in song, dance and drama can all be applied, not to amuse the white audience, but to inspire and direct the acting Negro group itself. I can conceive no more magnificent or promising crusade in modern times.

To achieve this end, black people must be re-educated in educational institutions oriented to black people:

> There has been a larger movement on the part of the Negro intelligentsia toward racial grouping for the advancement of art and literature. There has been a distinct plan for reviving ancient African art through an American Negro art movement, and more specially a thought to use the extremely rich and colorful life of the Negro in America and elsewhere as a basis for painting, sculpture, and literature. This has been partly nullified by the fact that if these new artists expect support for their art from the Negro group itself, that group must be deliberately trained and schooled in art appreciation and in willingness to accept new canons of art and in refusal to follow the herd instinct of the nation.

In two decades of conscious and unconscious questing for a Black Aesthetic, W.E.B. Du Bois experienced many difficulties in shaping and applying an idea which, he sensed, was sound. Some of the difficulties resulted from his personal limitations: his failure to clarify criteria, his dependence upon undefined abstractions, his inability to harmonize his awareness of the utilitarian value of literature for a specific group with his concern for the creation of Truth and Beauty, his fallacious assumption that his aesthetic was necessarily the aesthetic of most black people. Perhaps the major reason for his lack of success, however, is that, with this idea as with many others, Du Bois was twenty-five to fifty years ahead of those twelve million blacks he wanted to lead from self-respect to pride to achievement.

Today, a Black Arts movement exists; and, many black writers and educators are seriously defining the dimensions of a Black Aesthetic. Even today, however, when one considers the work of some self-identified Black Arts dramatists and poets who picture only the vice, squalor, contemptibility, and failure of black communities, one imagines Du Bois, in some afterworld he could not envision, muttering unhappily, "No. No. No! Will they never understand? To be black is to be beautiful and strong and proud."

WILSON J. MOSES

The Poetics of Ethiopianism:
W.E.B. Du Bois and Literary Black Nationalism

Du Bois's position with respect to Black Nationalism has been described
as ambivalent, reflecting his admitted double-consciousness as both a black
man and an American, his "two souls, two thoughts, two unreconciled
strivings; two warring ideals in one dark body." This often-quoted line
registers the double-consciousness manifested in the thought of many Afro-
Americans, and, indeed, many Western intellectuals who have attempted to
be at once culturally nationalistic, and yet loyal to a more broadly conceived
"Western Civilization." Du Bois's early work struggles to fuse two
complementary but substantially different mythological traditions. The first
of these is "Ethiopianism," a literary religious tradition common to English-
speaking Africans, regardless of nationality. The other is the European
tradition of interpretive mythology, transplanted to America by its European
colonizers.

The "Ethiopian" tradition sprang organically out of certain shared
political and religious experiences of English-speaking Africans during the
late eighteenth and early nineteenth centuries. It found expression in the
slave narratives, in the exhortations of conspiratorial slave preachers, and in
the songs and folklore of the slaves of the Old and the peasants of the New
South. On a more literary level, it appeared in the sermons and political
tracts of the sophisticated urban elite. The name "Ethiopianism" is assigned

From *American Literature* 47, no. 3 (1975). © 1975 by Duke University Press.

to this tradition because early black writers and even some of their white allies often referred to an inspiring Biblical passage, "Princes shall come out of Egypt; Ethiopia shall soon stretch out her hands unto God" (Psalms, 68:31). The verse was seen by some as a prophecy that Africa would "soon" be saved from the darkness of heathenism, and it came to be interpreted as a promise that Africa would "soon" experience a dramatic political, industrial, and economic renaissance. Others have insisted that the real meaning of the scripture is that some day the black man will rule the world. Such a belief is still common among older black folk today.

The "Ethiopian" prophecy seems to have been commonly known among free black people before the Civil War. In 1858, the African Civilization Society quoted the full verse in its constitution, along with an interpretation by Henry Highland Garnet. According to Garnet Ethiopia would "soon stretch forth her hands,"—"soon" meaning shortly after the work was taken up. The responsibility for seeing to it that the prophecy was fulfilled rested upon the Africans themselves. The signers of the constitution included the leading black nationalists of the day, among them, Daniel Alexander Payne, a bishop of the African Methodist Episcopal Church, and Robert Hamilton, who was later to found *The Anglo-African Magazine*. The quotation appeared in any number of documents published by free Africans in the northern states, and it seems unlikely that many literate free Africans were unfamiliar with it.

At times the verse was directly quoted; at times it was referred to thematically. An early eloquent articulation of the Ethiopian theme was made by Alexander Crummell, an Episcopal priest, who eventually inspired Du Bois. Crummell often used the direct quotation in sermons; but sometimes, as in his 1846 *Eulogium on the Life and Character of Thomas Clarkson*, the reference was indirect:

> Amid the decay of nations a rekindled light starts up in us. Burdens under which others expire, seem to have lost their influence upon us; and while *they* are "driven to the wall" destruction keeps far from us its blasting hand. We live in the region of death, yet seem hardly mortal. We cling to life in the midst of all reverses; and our nerveful grasp thereon cannot easily be relaxed. History reverses its mandates in our behalf—our dotage is in the past. "Time writes not its wrinkles on our brow."

Another example of this indirect "Ethiopianism" was Daniel Alexander Payne's oration "To the Colored People of the United States," delivered in 1862 as the Civil War approached what seemed to Payne a climax of apocalyptic proportions.

It is said that he is the God of the white man, and not of the black. This is horrible blasphemy—a *lie* from the pit that is bottomless—believe it not—no—never. Murmur not against the Lord on account of the cruelty and injustice of man. His almighty arm is already stretched out against slavery—against every man, every constitution, and every union that upholds it. His avenging chariot is now moving over the bloody fields of the doomed south, crushing beneath its massive wheels the very foundations of the blasphemous system. Soon slavery shall sink like Pharoah—even like the brazen-hearted tyrant, it shall sink to rise no more forever.

The theme also appeared in verse, as in Frances Ellen Watkins Harper's "Ethiopia,"

> Yes, Ethiopia yet shall stretch
>   Her bleeding hands abroad;
> Her cry of agony shall reach
>   Up to the throne of God.

Paul Laurence Dunbar's "Ode to Ethiopia," addressed not to Ethiopia the nation but to the "Mother Race," recounted the past and present struggles of the Afro-Americans and predicted their future triumph:

> Go on and up! Our souls and eyes
> Shall follow thy continuous rise;
>   Our ears shall list thy story
> From bards who from thy root shall spring
> And proudly tune their lyres to sing
>   Of Ethiopia's glory.

Thus the Rising Africa Theme became a tradition of reinterpreting the Biblical passage to speak to the experiences of the Anglo-African peoples. But "Rising Africa" is only one aspect of "Ethiopianism"; the balancing theme looks to the Decline of the West. The rise in the fortunes of Africa and all her scattered children would be accompanied by God's judgment upon the Europeans. A powerful expression of this belief occurred in *David Walker's Appeal*, published in 1829. In this volume, one of those forgotten American classics nonetheless well known in its time, and a book of importance to the legal and intellectual history of the United States, Walker warned of the impending doom of Western civilization. It would come as a judgment upon Christian sin in enslaving the Africans. "I tell you Americans! that unless you speedily alter your course, *you* and your Country are gone!!!"

"Ethiopianism," with its two thematic components, Rising Africa and Decline of the West, provided one element of Anglo-African literary tradition on which Du Bois mythmaking is based. Here is a typical example of a poem in the Ethiopian tradition. It was published in the tenth Atlanta University Publication in 1905, over a pseudonym, "The Moon." Probably Du Bois, who edited the Atlanta publications and also edited a periodical called *The Moon* was the author:

> "Ethiopia, my little daughter, why hast thou lingered and loitered in the Sun? See thy tall sisters, pale and blue of eye—see thy strong brothers, shrewd and slippery haired—see what they have done! Behold their gardens and their magic, their halls and wonder wheels! Behold their Gold, Gold, Gold!"
>
> "Flowers, O Mother Earth, I bring flowers, and the echo of a Song's song. Aye and the blue violet Humility, the mystic image flower of Heaven. And Mother, sweet Mother, in these great and misty years, I have seen Sights and heard Voices; Stories and Songs are quick within me—If I have loitered, sun-kissed, O forgive me, Mother yet chide me not bitterly—I too have lived."

The typically "Ethiopian" element of this poem is its assumption that Caucasians and Ethiopians are separate varieties of humanity with distinct destinies competing for honor in the eyes of history and the world. The characters of this poem represent historical forces, not real human beings. The argument is that Africans are a special people with special gifts and that blacks are in some ways superior to whites. To the African genius are attributed such traits as tropical dreaminess, feminine aestheticism, and a childlike love of nature. The Europeans of the first stanza are assigned their own traditional qualities by the use of such words as "pale," "strong," "shrewd," and "slippery."

The dreamy little Ethiopia is a minor avatar of the sleeping titaness who looms in "The Riddle of the Sphinx":

> Dark Daughter of the lotus leaves that watch the Southern Sea!
> Wan spirit of a prisoned soul a-panting to be free!
>   The muttered music of thy streams, the whisper of the
> deep,
>   Have kissed each other in God's name and kissed a world to
> sleep.

This woman is a personification of Africa, a sleeping world, a giantess, raped by pygmies while she sleeps. "The burden of white men bore her back and the white world stifled her sighs." The poet describes the ascendency of the West, based upon Mediterranean culture, and predicts its eventual going under:

> down
>   down
>   deep down,
> Till the devil's strength be shorn.
> Till some dim, darker David, a-hoeing of his corn,
> And married maiden, mother of God,
> Bid the black Christ be born!

In summary, Ethiopianism may be defined as the effort of the English-speaking Black or African person to view his past enslavement and present cultural dependency in terms of the broader history of civilization. It serves to remind him that this present scientific technological civilization, dominated by Western Europe for a scant four hundred years, will go under certainly—like all the empires of the past. It expresses the belief that the tragic racial experience has profound historical value, that it has endowed the African with moral superiority and made him a seer. Du Bois's poetry, while highly original, is nonetheless a product of this tradition, and therefore traditional. T. S. Eliot's poetry, by way of comparison, works within the European tradition of interpretive mythology although it is clearly innovative.

European interpretive mythology is the second of the two traditions basic to Du Bois's mythmaking. In *The Survival of the Pagan Gods*, a study of classical mythology in the Renaissance, Jean Seznec discusses the medieval practice of examining Greco-Roman mythology with the intention of either discovering within it, or assigning to it, Christian meaning. He discusses the ancient origins of this practice among the pre-Christian Greeks and Romans, who, attempting to understand the meanings of stories that were already very old, developed theories of interpretation in order to render myths intelligible. This tradition, once revived in the Middle Ages, endured throughout the Renaissance, and as Douglas Bush has shown, became a mode functional to English and American poetry.

How can it be known that Du Bois was aware of the tradition of interpretive mythology and that he consciously wrote in this tradition? In Chapter VIII of *The Souls of Black Folk*, in the section titled "Of the Quest of the Golden Fleece," Du Bois demonstrated his awareness of this kind of writing and his desire to experiment with it:

Have you ever seen a cotton-field white with harvest,—its golden fleece hovering above the black earth like a silvery cloud edged with dark green, its bold white signals waving like foam of billows from Carolina to Texas across that Black and human Sea? I have sometimes half-suspected that here the winged ram Chrysomallus left that Fleece after which Jason and his Argonauts went vaguely wandering into the shadowy East three thousand years ago; and certainly one might frame a pretty and not far-fetched analogy of witchery and dragon's teeth, and blood and armed men, between the ancient and the modern Quest of the Golden Fleece in the Black Sea.

In an earlier chapter of the same book, "Of the Wings of Atalanta," Du Bois had demonstrated his skill at updating mythology and adapting it to the needs of his times. *The Quest of the Silver Fleece*, in 1911, brought to maturity the ideas briefly outlined in the parent essay. In this novel he created a universe in which the ideology of progressive socialism and the traditionalism of Christian black nationalism work harmoniously within the framework of a Greek myth.

The Quest of the Silver Fleece is a story of witchcraft and voodoo magic. Zora, the heroine of the tale, makes her first appearance as an elfin child, personifying the supposedly preternatural traits of the primitive mind. "We black folks is got the *spirit*," she says. White folk may think they rule, but, "We'se lighter and cunninger; we fly right through them; we go and come again just as we wants to." Elspeth, the mother of Zora, is a malevolent black witch, who sows a wondrous cotton crop in a scene reminiscent of Cadmus's planting the dragon's teeth. The cotton crop is first stolen by the aristocratic Cresswell family, then woven into a wedding dress, and perhaps it is the magic of Medea (Elspeth-Zora) that begins to eat away at the vitality of Cresswell's bride. By the end of the story, Zora matures from elf-child to Ethiopian queen, who appears as a haunting "mirage of other days," ensconced in a "setting of rich, barbaric splendor."

A good clue to the meaning of any obscure poetic system may sometimes be found by examining its employment of traditional devices, and this method is useful in dealing with a poet like Du Bois. So typical was Ethiopianism of Du Bois's rhetoric that George Schuyler's satirization of his speaking style, while grotesque, was apt nonetheless. "I want to tell you that our destiny lies in the stars. Ethiopia's fate is in the balance. The Goddess of the Nile weeps bitter tears at the feet of the Sphinx. The lowering clouds gather over the Congo and the lightning flashes o'er Togoland. To your tents, O Israel! The hour is at hand." Among Du Bois's longer and more difficult poems is "Children of the Moon," which blends the Ethiopian and Western mythological traditions. It tells the story of a despairing woman who finds a "highway to the moon," at the end of which lies

>   a twilight land,
> Where, hardly-hid, the sun
> Sent softly-saddened rays of
> Red and brown to burn the iron soil
> And bathe the snow-white peaks
> In mighty splendor.

There she discovers a race of black men but no women:

> Black were the men,
> Hard-haired and silent-slow,
> Moving as shadows,
> Bending with face of fear to earthward;
> And women there were none.

Under her guidance the men build a tower which she climbs to "stand beneath the burning shadow of [a] peak, Beneath the whirring of almighty wings," where she hears a voice from "near-far" saying:

> "I am Freedom —
> Who sees my face is free —
> He and his."

The god reveals his name, but "who shall look and live?" Not daring, at first, to look, the goddess is persuaded in the end by "the sobbing of small voices—down, down far into the night," to climb:

> Up! Up! to the blazing blackness
> Of one veiled face.
> And endless folding and unfolding,
> Rolling and unrolling of almighty wings.

And then the poem moves to its climax:

> I rose upon the Mountain of the Moon
> I felt the blazing glory of the Sun;
> I heard the Song of Children crying, "Free!"

I saw the face of Freedom—
And I died.

The poem calls to mind the Egyptian myth in which Isis, the Nile goddess, ascends the heavens to do battle with Ra, the sun god, to force him to reveal his name.

In order to create the world of "Children of the Moon," Du Bois drew not only upon his knowledge of black Christian nationalism but also upon Greek and Egyptian mythology. The narrator is reminiscent of Isis, the moon goddess, patroness and teacher, Magna Mater of ancient Egypt, and Isis represents the Nilotic Africans whom Du Bois believed to have brought the Egyptians the civilizing arts. She was conceived by Du Bois as a black woman. Born a woman, Isis was later elevated, according to the mythographers, to divine status. The goddess is an appropriate symbol of the spirit of black civilization within Du Bois's poetic system. She becomes the Great Mother of Men in the Moon—black people—as Isis was the nourishing mother of ancient Egypt. "Isis, the mother," said Du Bois, "is still titular goddess, in thought if not in name, of the dark continent."

Du Bois provided one clue to the mythology of "Children of the Moon" when he spoke, in a later essay, of Ethiopian history as "the main current of Negro culture, from the Mountains of the Moon to the Mediterranean, blossoming on the lower Nile, but never severed from the Great Lakes of Inner Africa." The Children of the Moon are described as "moving shadows." They live in a "twilight land," and they labor beneath the "burning shadow" of a peak. One suspects that this land in which they live is to be associated with Ethiopia, the land of shadows, mentioned in Isaiah and referred to as "Ethiopia, the shadowy," in *The Souls of Black Folk*. Throughout the tradition references to Ethiopia were meant to include all African peoples, of course.

Du Bois's interest in Ethiopian rhetoric made itself felt in much of his writing, as for example, in the herald's oration in the lost pageant *Star of Ethiopia*:

> Hear ye, hear ye! All them that come to know the truth and listen to the tale of the Wisest and Gentlest of the Races of Men whose faces be Black. Hear ye, hear ye! And learn the ancient Glory of Ethiopia, All-Mother of men, whose wonders men forgot. See how beneath the Mountains of the Moon, alike in the Valley of Father Nile and in ancient Negro-land and Atlantis the Black Race ruled and strove and fought and sought the Star of Faith and Freedom even as other races did and do. Fathers of

Men and Sires of Children golden, black and brown, keep silence
and hear this mighty word.

The Mountains of the Moon referred to in the above passage and in
"Children of the Moon" are a semi-fictitious range, first mentioned in
Ptolemy's *Geographica*. Recent scholarship associates them with the
Ruwenzori Range. The Children of the Moon are blacks from central Africa,
the area of the Nile-Congo watershed. They can be seen either as Congolese
or Nilotics, therefore, which makes them symbolic of two of the great
branches of African people: not only those who went down the Nile to Egypt
but also those who followed the Congo, which "passed and rose red and
reeking in the sunlight—thundered to the sea—thundered through the sea in
one long line of blood, with tossing limbs and echoing cries of pain." The
Children of the Moon symbolized not only the ancient Ethiopians but
twentieth-century Afro-Americans as well. And the moon goddess is no
more Isis than she is the afflicted womanhood of Harlem.

The tedious tower building in "Children of the Moon" parallels the tower
building in "Star of Ethiopia." "Hear ye, hear ye! All them that dwell by the
Rivers of Waters and in the beautiful, the Valley of Shadows, and listen to the
ending of this tale. Learn Sisters and Brothers, how above the Fear of God,
Labor doth build on Knowledge; how Justice tempers Science and how Beauty
shall be crowned in Love beneath the Cross. Listen, O Isles, for all the pageant
returns in dance and song to build this Tower of Eternal Light beneath the
Star." The Tower of Eternal Light, built in "Star of Ethiopia," like the tower
that the Children of the Moon build is reminiscent of Obelisk, which the
Egyptians saw as representing a petrified sun's ray. It leads upward towards the
sun, for which the Egyptians used the symbol of a winged disk. In 1911, an
adaption of the symbol, in which the solar disk is replaced by the face of a black
man, was printed on the cover of the *Crisis*, the official organ of the National
Association for the Advancement of Colored People, edited by Du Bois. The
black face surrounded by wings is, of course, the terrible vision that the goddess
finally approaches in "Children of the Moon." The wings are the wings of
Ethiopia, mentioned by Isaiah in one of Du Bois's favorite Biblical passages:

Ah! Land of the buzzing wings
Which lies beyond the rivers of Ethiopia,
That sends ambassadors by sea,
In papyrus vessels on the face of the waters:
To a nation tall and sleek,
To a nation dreaded near and far,
To a nation strong and triumphant.

The narrator climbs the Tower up to the sun in much the same way that Isis ascended the heavens, when only a woman, to force the Sun God to unveil his secrets. To lift the veil of Isis is to read the meaning of some obscure riddle. Proclus, the Greek Neoplatonic philosopher, describes a statute of Isis bearing the following inscription: "I am that which is, has been, and shall be. My veil no one has lifted. The fruit I bore was the Sun." What lies behind the veil of this poem? What does the woman see when the wings unveil the face? Perhaps she sees the face of blazing blackness, the eclipse of the West. Perhaps she sees her own reflection, the face of Isis, the African, "Star of Ethiopia, All-Mother of Men, who gave the world the Iron Gift of Faith, the Pain of Humility and Sorrow Song of Pain, and Freedom, Eternal Freedom, underneath the Star." Du Bois's poetry often unveils the face of a black god as in the story of the King in the land of the Heavy Laden, who summons his only loyal servant, a woman, to go forth in battle against "the heathen." Smiling, the King commands:

> "Go smite me mine enemies, that they cease to do evil in my sight. . . ."
> "Oh King," she cried, "I am but a woman."
> And the King answered: "Go, then, Mother of Men."
> And the woman said, "Nay, King, but I am still a maid."
> Whereat the King cried: "O maid, made Man, thou shalt be Bride of God."
> And yet the third time the woman shrank back at the thunder in her ears, and whispered: "Dear God, I am black!"
> The king spake not, but swept the veiling of his face aside and lifted up the light of his countenance upon her and lo! it was black.
> So the woman went forth on the hills of God to do battle for the King, on that drear day in the land of the Heavy Laden, when the heathen raged and imagined a vain thing.

The King is a personification of God, it seems clear; like the "Thing of Wings," he is a veiled godhead. The "Thing of Wings," finally seen as "the blazing blackness / Of one veiled Face," is also a black God. The veil is not only a barrier; it is a symbol of the challenge that this barrier provides. Blackness, or the veil, stands between black folk and the full promise of America, but the veil will be put aside for those who are brave enough to see what lies beyond it. In other words, as Ralph Ellison put it, "Black will make you, or black will un-make you."

The veil is often but not always symbolic of black skin. It represents the limits within which the souls of black folk are confined, but veils also represent the limitations that white folk have placed upon their own vision. Possibly Du Bois borrowed the image from Thomas Jefferson, who spoke of "that immovable veil of black which covers all the emotions of the [black] race." But Du Bois gives things an ironic twist by persistently insisting that the veil is a gift that, like an infant's caul, endows its bearer with second sight.

Du Bois was fascinated by mystic symbolism. As Kelly Miller observed, he was poetic, "his mind being cast in a weird and fantastic mold." He enjoyed ritual, as he tells us himself, in describing his solitary twenty-fifth birthday celebration: "The night before I had heard Schubert's beautiful Unfinished Symphony, planned my celebration and written to Grandma and Mabel and had a curious little ceremony with candles, Greek wine, oil, and song and prayer." The mysticism of the Sphinx seems to have had real meaning for him as it has had, not only for Garveyites, but for the middle-class Africans and Afro-Americans who have pledged secret societies. Charles Wesley's official *History of Alpha Phi Alpha* recognizes the tendency of middle-class blacks to experiment with the Ethiopian tradition in poetry.

> Ask not culture for self alone;
> Let thy brother share thy gain.
> Perfect self is not our aim, but
> Homage to God, love for brother
> And high o'er all, the Ethiopian.
>   J. H. Boags and R. H. Ogle, 1909

> Mighty Sphinx in Egypt standing
> Facing Eastward toward the sun.
> Glorified and e'er commanding
> Your children bravely on.
> Be to us a bond of union
> Held fast by Peace and Right.
> . . . .
> Ethiopia Home of Sages
> Thou art still our noblest pride
> We, thy sons, through future ages
> Will take thee for our guide
> Trusting through thy bondless wisdom
> To reach virtue's supernal heights.
>   W. A. Scott, 1915

Such poetry allows an identification with symbols of stability, permanency, and high culture. English-speaking, middle-class Afro-Americans during the late Victorian and Edwardian periods needed an opportunity to be proud of their Africanness, just as Garveyites would a decade later.

Du Bois's Ethiopianism was really typical of the thinking of black middle-class intellectuals during the first two decades of the twentieth century. Of course, Du Bois was in a position to encourage Ethiopianism by publishing the verse of young poets who were interested in the tradition. Langston Hughes's poem, "The Negro Speaks of Rivers," often reprinted with the dedication, "To W.E.B. Du Bois," first appeared in the *Crisis* of June, 1921, and was possibly inspired by Du Bois's "The Story of Africa," which appeared in that same journal some seven years earlier. The similarities are, in any case, striking.

Thus is it possible to speak of at least one black literary tradition, the "Ethiopian," borrowing a term from Afro-Atlantic political studies and adding it to American literary history. This tradition is manifested in the work of major poets, minor poets, and unsophisticated versifiers. It rested upon a view of history as outlined in Walker's *Appeal* and stated more calmly in such essays as Alexander Crummell's "The Destined Superiority of the Negro." W.E.B. Du Bois is the central figure in this tradition. The most traditional of Afro-American poets, he was yet the most innovative within the tradition. There is a difference in degree of sophistication—but not in sentiment expressed—between Du Bois's "Riddle of the Sphinx" and the following lines by Marcus Garvey:

> Out of cold old Europe these white men came,
> From caves, dens and holes, without any fame,
> Eating their dead's flesh and sucking their blood,
> Relics of the Mediterranean flood.

Whether there are other Afro-American literary traditions and what, if any, effects the content of Afro-American literature may have had upon the forms employed must be the subject of future studies.

Can Du Bois the social scientist be reconciled with Du Bois the poet and prophet of race? How could a man so well trained in social science have allowed the Ethiopian tradition, rooted in nineteenth-century *Volksgeist* mythologies, to dominate his thought?

As a youth Du Bois was romantically involved with the idea of social science, which he naively believed might yield a science of racial advancement. He was infatuated, like many other young men of his generation with the notion of a "science of man." But Du Bois's theories of social change were not always consistent. Sociology became relatively less important with the passage of years until by 1910 it was no longer Du Bois's chief concern. Though he was capable of writing perfectly good sociology, it does not appear that he wanted to. He turned—and it would seem with more satisfactory results—to the power of imagination as his chief instrument for changing public morality. He became a crusading journalist, a novelist, and a poet of Ethiopianism, dedicated to embodying his view of history in mythical form.

ARNOLD RAMPERSAD

W.E.B. Du Bois as a Man of Literature

What Henry James wrote of Nathaniel Hawthorne is equally true of W.E.B. Du Bois: "our author," James wrote, "must accept the awkward as well as the graceful side of his fame; for he has the advantage of pointing a valuable moral." Hawthorne's moral was that "the flower of art blooms only where the soil is deep, that it takes a great deal of history to produce a little literature, that it needs a complex social machinery to set a writer in motion." Du Bois's reputation as a man of literature is surely the "awkward" side of such fame as he possesses, and one meaning of his awkward side is essentially the same as Hawthorne's (as James saw it), with an important difference. The flower of art will bloom only where there is liberty or the memory of liberty. Du Bois understood the need for justice in the growth of the flower of art: "The time has not yet come," he wrote in 1913, "for the great development of American Negro literature. The economic stress is too great and the racial persecution too bitter to allow the leisure and the poise for which literature calls." Or, as James went on in the famous passage about Hawthorne, "American civilization has hitherto had other things to do than to produce flowers. . . ."

The other, more graceful sides of Du Bois's reputation vary with the attitude of each observer but rest somewhere in his pioneering and persisting works of history and sociology and his decades of crusading journalism

From *American Literature* 51, no. 1 (March 1979). © 1979 by Duke University Press.

against neoslavery in the South and in some respects similar oppression in the North. Trained at Fisk, Harvard, and the University of Berlin, he produced essays, monographs, and books of history and sociology that gave him by themselves the most prominent place among black American thinkers, so that the NAACP could write with justification in 1934 that "he created, what never existed before, a Negro intelligentsia, and many who have not read a word of his writings are his spiritual disciples and descendants." Certainly of Afro-American writers and the Afro-American theme one may claim of Du Bois what has been written of the English sociologists Sidney and Beatrice Webb—that every creative writer who has touched on the field of sociology has, directly or indirectly, been influenced by them.

But Du Bois ventured into the field of belles-lettres. And not by accident but as part of the plan of his life. On his twenty-fifth birth-night (1893) he confided solemnly to his journal that "these are my plans: to make a name in science, to make a name in art and thus to raise my race." A bibliography of his writings runs to some two thousand entries, out of which it is difficult to separate those completely untouched by his love of art. But there are poems enough for a slender volume, a multitude of partly personal, impressionistic essays, some verse drama, autobiographies, five novels— including a trilogy composed near his ninetieth birthday. Great reputations have been made of a smaller volume of writing, but most of this work has contributed little to Du Bois's fame. Indeed, his basic competence as a man of literature has been challenged. An angry Claude McKay, singed by a Du Bois review of his first novel, informed him that "nowhere in your writings do you reveal any comprehension of aesthetics." The poet, novelist, and critic Arna Bontemps thought Du Bois unimaginative in that he leaned toward "the tidy, the well-mannered, the Victorian" in his choice of literature. His first biographer Francis Broderick barely mentioned this belletristic writing and declared that Du Bois wanted "a literature of uplift in the genteel tradition." His second biographer, Elliott M. Rudwick, mentions the creative work not at all. And though Du Bois called his second novel "my favorite book" among the two dozen or more he published, a major historian of the black novel in America dismissed him as a "Philistine."

Du Bois himself did not show great pride in this aspect of his work; he was apologetic on the very few occasions he wrote of his efforts in literature. His first novel was "really an economic study of some merit"—the sum total of his commentary on the work; he was hesitant to write "mere" autobiography; *Dark Princess* was his favorite book but that remark is all he ever ventured about the novel; his poems were "tributes to Beauty, unworthy to stand alone." Nor was he always complimentary about actual achievement in black literature. In 1913 he saw the body as "large and creditable [though] only here and there work that could be called first-class." In 1915 a five-point plan for the future of the race included "a revival of art and literature," presumably moribund. In 1926, surveying the field for the *Encyclopedia Britannica* he judged that "all these things are beginnings rather than fulfillments," though they were certainly significant beginnings. In 1933 he mourned that the so-called "Harlem Renaissance" had "never taken real and lasting root" and that "on such an artificial basis no real literature can grow." Somewhere around 1960 one of his fictional characters looked in vain for recent work of major artistic quality: "In the last decade we have not produced a poem or a novel, a history or play of stature—nothing but gamblers, prizefighters and jazz. . . . Once we could hear Shakespeare in Harlem."

But with these splashings of cold water there was an equally cool and lucid sense of the potential of black writing, so that Du Bois could write in April 1920 that "a renaissance of American Negro literature is due," and observe in the decade that followed, almost from the day of his prediction, the accuracy of his insight. Nor is there any lack of evidence that Du Bois was highly regarded as a man of literature, from the early praise of William and Henry James and the reverence in which he was held by black poets such as James Weldon Johnson and Langston Hughes, to the radical socialist magazine *The Messenger*, which in 1919 damned Du Bois with praise of him as "the leading litterateur of the race." But more important than testimonies is a survey of his somewhat motley collection of essays, poems, novels, and other work for the ways in which he helped to shape modern Afro-American writing. For Du Bois, maturing in the most repressive period of black American history, took unto himself the primary responsibility of the would-be mythmaker, applying a luminous imagination and intelligence to "Adam's task, of giving names to things." It is only slight exaggeration to say that wherever the Afro-American subsequently went as a writer, Du Bois had been there before him, anticipating both the most vital ideas of later currency and the very tropes of their expression. Some of these anticipations are slighter than others, but none is trivial to anyone who knows black literature. Collectively they underscore Du Bois's significance and raise challenging questions about the relationship of politics, art, and the individual imagination.

If free verse became the basic medium of black poetry—and it did—Du Bois was, as far as I know, the first black poet publicly to break with rhyme and blank verse in "A Litany of Atlanta." The theme of Africa as a proper and necessary object of black celebration was introduced into black verse by Du Bois in his "Day in Africa." He was the first to celebrate the beauty of human blackness in his "Song of the Smoke." "The Burden of Black Women" is the first published poem to dwell on hatred as the consequence of the white destruction of crucial institutions, particularly marriage and motherhood, in black culture. Du Bois was the first black poet simultaneously to love trees and turn his back on what Nikki Gioivanni called "tree poems"—the first, in other words, to resist the concept of poetry as escape from social and political reality. If *Native Son* dramatized the black capacity for violent protest and in so doing, as Irving Howe claimed, changed American culture "forever," Du Bois's John Jones in 1903 and Matthew Towns in 1928 had struck earlier blows against white Americans long before Bigger rebelled. Arthur P. Davis has noted that in *The Quest of the Silver Fleece* Du Bois ended the poisonous reign of near-white heroines in black fiction with his characterization of Zora; the novel is the first *Bildungsroman* in Afro-American fiction, as Addison Gayle points out, and the first black novel to present and analyze economics as a significant factor in American culture in the significant manner of Cable, Dreiser, and Dos Passos. In its portrait of the manipulative Carolyn Wynn Du Bois published in 1911 the first truly psychological study of a character in black fiction—not, as Robert Bone argues, the hero of Johnson's *The Autobiography of an Ex-Colored Man* (1912). *Dark Princess* (1928) is the first work of art, as far as I know, to identify and promulgate the doctrine of the third world.

And when Du Bois wrote in the *Atlantic Monthly* in 1897 of the "Strivings of the Negro People" and declared the irrevocable twoness of the black American, he laid the foundation of all future literary renditions of the subject. True to his gift he both analyzed and simultaneously provided the metaphor appropriate to his analysis. The metaphor was the Veil, anticipatory of the central image of Ellison's *Invisible Man*, for "the Negro is a sort of seventh son, born with a veil, and gifted with second sight in this American world—a world which yields him no true self-consciousness, but only lets him see himself through the revelation of the other world." The crucial analysis followed: "It is a peculiar sensation, this double-consciousness, this sense of always looking at one's self through the eyes of others, of measuring one's soul by the tape of a world that looks on in amused contempt and pity. One ever feels his twoness,—an American, a Negro; two souls, two thoughts, two unreconciled strivings; two warring ideals in one dark body, whose dogged strength alone keeps it from being torn asunder."

If one excludes from consideration a personal desire for fame, there are perhaps four important aspects to Du Bois's enormous concern with the development of black literature in America—and his own part in it (he understood by the middle of his teenage years that—as he told Barrett Wendell at Harvard in 1890,—he had "something to say to the world" and was determined to prepare himself "in order to say it well"). First, Du Bois believed that the production of a body of great literature and other art was the necessary basis for the entrance of Afro-America into the polity of civilized peoples, a notion based on the concept of distinct racial "gifts" then accepted by a host of scientists and social observers attempting to understand the meaning of race. He argued in 1926 that "until the art of the black folk compels recognition they will not be rated as human" (he might have argued instead that until they were rated as human, their art would not be appreciated). He believed, following the line of the more liberal sociologists and anthropologists (but using, nevertheless, the concepts of the same highly suspect racial science) that "the Negro is primarily an artist," though he knew that "the usual way of putting this is to speak disdainfully of his sensuous nature."

Secondly, Du Bois unquestionably saw the art of literature as important in the almost one-sided war of propaganda waged against the black at the turn of the century in books such as Charles Carroll's *The Negro a Beast* (1900), Shufeldt's *The Negro: A Menace to American Civilization* (1907), and Thomas Dixon, Jr.'s *The Leopard's Spots* (1902) and *The Clansman* (1905), the latter filmed eventually by D. W. Griffith as *Birth of a Nation*. But if he declared in 1926 that "all art is propaganda and ever must be, despite the wailing of the purists," he also repeatedly defended the need for candor and artistic freedom. Any mention of black life in America, he noted, had caused for a hundred years "an ugly picture, a dirty allusion, a nasty comment or a pessimistic forecast. The result is that the Negro today," he wrote in 1924 in defense of Eugene O'Neill, "fears any attempt of the artist to paint Negroes. He is not satisfied unless everything is perfect and proper and beautiful and joyful and hopeful . . . lest his human foibles and shortcomings be seized by his enemies for the purposes of the ancient and hateful propaganda." Du Bois knew of black folk, as he wrote two years later, that "we can afford the Truth. White folk today cannot." The black should be set before the world, he wrote in 1915, "as both a creative artist and a strong subject for artistic treatment." But it is important to insist that Du Bois was no part of the clamor by certain middle-class and aristocratic members of the black intelligentsia for a literature set in the middle-class, to show whites that some blacks, at least, were capable of refinement—although it was a call in which his sometime (1919–1926) literary editor on *The Crisis*, Jessie Fauset, was partly complicitous, and with which he appeared to some observers to be in agreement.

Thirdly, Du Bois sought out the power of art because of an increasing sense of the limitation of empirical social science and academic historiography. In 1896 he could congratulate himself on complying with

"the general principles laid down in German universities" when he prepared
his first book, on the African slave trade; in *The Philadelphia Negro* (1899) he
intoned that the social scientist "must ever tremble lest some personal bias,
some moral conviction or some unconscious trend of thought due to
previous training, has to a degree distorted the picture in his view." But
under the pressure of grave social forces he had already begun to doubt—as
he stated in 1898—that empirical research into society would "eventually
lead to a systematic body of knowledge deserving the name of science." In
1903 he deplored the tendency of inferior sociology to lapse into "bad
metaphysics and false psychology"; the next year he declared that sociologists
were "still only groping after a science." The goals of social research, and his
methods and approaches, became less scholarly, more political, more
imaginative. A volume of social study published by him in 1906 did not seek
"definite conclusions. Its object is rather to blaze the way and point out a few
general truths."

And fourthly, Du Bois's turn toward art was empowered by perhaps the
central factor of his overall career—his perception of the need for action, not
subservience or contemplation, in the face of American racism. The growth
of Du Bois's practice of art coincided with the growth of his political
activism, beginning with his return to the South as an adult in 1897 and
reaching its first decisive point with his 1903 challenge to the authority of
Booker T. Washington, the most powerful black leader of the age. From this
step eventually came Du Bois's founding of the radical Niagara Movement
(radical in its demands of civil rights and other basic freedoms), and his
leadership of the movement in the years between 1905 and 1910, when he
felt professionally the weight of Booker T. Washington's antagonism. This
period ended with his departure from the university for the fledgling
NAACP in 1910, to become editor of its crusading monthly magazine *The
Crisis*. His turn to art in the course of these thirteen or so years was not for
relief from the hurly-burly of political action but was an aspect of political
action itself. And such achievements in form and theme as he accomplished
are testimony, in the context of black American literature, to the acuteness of
Lukács's observation that "new styles, new ways of representing reality,
though always linked to old forms and styles, never arise from any immanent
dialectic within artistic forms. Every new style is socially and historically
determined and is the product of a social development."

For it is clear that Du Bois showed no great potential for achievement
in art much beyond skilled mediocrity and imitativeness until he experienced
the goad of Southern racism. He showed very little interest in the discussion
of theoretical issues pertaining to art and the process of imagination and
literary creation. His pronouncements on literature are generally negligible

in depth and scope; one must recover, from observation of his literary practice, the factors that pertained to his performance as a man of literature. And what empowered Du Bois as an Afro-American mythmaker and distinguished him from more superficially gifted and involved artists was a combination of great intellect, greater energy, and—above all—a capacity for feeling the political experience so intensely that its purposes were subsumed, as it were, into every fibre of his intellectual being at least as intensely as the famous poet contemplating the sparrow in the gravel; and allowing that intensity to inspire art and scholarship out of imitation and mediocrity and into the world of action.

Du Bois himself dated the time of his turn toward action. The year was 1897. With his doctoral thesis published as the first volume in the Harvard Historical Studies and the research completed for perhaps his greatest work of scholarship, *The Philadelphia Negro*, he set out to create the mechanism for a one-hundred-year empirical study of black life divided into ten great subjects, each subject the focus of study for one year, every ten years the cycle repeating itself. His base was the classroom and his study at Atlanta University. Du Bois recollected how he came to change the basic course of his life:

> At the very time when my studies were most successful, there cut across this plan which I had as a scientist, a red ray which could not be ignored. I remember when it first, as it were, startled me to my feet: a poor Negro in central Georgia, Sam Hose, had killed his landlord's wife. I wrote out a careful and reasoned statement concerning the evident facts and started down to the Atlanta *Constitution* office, carrying in my pocket a letter of introduction to Joel Chandler Harris. I did not get there. On the way news met me: Sam Hose had been lynched, and they said that his knuckles were on exhibition at a grocery store farther down on Mitchell Street, along which I was walking. I turned back to the University. I began to turn aside from my work. I did not meet Joel Chandler Harris nor the editor of the *Constitution*.

The impact on his art of this heightened degree of Du Bois's understanding of the meaning of action, power, and the political was firm and accruing, but also gradual and sometimes wayward. For he embarked on this radical passage without any congeries of beliefs that might be called ideology in any strict sense of the term; indeed, he proceeded with two biases that on one level appeared to contradict each other as well as ideology itself, but which were, on another, more functional level, its surrogates. First, he retained his respect for empirical sociology and academic historiography; secondly, he deepened his racial or nationalistic commitment to the black folk of America, laying the foundation and developing the basic dialectical superstructure for all subsequent black nationalist pleading. Simultaneously he suppressed the socialist methodology he had learned as a student in Germany, though by the end of the first decade of the century he would identify himself as a quasi-socialist, and then briefly join the American Socialist Party. Socialist analysis—socialist fervor—was resisted both by scholarship as he understood its demands and by the exclusive tendencies of black nationalism. But Du Bois's black nationalism was further tempered by the fact that the essence of his politics was his demand for the *integration* of black into American society, a demand that took precedence as an idea and as a shaper myth and image over the insistent nationalism that formed the basis of his argument that blacks should enjoy all the rights of the typical American citizen.

The absence of an ideologically consistent core of beliefs—the presence of this noble confusion—encouraged Du Bois to develop, especially in his essays between 1897 and 1903 (when *The Souls of Black Folk* appeared) a dazzling variety of metaphoric, ironic, pietistic, and sentimental rhetorical strategies appropriate to liberal intellection and liberal discourse. Much later in life, essentially a communist without a party card, Du Bois regretted that too much sentiment and moralizing, too little Marx and Freud, had informed his early work. The evidence is there, though, that he was aware of a problem even as he wrote. In 1904, writing about *The Souls of Black Folk*, he innocently admitted "the style and workmanship" of his book did not make its meaning altogether clear, that the collection conveyed "a clear message" but that around this center floated "a penumbra" of subjectivity, vagueness, and half-veiled allusions. "In its larger aspects," he said, groping to understand what he had wrought, "the style is tropical—African."

The aching ideological contradictions—in other words, the *charm* of these moving and important early essays—gave way to more rigid ideas and forms. The next collection of essays, *Darkwater: Voices from Within the Veil* (1920), would draw the wish from one reviewer, a longtime acquaintance of Du Bois, that the author would walk "more in the manner of the Nazarene." Here and in *The Negro* (1915), a survey of the African peoples on the continent and elsewhere, there is a disjunction between analysis and art, as there is in the many dramatized editorials that gave bite to the *Crisis* magazine. Du Bois had consciously become, as he admitted, a propagandist. While it is partly true that with the publication of *The Negro* Du Bois became, as Wilson Moses put it, "a poet of Ethiopianism, dedicated to embodying his view of history in mythical form," no significant formal poetry emerged from this aspect of his writing; he essentially preserved the approach to historiography of writers like Macaulay and Carlyle, for whom the writing of history was a dramatic art. In Du Bois's grand study of the postbellum South, *Black Reconstruction in America* (1935), most of the "artistic" passages can be excised from the text without the slightest modification of the argument and spirit of the work. As a historian Du Bois was showing a certain imaginative stylistic range; as a poet, however, despite the clear passion he brought to both tasks, he seems to have been relatively uninspired.

The poetry and fiction that Du Bois wrote during his first years of radical commitment are another matter. The bulk of his significant poetry was composed during his leadership of the Niagara Movement, after his decision to join the radical ranks and before the NAACP rescued him from the wilderness of deepening alienation and confusion. The art of this period—1905 to 1910—reflects an intellectual and spiritual turmoil distinctly different from that of *The Souls of Black Folk*. The emblem of this period might well show Du Bois in anguish on a train returning to Atlanta in the last week of September 1906, uncertain of the fate of his wife and daughter, as well as of his work and the university, in the worst race riot in the South in the first decade of the century. On this train journey Du Bois wrote "A Litany of Atlanta."

> We raise out shackled hands and charge thee, God
> by the bones of our stolen fathers, by the tears
> of our dead mothers, by the very blood of Thy
> crucified Christ: What meaneth this? Tell us the
> plan; give us the sign!

"Surely," the poet asks, "thou, too, art not white, O Lord, a pale, bloodless, heartless thing!" Or is God dead? But the poet recoils from "these wild, blasphemous words":

> Thou art still the God of our black fathers and in
> Thy Soul's Soul sit some soft darkenings, some
> shadowing of the velvet night.
> But whisper—speak—call, great God, for Thy
> silence is white terror to our heart! The way, O
> God, show us the way and point us the path!

The thou's and thy's and art's should not obscure the importance of the poem, or its power, for in the fire of the political moment so replete with personal meaning Du Bois severed the ancient link between black poetry and rhyme or blank verse, as well as to the three dominant modes of Afro-American verse of the age—the poetry of social uplift by writers such as Frances E. W. Harper, the Afro-Georgian lyricism of Braithwaite, Dunbar, and others, and the immensely popular dialect tradition, with its poles of maudlin pathos, on one hand, and low comedy, on the other—"the range between appetite and emotion, with certain lifts far beyond and above it," that William Dean Howells told us is the range of the black race.

With "A Litany of Atlanta" Du Bois opened the way for a black poetry of secularism, skepticism, and cultural authenticity, a poetry that surfaced swiftly and importantly again in his own works with "Song of the Smoke," where for the first time an Afro-American poet unambiguously praised blackness of skin and the potential of the race compared to the white overlords:

> I will be black as blackness can—
> The blacker the mantle, the mightier the man!
> For blackness was ancient ere whiteness began.

And in "The Burden of Black Women," later retitled "The Riddle of the Sphinx," the hatred authentic to the black experience of life in America but anathema to the tropes of liberal discourse surfaced for the first time in published verse:

> The white world's vermin and filth:
> All the dirt of London,
> All the scum of New York
> Valiant spoilers of women
> . . . .
> Bearing the white man's burden
> Of Liquor and Lust and Lies.
> . . . .
> I hate them, Oh!
> I hate them well,
> I hate them, Christ!
> As I hate Hell,
> If I were God
> I'd sound their knell
> This day!

Not all the verse of this period, no matter how politically charged the theme, marked a significant achievement in Du Bois's efforts to poeticize the black experience and predicament. "A Day in Africa" introduces a new element into black poetical consciousness—Africa as an object of veneration for black Americans—but its ideas are confused and its language reflects this confusion:

> I leaped and danced, and found
> My breakfast poised aloft,
> All served in living gold.
> In purple flowered fields I wandered
> Wreathed in crimson, blue and green.
> My noon-tide meal did fawn about my feet
> In striped sleekness.
> I kissed it ere I killed it.

A "wild new creature" threatens the persona, who poises his spear in defiance. But the black warrior sees fear in the eyes of the animal (the white interloper in Africa) and refuses to kill it. Africa is color, freedom, sensual ease, courage, mercy. Yet the poem is an almost total failure; its form is overburdened by Du Bois's nearly absolute ignorance of his subject, Africa, whose history he had just begun to study after being awakened to its complexity by Franz Boas in 1906, when the anthropologist spoke at Atlanta University. Du Bois would not see Africa until 1923. Unlike the other three quoted poems, "A Day in Africa" is comparatively unmotivated except in the most abstract of ways. One is reminded again, first, that the apprehension of the need for action is hardly in itself ideology, and that still less is it automatically art when applied to the forms of art. The process and the difficulty of art are not abbreviated by the call to action. The firing of the radical imagination only further complicates the task of persuasion that the radical literateur undertakes. The problem of accommodating political thought within the scope of the imagination is still further subsumed into the creative writer's ultimate problem, at once commonplace and yet urgent— the problem of rhetoric.

Unable to achieve a consistent and credible equipoise between ideology and form, Du Bois found his final achievement as a poet in his position as pioneer, as bridge between often inspired imitation and later poetical authenticity in black literature. One clue to Du Bois's problems of equipoise lies in the fact that the dominant formal referent in his poetry is religion—and Du Bois, once his Congregationalist faith died, was never born again. A list of some of his titles shows his concern: A Litany of Atlanta, The Prayer of the Bantu, The Prayers of God, Hymn to the Peoples, Christ of the Andes; in addition to which he wrote parables featuring a black Christ and in other ways relied on religious constructs for intellectual deliverance. Religion in Du Bois's work has distinctly earthly correspondences; "the impenetrable meaning of human suffering matches the inscrutability of God; Christ is the incarnation of all human hope; Heaven is the world beyond the Veil; and life is Hell." And yet the use of religion is symptomatic of the poet's problems in representing ideas often in conflict with each other but striving for integration. The justification for the use of religion in this way did not come from the place of religion in Du Bois's life, or in the culture of the black folk, but from the historic role of religion in white culture. Thus Du Bois was attempting to fuse political passion within the traditional vehicles of a white spirituality whose effectiveness, indeed, whose very existence he was simultaneously calling into question. The use of the traditional vehicles gives a superficial monumentality to the tenor of his message, but a full union is not possible.

The change in Du Bois's art between the earlier essays of *The Souls of Black Folk* and the poems is reflected significantly in the distance between Du Bois's first important piece of published fiction, the short story "Of the Coming of John" in *Souls* and the later novels—but especially so in the case of his first novel *The Quest of the Silver Fleece*. In the short story a young black man leaves his small Southern town and becomes educated—and alienated from his fellow blacks, the whites, and himself; he returns home, is ostracized as a remote and possibly radical man, reacts blindly when he finds his sister struggling with a playful would-be white seducer, kills the man, and then possibly kills himself as a lynch mob closes in. In *The Quest of the Silver Fleece* a young black man discovers education, goes North to work and becomes involved in politics, almost succumbs to corruption, but returns home to rally his people in their struggle for education and a better life, prepared at the end to fight physically for their rights. In *Dark Princess* a young black man, embittered by racism, goes to Europe and becomes involved in a plot for an uprising of the darker people against white colonialism. He returns to the United States to report on the state of black culture, becomes involved in politics, almost succumbs to corruption, but is rescued in time; he atones for his sins by hard work and at the end of the novel is a changed man, dedicated to duty and willing to fight for his beliefs. In the *Black Flame* trilogy (1957, 1959, 1961) a young black man embarks on a life of service to his race as a teacher. Intellectually ungifted but patient and honorable, he is shaped in his life and career by the major events of black American history and by the culture of the South, where he lives almost all his life. He dies in the 1950's in his eighty-eighth year, witness to the first cracks in the wall of segregation but tragically uncertain of the value of his life of service. The trilogy also consistently dramatizes the major personalities and passages of his lifetime—Southern, national, international—with capitalism as the formidable villain of this complementary story, and rising socialism as its struggling hero.

The ideological shifting in the works and its effect upon form are noteworthy. In the first story, "Of the Coming of John," the central drama is the struggle between the divided souls of the young black aspirant to culture in a racist world; and in spite of the violence of murder and possible suicide, pathos—not tragedy—marks the dramatic depth of the tale. The black folk is defined by its ignorance, the white folk by its reaction. The drama takes place in a world of political stasis that immobilizes time and history; society is essentially indecipherable, and the logical inference is an encompassing pessimism. The warring souls of the black, the story seems to say, must forever war, the contradictions therein are both endemic and permanent. Black alienation follows directly from education in racist America, and is worse than inevitable or pathological—black alienation is useless. The only way out of the gloom is perhaps through the wisdom and humanity of the narrator, a nameless professor at the college attended by John; but he or she, who might well be white, is baffled and quite concerned, but impotent. The black man must endure; the world prevails.

This depiction presented Du Bois with few formal problems. But he was never again to make pathos the focus of his art or to accept pessimism as the resolution of a black fiction—not because the situation of blacks never seemed rather hopeless to him or because blacks themselves were never pessimistic, but because he developed a different sense of the functioning of the world and history and a different sense of the potential of blacks and humanity in general. From this sense derived a different sense of the moral and political function of art and a different attitude toward form. The heroes of *Quest of the Silver Fleece* and *Dark Princess* are at first baffled and confused, as John was in the first story; but the burden of their stories is the resolution of bafflement and confusion, with the end of the stories presenting morally and politically earnest heroes and heroines preparing to swim boldly in a world that is still deep but now fathomable. The process shifts from one work to another but the basic pattern is the same. The baffled, divided hero is, in a sense, *reborn* into psychological monism or harmony, which is tantamount to moral and political zeal. This rebirth comes through education both from learned books and from manual labor, reuniting body and mind, intellect and muscle, as the souls are reunited. The hero discovers the way and atones for his sins, accepting duty and work as first principles of life, with love as its crowning glory. The immoral stasis of the world in "Of the Coming of John" gives way to the exposition of culture as process, and history and the world as both scrutable and stimulant to optimism. And the

formal simplicity of the short story gives way to a formal complication that
Du Bois strove with only limited success to manage.

Writing in *The World and Africa* just after World War II about the
decline of western culture in the late nineteenth century, Du Bois deplored
the fact that "art, in building, painting and literature, became cynical and
decadent. Literature became realistic and therefore pessimistic." Though
this was written when he was very close to communism, it is consistent with
his attitudes toward fiction during the greater part of his life, or once he had
become politically alert and committed to action. Art and pessimism were,
for him, incompatible if art were to succeed. All art, he said in 1926,
attacking the "art for art's sake" movement among certain black writers, is
propaganda—and black art must be propaganda "for gaining the right of
black folk to love and enjoy." But his purpose was broader than is apparent
in such a crude statement. It was "the bounden duty of black America" to
create, preserve, and realize "Beauty" for America, for the aim of art and
political struggle was not black power in isolation but a philosophically
reconstructed universe. The tools in the creation of beauty had always been
and must be, he said, truth—"the highest hand-maid of imagination . . . the
one great vehicle of universal understanding"; and goodness, "in all its
aspects of justice, honor and right—not for sake of an ethical sanction but as
the one true method of gaining sympathy and human interest." Thus, Du
Bois went on, "the apostle of Beauty . . . becomes the apostle of Truth and
Right not by choice but by inner and outer compulsion."

These terms such as Truth and Beauty and Right are vague enough for
us to miss the order of the process Du Bois is describing, but they are
significant; indeed, they also suggest quaint ways in which he would, as a
practicing writer, oppose realism. In both *Quest of the Silver Fleece* and *Dark
Princess* (but *not* in *The Black Flame* decades after) the most terribly stilted
language surfaces during decisive emotional or philosophical moments, and
appears in the midst of otherwise conventionally mimetic dialogue and
narration that show Du Bois to have some definite ability—not mere
potential—as a novelist. But the failings of his work are there; though one
finds depth of characterization in both novels, many more of the performers
are types of humanity rather than creations credible outside of their
ideological burden in the particular piece. There is, too, a fair amount of
what one must regard as melodramatic and unsatisfying effects, notably in
the end of *Dark Princess*, where a typical masque-like scene, replete with
symbolism, supplants the otherwise sober auditing of the account. Such
effects represent Du Bois's conscious choices as an artist, and it would be a
mistake to consider them other than bad choices. They were, however,
generated by his philosophy of art and by the fact that there was but one

genre into which his story could fit. That genre was not finally the novel, which is what he called *Quest of the Silver Fleece*, or the romance, which is the way he identified *Dark Princess*, but the epic.

Epic in more than one sense—but literally so, in that the mature Du Bois fiction is the gravely serious story, recited in at times too lofty a tone and language, of a young (black) man of quality embarking on the most perilous of journeys within a grand landscape, on the success of which depends the future salvation of his race or nation—salvation on a relatively small scale in *Quest of the Silver Fleece*, on a worldwide scale in *Dark Princess*. What drove Du Bois to the epic form was that ecstatic optimism with which both novels end, an optimism that was the richest dividend of his awakened political consciousness. Applied to his writing, this optimism was compounded by his nostalgia for a vanished innocence within both a mythic Africa and humanity as a whole, by his sense of the potential of Africans and all humanity, and finally by his sense of the history of the world as the history of process. This sense enabled Du Bois to share vicariously in the intellectual and social homogeneity out of which the epic first sprang.

The realism to which Du Bois objected was close to that of such writers as Zola, the earlier Dreiser, and Frank Norris—and the differences between his sense of the epic and theirs is considerable. Their pessimism is formally exemplified in their worship of the fact, the detail, the superficial information of "that harsh, blunt, colorless tool called realism," as Norris himself put it in attempting to transcend its limitations. Du Bois had not turned his back on statistical sociology in order to create art based on accepting the surface as the substance of things; his politics did not allow him to be pessimistic; and his understanding of history and society diverted him—though not always—from those fallacies of naturalism and supernaturalism by which other writers complicated their art but betrayed their philosophical helplessness. Nor could he develop a highly symbolic art which would reflect a contemplative attitude to a mysterious universe and thus deflect the epic thrust of his socially centered narrative. There are two looming symbols in his first novel—cotton (the silver fleece of the title) and a great swamp. The swamp stands for the immoral past of the preliterate black; the best cotton grows where the swamp has been cleared, a task that requires unity and character on the part of the black folk. Thus literally one symbol is a transcendence of the other, and because the cotton is stripped of its monetary and inhuman significance and reidentified with human work and thought and character, it carries within itself as a symbol the force of its own self-transcendence, since its power as a symbol derives from its part in the world of human action.

The major formal tension in Du Bois's fiction, and the source of its major shortcomings, arises from the crucial relationship of the narration to history on one hand and to the particular, chosen moment on the other; between the depiction of historical process and the depiction of its immediate product; between—if you will—life, and the chosen slice of life. Characters fail as art when they take their total essence from history; they tend to succeed when they take their essence more from the historical moment, which is itself governed—but distantly—by history. In *The Black Flame*, hastily written as Du Bois neared death, Du Bois tried to show his understanding at last of this division. The trilogy tells two stories—the epic of history, and the counterepic or antiepic of the black hero as epiphenomenon; counterepic, because the black hero no longer triumphs in his own lifetime, but ends his life apparently inconclusively. The great achievement of this flawed work comes from the ironic interplay between the march of dialectic, crudely related, and the crawling and stumbling of humans defined by their failures as well as their modest virtues.

Du Bois claimed that his life had its significance only because he was part of the great problem of race, and that he had done little to change his day. Perhaps. Within black America, though, his achievement was incomparable. Though he never attained competence as a great poet or novelist, his efforts in those roles combine with his other works to extend our understanding of the history and character of his people and, indeed, of humanism itself. In spite of his failures as a formal artist there lingers about him more than a trace of what Lukács found in a far greater nineteenth-century writer—glimpses still of "the gloomy magnificence of primary accumulation in the field of culture."

ANTHONY APPIAH

The Uncompleted Argument: Du Bois and the Illusion of Race

Introduction

Contemporary biologists are not agreed on the question of whether there are any human races, despite the widespread scientific consensus on the underlying genetics. For most purposes, however, we can reasonably treat this issue as terminological. What most people in most cultures ordinarily believe about the significance of "racial" difference is quite remote, I think, from what the biologists *are* agreed on. Every reputable biologist will agree that human genetic variability between the populations of Africa or Europe or Asia is not much greater than that within those populations; though *how much* greater depends, in part, on the measure of genetic variability the biologist chooses. If biologists want to make interracial difference seem relatively large, they can say that "the proportion of genic variation attributable to racial differences is . . . 9–11%." If they want to make it seem small, they can say that, for two people who are both Caucasoid, the chances of difference in genetic constitution at one site on a given chromosome are currently estimated at about 14.3 percent, while for any two people taken at random from the human population, they are estimated at about 14.8 percent. (I will discuss why this is considered a measure of genetic difference in section 2.) The

From *Critical Inquiry* 12, no. 1 (Autumn 1985). © 1985 by The University of Chicago.

statistical facts about the distribution of variant characteristics in human populations and subpopulations are the same, whichever way the matter is expressed. Apart from the visible morphological characteristics of skin, hair, and bone, by which we are inclined to assign people to the broadest racial categories—black, white, yellow—there are few genetic characteristics to be found in the population of England that are not found in similar proportions in Zaire or in China; and few too (though more) which are found in Zaire but not in similar proportions in China or in England. All this, I repeat, is part of the consensus. A more familiar part of the consensus is that the differences between peoples in language, moral affections, aesthetic attitudes, or political ideology—those differences which most deeply affect us in our dealings with each other—are not biologically determined to any significant degree.

These claims will, no doubt, seem outrageous to those who confuse the question of whether biological difference accounts for our differences with the question of whether biological similarity accounts for our similarities. Some of our similarities as human beings in these broadly cultural respects—the capacity to acquire human languages, for example, or, more specifically, the ability to smile—*are* to a significant degree biologically determined. We can study the biological basis of these cultural capacities and give biological explanations of our exercise of them. But if biological difference between human beings is unimportant in these explanations—and it is—then racial difference, as a species of biological difference, will not matter either.

In this essay, I want to discuss the way in which W.E.B. Du Bois—who called his life story the "autobiography of a race concept"—came gradually, though never completely, to assimilate the unbiological nature of races. I have made these few prefatory remarks partly because it is my experience that the biological evidence about race is not sufficiently known and appreciated but also because they are important in discussing Du Bois. Throughout his life, Du Bois was concerned not just with the meaning of race but with the truth about it. We are more inclined at present, however, not to express our understanding of the intellectual development of people and cultures as a movement toward the truth; I shall sketch some of the reasons for this at the end of the essay. I will begin, therefore, by saying what I think the rough truth is about race, because, against the stream, I am disposed to argue that this struggle toward the truth is exactly what we find in the life of Du Bois, who can claim, in my view, to have thought longer, more engagedly, and more publicly about race than any other social theorist of our century.

"The Conservation of Races"

Du Bois's first extended discussion of the concept of race is in "The Conservation of Races" (1897), a paper he delivered to the American Negro Academy in the year it was founded. The "American Negro," he declares, has "been led to . . . minimize race distinctions" because "back of most of the discussions of race with which he is familiar, have lurked certain assumptions as to his natural abilities, as to his political, intellectual and moral status, which he felt were wrong." Du Bois continues: "Nevertheless, in our calmer moments we must acknowledge that human beings are divided into races," even if when we "come to inquire into the essential difference of races we find it hard to come at once to any definite conclusion." For what it is worth, however, the "final word of science, so far, is that we have at least two, perhaps three, great families of human beings—the whites and Negroes, possibly the yellow race."

Du Bois is not, however, satisfied with the final word of nineteenth-century science. For, as he thinks, what matter are not the "grosser physical differences of color, hair and bone" but the "differences—subtle, delicate and elusive, though they may be—which have silently but definitely separated men into groups."

> While these subtle forces have generally followed the natural cleavage of common blood, descent and physical peculiarities, they have at other times swept across and ignored these. At all times, however, they have divided human beings into races, which, while they perhaps transcend scientific definition, nevertheless, are clearly defined to the eye of the historian and sociologist.
>
> If this be true, then the history of the world is the history, not of individuals, but of groups, not of nations, but of races. . . . What, then, is a race? It is a vast family of human beings, generally of common blood and language, always of common history, traditions and impulses, who are both voluntarily and involuntarily striving together for the accomplishment of certain more or less vividly conceived ideals of life.

We have moved, then, away from the "scientific"—that is, biological and anthropological—conception of race to a sociohistorical notion. Using this sociohistorical criterion—the sweep of which certainly encourages the thought that no biological or anthropological definition is possible—Du Bois considers that there are not three but eight "distinctly differentiated races, in the sense in which history tells us the word must be used." The list is an odd one: Slavs, Teutons, English (both in Great Britain and America), Negroes (of Africa and, likewise, America), the Romance race, Semites, Hindus and Mongolians.

> The question now is: What is the real distinction between these nations? Is it the physical differences of blood, color and cranial measurements? Certainly we must all acknowledge that physical differences play a great part. . . . But while race differences have followed mainly physical race lines, yet no mere physical distinctions would really define or explain the deeper differences— the cohesiveness and continuity of these groups. The deeper differences are spiritual, psychical, differences—undoubtedly based on the physical, but infinitely transcending them.

Each of the various races is

> striving, . . . in its own way, to develop for civilization its particular message, its particular ideal, which shall help to guide the world nearer and nearer that perfection of human life for which we all long, that "one far off Divine event."

For Du Bois, then, the problem for the Negro is the discovery and expression of the message of his or her race.

> The full, complete Negro message of the whole Negro race has not as yet been given to the world.
> The question is, then: how shall this message be delivered; how shall these various ideals be realized? The answer is plain: by the development of these race groups, not as individuals, but as races. . . . For the development of Negro genius, of Negro literature and art, of Negro spirit, only Negroes bound and welded together, Negroes inspired by one vast ideal, can work out in its fullness the great message we have for humanity.
> For this reason, the advance guard of the Negro people—the eight million people of Negro blood in the United States of America—must soon come to realize that if they are to take their just place in the van of Pan-Negroism, then their destiny is *not* absorption by the white Americans.

Du Bois ends by proposing his Academy Creed, which begins with words that echo down almost a century of American race relations:

1. We believe that the Negro people, as a race, have a contribution to make to civilization and humanity, which no other race can make.

2. We believe it the duty of the Americans of Negro descent, as a body, to maintain their race identity until this mission of the Negro people is accomplished, and the ideal of human brotherhood has become a practical possibility.

What can we make of this analysis and prescription?

On the face of it, Du Bois' argument in "The Conservation of Races" is that "race" is not a scientific—that is, biological—concept. It is a sociohistorical concept. Sociohistorical races each have a "message" for humanity—a message which derives, in some way, from God's purpose in creating races. The Negro race has still to deliver its full message, and so it is the duty of Negroes to work together—through race organizations—so that this message can be delivered.

We do not need the theological underpinnings of this argument. What is essential is the thought that through common action Negroes can achieve, by virtue of their sociohistorical community, worthwhile ends which will not otherwise be achieved. On the face of it, then, Du Bois' strategy here is the antithesis in the classic dialectic of reaction to prejudice.

The thesis in this dialectic—which Du Bois reports as the American Negro's attempt to "minimize race distinctions"—is the denial of difference. Du Bois' antithesis is the acceptance of difference, along with a claim that each group has its part to play; that the white race and its racial Other are related not as superior to inferior but as complementaries; that the Negro message is, with the white one, part of the message of humankind.

I call this pattern the classic dialectic for a simple reason: we find it in feminism also—on the one hand, a simple claim to equality, a denial of substantial difference; on the other, a claim to a special message, revaluing the feminine Other not as the helpmeet of sexism, but as the New Woman.

Because this *is* a classic dialectic, my reading of Du Bois' argument is a natural one. I believe that it is substantially correct. But to see that it is correct, we need to make clear that what Du Bois attempts, despite his own claims to the contrary, is not the transcendence of the nineteenth-century scientific conception of race—as we shall see, he relies on it—but rather, as the dialectic requires, a revaluation of the Negro race in the face of the sciences of racial inferiority. We can begin by analyzing the sources of tension in Du Bois' allegedly sociohistorical conception of race, which he explicitly sets over against the scientific conception. The tension is plain enough in his references to "common blood"; for this, dressed up with fancy craniometry, a dose of melanin, and some measure for hair-curl, is what the scientific notion amounts to. If he has fully transcended the scientific notion, what is the role of this talk about "blood"?

We may leave aside for the moment the common "impulses" and the voluntary and involuntary "strivings." These must be due either to a shared biological inheritance, "based on the physical, but infinitely transcending" it; to a shared history; or, of course, to some combination of these. If Du Bois' notion is purely sociohistorical, then the issue is common history and traditions; otherwise, the issue is, at least in part, a common biology. We shall know which only when we understand the core of Du Bois' conception of race.

The claim that a race generally shares a common language is also plainly inessential: the "Romance" race is not of common language nor, more obviously, is the Negro. And "common blood" can mean little more than "of shared ancestry," which is already implied by talk of a "vast family." At the center of Du Bois' conception, then, is the claim that a race is "a vast family of human beings, . . . always of common history [and] traditions." So, if we want to understand Du Bois, our question must be: What is a family of common history?

We already see that the scientific notion, which presupposes common features in virtue of a common biology derived from a common descent, is not fully transcended. A family can, it is true, have adopted children, kin by social rather than biological law. By analogy, therefore, a vast human family might contain people joined not by biology but by an act of choice. But it is plain that Du Bois cannot have been contemplating this possibility: like all of his contemporaries, he would have taken for granted that race is a matter of birth. Indeed, to understand the talk of "family," we must distance ourselves from its sociological meaning. A family is almost always culturally defined only through either patrilineal or matrilineal descent. But if an individual drew a "conceptual" family tree back over five hundred years and assumed that he or she was descended from each ancestor in only one way, it would have more than a million branches at the top. Although, in such a case, many individuals would be represented by more than one branch—that far back we are all going to be descended from many people by more than one route—it is plain that either a matrilineal or patrilineal conception of our family histories drastically underrepresents the biological range of our ancestry. Biology and social convention go startlingly different ways. Let's pretend, secure in our republicanism, that the claim of the queen of England to the throne depends partly on a single line from one of her ancestors nine hundred years ago. If there were no overlaps in her family tree, there would be more than fifty thousand billion such lines, though there have never been that many people on the earth; even with reasonable assumptions about overlaps, there are millions of such lines. We chose one line, even though most of the population of England is probably descended from William the Conqueror by *some* uncharted route. Biology is democratic: all parents are equal. Thus, to speak of two people as being of common ancestry requires that, before some historical point in the past, a large proportion of the branches in their respective family trees coincided.

Already, then, Du Bois requires, as the scientific conception does, a common ancestry (in the sense just defined) with whatever—if anything—that ancestry biologically entails. But apparently this does not commit him to the scientific conception, for there are many groups of common ancestry—ranging from humanity in general to narrower groups such as the Slavs, Teutons, and Romance people taken together—which do not, for Du Bois, constitute races. Thus, Du Bois' "common history," which must be what is supposed to distinguish Slav from Teuton, is an essential part of his conception. The problem is whether a common history can be a criterion which distinguishes one group of human beings—extended in time—from another. Does adding a notion of common history allow us to make the distinctions between Slav and Teuton or between English and Negro? The answer is no.

Consider, for example, Du Bois himself. As the descendant of Dutch ancestors, why doesn't his relation to the history of Holland in the fourteenth century (which he shares with all people of Dutch descent) make him a member of the Teutonic race? The answer is straightforward: the Dutch were not Negroes; Du Bois is. But it follows from this that the history of Africa is part of the common history of Afro-Americans not simply because Afro-Americans descended from various peoples who played a part in African history but rather because African history is the history of people of the same race.

My general point is this: in order to recognize two events at different times as part of the history of a single individual, we have to have a criterion for identity of the individual at each of those times, independent of his or her participation in the two events. In the same way, when we recognize two events as belonging to the history of one race, we have to have a criterion for membership in the race at those two times, independent of the participation of the members in the two events. To put it more simply: sharing a common group history cannot be a criterion for being members of the same group, for we would have to be able to identify the group in order to identify *its* history. Someone in the fourteenth century could share a common history with me through our membership in a historically extended race only if something accounts both for his or her membership in the race in the fourteenth century and for mine in the twentieth. That something cannot, on pain of circularity, be the history of race. Whatever holds Du Bois' races together conceptually cannot be a common history; it is only because they are bound together that members of a race at different times can share a history at all. If this is true, Du Bois' reference to a common history cannot be doing any work in his individuation of races. And once we have stripped away the sociohistorical elements from Du Bois' definition of race, we are left with the true criterion.

Consequently, not only the talk of language, which Du Bois admits is neither necessary (the Romance race speaks many languages) nor sufficient (Afro-Americans and Americans generally speak the same language) for racial identity, must be expunged from the definition; now we have seen that talk of common history and traditions must go too. We are left with common descent and the common impulses and strivings that I put aside earlier. Since common descent and the characteristics which flow from it are part of the scientific conception of race, these impulses are all that remain to do the job that Du Bois had claimed for a sociohistorical conception: namely, to distinguish his conception from the biological one. Du Bois claims that the existence of races is "clearly defined to the eye of the historian and sociologist." Since biology acknowledges common ancestry as a criterion, whatever extra insight is provided by sociohistorical understanding can be gained only by observing the common impulses and strivings. Reflection suggests, however, that this cannot be true. For what common impulses— whether voluntary or involuntary—do the Romance people share that the Teutons and the English do not?

Du Bois had read the historiography of the Anglo-Saxon school, which accounted for the democratic impulse in America by the racial tradition of the Anglo-Saxon moot. He has read American and British historians in earnest discussion of the "Latin" spirit of Romance peoples; and perhaps he had believed some of it. Here perhaps may be the source of the notion that history and sociology can observe the differing impulses of races.

In all these writings, however, such impulses are allegedly discovered to be the a posteriori properties of racial and national groups, not criteria of membership in them. It is, indeed, because the claim is a posteriori that historical evidence is relevant to it. And if we ask what common impulses history has detected which allow us to recognize the Negro, we shall see that Du Bois' claim to have found a criterion of identity in these impulses is mere bravado. If, without evidence about his or her impulses, we can say who is a Negro, then it cannot be part of what it is to be a Negro that he or she has them; rather, it must be an a posteriori claim that people of a common race, defined by descent and biology, have impulses, for whatever reason, in common. Of course, the common impulses of a biologically defined group may be historically caused by common experiences, common history. But Du Bois' claim can only be that biologically defined races happen to share, for whatever reason, common impulses. The common impulses cannot be a criterion of group membership. And if that is so, we are left with the scientific conception.

How, then, is it possible for Du Bois' criteria to issue in eight groups, while the scientific conception issues in three? The reason is clear from the list. Slavs, Teutons, English, Hindus, and Romance peoples each live in a characteristic geographical region. (American English—and, for that matter, American Teutons, American Slavs, and American Romance people—share recent ancestry with their European "cousins" and thus share a relation to a place and certain languages and traditions.) Semites and Mongolians each inhabit a rather larger geographical region also. Du Bois' talk of common history conceals his superaddition of a geographical criterion: group history is, in part, the history of people who have lived in the same place.

The criterion Du Bois actually uses amounts to this: people are members of the same race if they share features in virtue of being descended largely from people of the same region. Those features may be physical—hence Afro-Americans are Negroes—or cultural—hence Anglo-Americans are English. Focusing on one sort of feature—"grosser . . . differences of color, hair and bone"—defines "whites and Negroes, possibly the yellow race" as the "final word of science, so far." Focusing on a different feature—language or shared customs—defines instead Teutons, Slaves, and Romance peoples. The tension in Du Bois' definition of race reflects the fact that, for the purposes of European historiography (of which his Harvard and University of Berlin training had made him aware), it was the latter that mattered; but for the purposes of American social and political life, it was the former.

The real difference in Du Bois' conception, therefore, is not that his definition of race is at odds with the scientific one. It is, rather, as the classic dialectic requires, that he assigns to race a moral and metaphysical significance different from that of his contemporaries. The distinctive claim is that the Negro race has a positive message, a message not only of difference but of value. And that, it seems to me, is the significance of the sociohistorical dimension: the strivings of a race are, as Du Bois viewed the matter, the stuff of history.

> The history of the world is the history, not of individuals, but of groups, not of nations, but of races, and he who ignores or seeks to override the race idea in human history ignores and overrides the central thought of all history.

By studying history, we can discern the outlines of the message of each race.

"Crisis": August 1911

We have seen that, for the purpose that concerned him most—understanding the status of the Negro—Du Bois was thrown back on the scientific definition of race, which he officially rejected. But the scientific definition (Du Bois' uneasiness with which is reflected in his remark that races "perhaps transcend scientific definition") was itself threatened as he spoke at the first meeting of the Negro Academy. In the later nineteenth century most thinking people (like too many even today) believed that what Du Bois called the "grosser differences" were a sign of an inherited racial essence which accounted for the intellectual and moral deficiency of the "lower" races. In "The Conservation of Races" Du Bois elected, in effect, to admit that color was a sign of a racial essence but to deny that the cultural capacities of the black-skinned, curly-haired members of humankind were inferior to those of the white-skinned, straighter-haired ones. But the collapse of the sciences of racial inferiority led Du Bois to deny the connection between cultural capacity and gross morphology—the familiar impulses and strivings of his earlier definition.

We can find evidence of his change of mind in an article in the August 1911 issue of the *Crisis*.

> The leading scientists of the world have come forward . . . and laid down in categorical terms a series of propositions which may be summarized as follows:
>   1. (a) It is not legitimate to argue from differences in physical characteristics to differences in mental characteristics. . . .
>   2. The civilization of a . . . race at any particular moment of time offers no index to its innate or inherited capacities.

These results have been amply confirmed since then. And we do well, I think, to remind ourselves of the current picture.

Human characteristics are genetically determined, to the extent that they are determined, by sequences of DNA in the chromosome—in other words, by genes. The region of a chromosome occupied by a gene is called a locus. Some loci are occupied in different members of a population by different genes, each of which is called an allele; and a locus is said to be polymorphic in a population if there is at least one pair of alleles for it. Perhaps as many as half the loci in the human population are polymorphic; the rest, naturally enough, are monomorphic.

Many loci have not just two alleles but several, and each has a frequency in the population. Suppose a particular locus has n alleles, which we can call 1, 2, and so on up to n; then we can call their frequencies x_1, x_2, ..., to x_n. If we consider two randomly chosen members of a population and look at the same locus on one chromosome of each of them, the probability that they'll have the same allele at that locus is just the probability that they'll both have the first allele (x_1^2), plus the probability that they'll both have the second (x_2^2), plus the probability that they'll both have the nth (x_n^2). We can call this number the expected homozygosity at that locus: for it is just the proportion of people in the population who would be homozygous at that locus—having identical alleles at that locus on each of the relevant chromosomes—provided the population is mating at random.

Now if we take the average value of the expected homozygosity for all loci, polymorphic and monomorphic (which, for some reason, tends to get labeled J), we have a measure of the chance that two people, taken at random from the population, will share the same allele at a locus on a chromosome taken at random. This is a good measure of how similar a randomly chosen pair of individuals should be expected to be in their biology *and* a good (though rough) guide to how closely the populations are genetically related.

I can now express simply one measure of the extent to which members of these human populations we call races differ more from each other than they do from members of the same race. For example, the value of J for Caucasoids—based largely on samples from the English population—is estimated to be about 0.857, while that for the whole human population is estimated at 0.852. The chances, in other words, that two people taken at random from the human population will have the same characteristic at a locus, are about 85.2 percent, while the chances for two (white) people taken from the population of England are about 85.7 percent. And since 85.2 is 100 minus 14.8 and 85.7 is 100 minus 14.3, this is equivalent to what I said in the introduction: the chances of two people who are both Caucasoid differing in genetic constitution at one site on a given chromosome are about 14.3 percent, while, for any two people taken at random from the human population, they are about 14.8 percent. The conclusion is obvious: given only a person's race, it is hard to say what his or her biological characteristics will be, except in respect of the "grosser" features of color, hair, and bone (the genetics of which are, in any case, rather poorly understood)—features of "morphological differentiation," as the evolutionary biologist would say. As Nei and Roychoudhury express themselves, somewhat coyly, "The extent of genic differentiation between human races is not always correlated with the degree of morphological differentiation."

To establish that race is relatively unimportant in explaining biological differences between people, where biological difference is measured in the proportion of differences in loci on the chromosome, is not yet to show that race is unimportant in explaining cultural difference. It could be that large differences in intellectual or moral capacity are caused by differences at very few loci and that, at these loci, all (or most) black-skinned people differ from all (or most) white-skinned or yellow-skinned ones. As it happens, there is little evidence for any such proposition and much against it. But suppose we had reason to believe it. In the biological conception of the human organism, in which characteristics are determined by the pattern of genes in interaction with environments, it is the presence of the alleles (which give rise to these moral and intellectual capacities) that accounts for the observed differences in those capacities in people in similar environments. So the characteristic racial morphology—skin and hair and bone—could only be a sign of those differences if it were (highly) correlated with those alleles. Furthermore, even if it were so correlated, the causal explanation of the differences would be that they differed in those alleles, not that they differed in race. Since there are no such strong correlations, even those who think that intellectual and moral character are strongly genetically determined must accept that *race* is at best a poor indicator of capacity.

But it was earlier evidence, pointing similarly to the conclusion that "the genic variation within and between the three major races of man . . . is small compared with the intraracial variation" and that differences in morphology were not correlated strongly with intellectual and moral capacity, which led Du Bois in the *Crisis* to an explicit rejection of the claim that biological race mattered for understanding the status of the Negro:

> So far at least as intellectual and moral aptitudes are concerned, we ought to speak of civilizations where we now speak of races. . . . Indeed, even the physical characteristics, excluding the skin color of a people, are to no small extent the direct result of the physical and social environment under which it is living. . . . These physical characteristics are furthermore too indefinite and elusive to serve as a basis for any rigid classification or division of human groups.

This is straightforward enough. Yet it would be too swift a conclusion to suppose that Du Bois here expresses his deepest convictions. After 1911, he went on to advocate Pan-Africanism, as he had advocated Pan-Negroism in 1897, and whatever Afro-Americans and Africans, from Ashanti to Zulu, share, it is not a single civilization.

Du Bois managed to maintain Pan-Africanism while officially rejecting talk of race as anything other than a synonym for color. We can see how he did this by turning to his second autobiography, *Dusk of Dawn*, published in 1940.

"Dusk of Dawn"

In *Dusk of Dawn*—the "essay toward an autobiography of a race concept"—Du Bois explicitly allies himself with the claim that race is not a scientific concept.

> It is easy to see that scientific definition of race is impossible; it is easy to prove that physical characteristics are not so inherited as to make it possible to divide the world into races; that ability is the monopoly of no known aristocracy; that the possibilities of human development cannot be circumscribed by color, nationality, or any conceivable definition of race.

But we need no scientific definition, for

> all this has nothing to do with the plain fact that throughout the world today organized groups of men by monopoly of economic and physical power, legal enactment and intellectual training are limiting with determination and unflagging zeal the development of other groups; and that the concentration particularly of economic power today puts the majority of mankind into a slavery to the rest.

Or, as he puts it pithily a little later,

> the black man is a person who must ride "Jim Crow" in Georgia.

Yet, just a few pages earlier, he has explained why he remains a Pan-Africanist, committed to a political program which binds all this indefinable black race together. The passage is worth citing extensively.

Du Bois begins with Countée Cullen's question, "What is Africa to me?" and answers,

> Once I should have answered the question simply: I should have said "fatherland" or perhaps better "motherland" because I was born in the century when the walls of race were clear and straight; when the world consisted of mut[u]ally exclusive races; and even though the edges might be blurred, there was no question of exact definition and understanding of the meaning of the word. . . .
>   Since then [the writing of "The Conservation of Races"] the concept of race has so changed and presented so much of

contradiction that as I face Africa I ask myself: what is it between us that constitutes a tie which I can feel better than I can explain? Africa is, of course, my fatherland. Yet neither my father nor my father's father ever saw Africa or knew its meaning or cared overmuch for it. My mother's folk were closer and yet their direct connection, in culture and race, became tenuous; still, my tie to Africa is strong. On this vast continent were born and lived a large portion of my direct ancestors going back a thousand years or more. The mark of their heritage is upon me in color and hair. These are obvious things, but of little meaning in themselves; only important as they stand for real and more subtle differences from other men. Whether they do or not, I do not know nor does science know today.

But one thing is sure and that is the fact that since the fifteenth century these ancestors of mine and their other descendants have had a common history; have suffered a common disaster and have one long memory. The actual ties of heritage between the individuals of this group, vary with the ancestors that they have in common [with] many others: Europeans and Semites, perhaps Mongolians, certainly American Indians. But the physical bond is least and the badge of color relatively unimportant save as a badge; the real essence of this kinship is its social heritage of slavery; the discrimination and insult; and this heritage binds together not simply the children of Africa, but extends through yellow Asia and into the South Seas. It is this unity that draws me to Africa.

This passage is affecting, powerfully expressed. We might like to be able to follow it in its conclusions. But we should not; since the passage seduces us into error, we should begin distancing ourselves from the appeal of its argument by noticing how it echoes an earlier text. Color and hair are unimportant save "as they stand for real and more subtle differences," Du Bois says here, and we recall the "subtle forces" that "generally followed the natural cleavage of common blood, descent and physical peculiarities" of "The Conservation of Races." There it was an essential part of the argument that these subtle forces—"impulses" and "strivings"—were the common property of those who shared a "common blood"; here, Du Bois does "not know nor does science" whether this is so. But if it is not so, then, on Du Bois' own admission, these "obvious things" are "of little meaning." If they are of little meaning, then his mention of them marks, on the surface of his argument, the extent to which he cannot quite escape the appeal of the earlier conception of race.

Du Bois' yearning for the earlier conception which he prohibited himself from using accounts for the pathos of the gap between the unconfident certainty that Africa is "of course" his fatherland and the concession that it is not the land of his father or his father's father. What use is such a fatherland? What use is a motherland with which your own mother's connection is "tenuous"? What does it matter that a large portion of his ancestors have lived on that vast continent, if there is no subtler bond with them than brute—that is, culturally unmediated—biological descent and its entailed "badge" of hair and color?

Even in the passage that follows Du Bois' explicit disavowal of the scientific conception of race, the references to "common history"—the "one long memory," the "social heritage of slavery"—only lead us back into the now familiar move of substituting a sociohistorical conception of race for the biological one; but that is simply to bury the biological conception below the surface, not to transcend it. Because he never truly "speaks of civilization," Du Bois cannot ask if there is not in American culture—which undoubtedly *is* his—an African residue to take hold of and rejoice in, a subtle connection mediated not by genetics but by intentions, by meaning. Du Bois has no more conceptual resources here for explicating the unity of the Negro race—the Pan-African identity—than he had in "The Conservation of Races" half a century earlier. A glorious non sequitur must be submerged in the depths of the argument. It is easily brought to the surface.

If what Du Bois has in common with Africa is a history of "discrimination and insult," then this binds him, by his own account, to "yellow Asia and . . . the South Seas" also. How can something he shares with the whole nonwhite world bind him to only a part of it? Once we interrogate the argument here, a further suspicion arises that the claim to this bond may be based on a hyperbolic reading of the facts. Du Bois' experience of "discrimination and insult" in his American childhood and as an adult citizen of the industrialized world was different in character from that experienced by, say, Kwame Nkrumah in colonized West Africa; it is absent altogether in large parts of "yellow Asia." What Du Bois shares with the nonwhite world is not insult but the *badge* of insult; and the badge, without the insult, is the very skin and hair and bone which it is impossible to connect with a scientific definition of race.

Concluding Unscientific Postscript

Du Bois died in Nkrumah's Ghana, led there by the dream of Pan-Africanism and the reality of American racism. If he escaped that racism, he never completed the escape from race. The logic of his argument leads naturally to the final repudiation of race as a term of difference and to speaking instead "of civilizations where we now speak of races." The logic is the same logic that has brought us to speak of genders where we spoke of sexes, and a rational assessment of the evidence requires that we should endorse not only the logic but the premises in the case of race, but it is all there in the scientific journals. Discussing Du Bois has been largely a pretext for adumbrating the argument he never quite managed to complete.

I think the argument worth making because I believe that we—scholars in the academy—have not done enough to share it with our fellow citizens. One barrier facing those of us in the humanities has been methodological. Under Saussurian hegemony, we have too easily become accustomed to thinking of meaning as constituted by systems of differences purely internal to our endlessly structured *langues*. Race, we all assume, is, like all other concepts, constructed by metaphor and metonymy; it stands in, metonymically, for the Other; it bears the weight, metaphorically, of other kinds of difference.

Yet, in our social lives away from the text-world of the academy, we take reference for granted too easily. Even if the concept of race *is* a structure of oppositions—white opposed to black (but also to yellow), Jew opposed to Gentile (but also to Arab)—it is a structure whose realization is, at best, problematic and, at worst, impossible. If we can now hope to understand the concept embodied in this system of oppositions, we are nowhere near finding referents for it. The truth is that there are no races: there is nothing in the world that can do all we ask "race" to do for us. The evil that is done is done by the concept and by easy—yet impossible—assumptions as to its application. What we miss through our obsession with the structure of relations of concepts is, simply, reality.

Talk of "race" is particularly distressing for those of us who take culture seriously. For, where race works—in places where "gross differences" of morphology are correlated with "subtle differences" of temperament, belief, and intention—it works as an attempt at a metonym for culture; and it does so only at the price of biologizing what *is* culture, or ideology. To call it "biologizing" is not to consign our concept of race to biology. What is present there is not our concept but our word only. Even the biologists who believe in human races use the term "race," as they say, "without any social implication." What exists "out there" in the world—communities of meaning, shading variously into each other in the rich structure of the social world—is the province not of biology but of hermeneutic understanding.

I have examined these issues through the writings of Du Bois, with the burden of his scholarly inheritance, and have tried to transcend the system of oppositions which, had Du Bois accepted it, would have left him opposed to the (white) norm of form and value. In his early work, Du Bois took race for granted and sought to revalue one pole of the opposition of white to black. The received concept is a hierarchy, a vertical structure, and Du Bois wished to rotate the axis, to give race a "horizontal" reading. Challenge the assumption that there can be an axis, however oriented in the space of values, and the project fails for loss of presuppositions. In his later work, Du Bois— whose life's work was, in a sense, an attempt at just this impossible project— was unable to escape the notion of race he had explicitly rejected. We may borrow his own metaphor: though he saw the dawn coming, he never faced the sun. And we must surely admit that he is followed in this by many in our culture today; we too live in the dusk of that dawn.

THOMAS C. HOLT

The Political Uses of Alienation:
W.E.B. Du Bois on Politics, Race, and Culture, 1903–1940

Certainly one of the most quoted passages in African-American letters is
found in the first of W.E.B. Du Bois's poignant and haunting collection of
essays, *The Souls of Black Folk*. Since it is the axiomatic text embracing key
themes I wish to explore in this essay, I will quote it in full.

> After the Egyptian and Indian, the Greek and Roman, the
> Teuton and Mongolian, the Negro is a sort of seventh son, born
> with a veil, and gifted with second-sight in this American
> world,—a world which yields to him no true self-consciousness,
> but only lets him see himself through the revelation of the other
> world. It is a peculiar sensation, this double-consciousness, this
> sense of always looking at one's self through the eyes of others,
> of measuring one's soul by the tape of a world that looks on in
> amused contempt and pity. One ever feels his twoness,—an
> American, a Negro; two souls, two thoughts, two unreconciled
> strivings; two warring ideals in one dark body, whose dogged
> strength alone keeps it from being torn asunder.
>
> The history of the American Negro is the history of this
> strife,—this longing to attain self-conscious manhood, to merge
> his double self into a better and truer self. In this merging he

From *American Quarterly* 42, no. 2 (June 1990). © 1990 by American Studies Association.

wishes neither of the older selves to be lost. He would not
Africanize America, for America has too much to teach the world
and Africa. He would not bleach his Negro soul in a flood of
white Americanism, for he knows that Negro blood has a
message for the world. He simply wishes to make it possible for
a man to be both a Negro and an American, without being cursed
and spit upon by his fellows, without having the doors of
Opportunity closed roughly in his face.

This poetic passage appeared in the essay "Of Our Spiritual Strivings,"
a slightly revised version of an earlier publication in the August 1897 issue of
Atlantic Monthly, which was, in turn, a reformulation of a paper presented in
March of that year to the American Negro Academy (a recently formed
organization of black intellectuals). Comparison of these texts suggests not
only the trajectory of Du Bois's thought, but the intellectual struggle it
entailed. The earliest version, "The Conservation of the Races," suggests not
only the social-biological reality of race—despite difficulties defining it—but
also the utility of racial differences for social progress, a theme to which Du
Bois would frequently return. In that essay Du Bois published his earliest
(and least poetic) formulation of the paradox of double-consciousness:

Here, then, is the dilemma, and it is a puzzling one, I admit. No
Negro who has given earnest thought to the situation of his
people in America has failed, at some time in life, to find himself
at these cross-roads; has failed to ask himself at some time: what,
after all, am I? Am I an American or am I a Negro? Can I be
both? Or is it my duty to cease to be a Negro as soon as possible
and be an American? If I strive as a Negro, am I not perpetuating
the very cleft that threatens and separates black and white
America? Is not my only possible practical aim the subduction of
all that is Negro in me to the American? Does my black blood
place upon me any more obligation to assert my nationality than
German, or Irish, or Italian blood would?

This "incessant self-questioning" stifles "action," "responsibility," and
"enterprise," leaving the best "energy," "talent," and "blood" of the race
paralyzed, thus surrendering the field of action to "every rascal and demagogue
who chooses to cloak his selfish deviltry under the veil of race pride."
       On the surface, both passages have as their theme the fundamental
duality of black life in America, the paradox of being so intimately a part of
the national culture and yet so starkly apart from it; or, as Du Bois puts it,

"an outcast and a stranger in mine own house." In the 1903 essay, alienation is material, cultural and spiritual. Blacks are builders of the economic infrastructure, yet dispossessed of its fruits; creators of one of its truly original native cultures, in story and song, yet culturally demeaned and maligned; faithful adherents to the nation's basic ideals and values, yet shunned, abused, and stigmatized as if an alien people.

Yet, the contrasts between these two formulations are also interesting. "The Conservation of Races" is addressed to a black audience; indeed, it is an exhortation to the "talented tenth" for self-appointed racial leadership. It begins with an assertion of the reality of racial differences, against which it is vain to protest; blacks are of a different "blood" and are aliens in their own land. The passage quoted comes in the middle of the essay, following another that poses for black intellectuals a choice between assimilation and the affirmation of racial solidarity and group action. It is a Hamlet-like portrait in which black intellectuals are poised at a crossroads, where they must choose between racial suicide and racial solidarity; hence, the exhortation *to conserve* the race. They are admonished to put aside the self-questioning, confusion, hesitation, and vacillation that thwarts resolution and action, leaving the race vulnerable to charlatans who only exploit race consciousness. In words that very well could have come from contemporary African-American conservatives like Glenn Loury or Thomas Sowell, Du Bois rails against black immorality, the breakdown of family, and the enemy within. "Unless we conquer our present vices they will conquer us," he thunders. It is worth noting that when he wrote this warning Du Bois was fresh from his study of the Philadelphia ghetto and that his tone here is consistent with *The Philadelphia Negro*.

By contrast, *Souls of Black Folk* marks Du Bois's conscious turn toward active political engagement. It is a sustained attack both on the sterile and pusillanimous leadership of Booker T. Washington and the materialist ethos of American capitalism to which Washington's philosophy was indebted. "Of Our Spiritual Strivings" sets forth the major themes to be explicated throughout the following essays. Although many of the themes of "Conservation of the Races" are present in this text, too, the tone is much different, and the paradox seems somehow deeper and more subtle. Possibly, this difference is because the essay is addressed primarily to a white audience. Yet, read against the texts and themes Du Bois would develop over the following forty years, "Strivings" also reflects a deeper, more subtle exploration of the dilemma originally posed in "Conservation," notwithstanding that only a few months separated their respective composition.

In "Strivings," blacks are not so much aliens as alienated. It is not cultural difference but cultural disfranchisement that shapes their struggle.

Their artisans, ministers, doctors, and artists are deprived both of the means to pursue their crafts to higher standards and the recognition of the worth of indigenous material and creativity. Although Du Bois writes of "the innate love of harmony and beauty that set the ruder souls of his people a-dancing and a-singing," for the most part, African-American culture appears as the product of a special experience—in this instance slavery and a hard freedom—rather than a special providence or provenance. Thus, if the *specialness* of black culture is a consequence of the uniqueness of black experience, it follows, too, that the culture is not a fixed entity, not a system or structure, not a grammar to be decoded. It is—like race, perhaps—contingent, contested, and historical.

Here, then, racial difference is more clearly a socially constructed phenomenon rather than a biological reality. It is not even a given of human consciousness but must be summoned there from the social environment. The passage quoted is the third paragraph of the essay, and it follows a description of Du Bois's *discovery*, as a child, of racial discrimination, when a young schoolmate insulted him. That insult stimulated a consciousness of his difference, and of himself in relation to his schoolmates that he had not felt before. Thereafter, the "sky was bluest when I could beat my mates at examination-time, or beat them at a foot-race, or even beat their stringy heads." He had to reconstitute his relation to his world, and in the process his consciousness of acting and being in that world. "Between me and the other world there is ever an unasked question: unasked by some through feelings of delicacy; by others through the difficulty of rightly framing it. . . . How does it feel to be a problem?" In its opening paragraphs, then, the 1903 essay frames the problematic question of how one achieves mature self-consciousness and an integrity or wholeness of self in an alienating environment. This problem would become the dominant focus—political and cultural—of Du Bois's life and work.

Introduced here, too, is the metaphor of the veil, a leitmotif in Du Bois's writing that summons multiple variations on the theme of sight and insight. Falling between the white and the blacks worlds, the veil obscures vision—vision of self and of other. The problem shifts subtly from being a matter of what we are—a race apart—to how we are seen, and how we see ourselves. The pain of prejudice springs not only from the cold stare of whites but also from one's invisibility to them. Equally important is the capacity for self-recognition because it forms the essential basis for action and struggle. In this essay, the emphasis is less on the black immorality and venality excoriated in "Conservation" than the unfathomable endurance and strength of an oppressed people. Blacks have gifts for the world—both current and potential. The goal is not social endogamy or black nationalism but to be "a co-worker in the kingdom of culture."

Neither is this essay merely a plea for tolerance and cultural pluralism. The suffering of "this historic race" gives it a claim to specialness, to have "a message for the world," and with that comes also the duty to change the world. More specifically, black intellectuals, "the talented tenth," have a special duty to their race, and the race could be the saviors of humankind. Thus, the struggle for black self-realization becomes, in turn, a struggle for all people.

Variations on these themes—suspended duality, unresolved paradox, perpetual alienation—appear throughout Du Bois's long and prolific career. His recognition of both the intractability and the efficacy of this double-consciousness is one reason that Du Bois has avoided interpretation by most scholars. His major biographers find him incomprehensible and inconsistent; they portray him lurching between the antithetical and contradictory goals of black nationalism and racial integration. There has been a persistent misreading of Du Bois and a misperception of the basic truths about the African-American experience that he did so much to disclose. Indeed, Du Bois's paradoxical positions may be taken as somehow emblematic of the African-American experience generally. By that I mean, African-Americans *live* a kind of paradox embodied in their very lives, which are shaped profoundly by conflicts of identity and purpose. Although this paradox of crosscutting racial and national identities articulates differently within different class strata, it marks the lives of all African-Americans because all experience racial alienation in some form—social, economic, or political.

For example, a sharecropper like Nate Shaw expounds an attachment to the American work ethic that is clearly inconsistent with his situation, one in which maximum work effort literally does not pay. He "accepts" that ideology, nonetheless, and organizes his life *as if it were true*, even as he understands that the opportunity it implies is an illusion. Shaw's "acceptance" is not a reflection of false consciousness, however, but a curious blend of pragmatism, hope, and fatalism, which has characterized the black response to an historical experience of extreme and arbitrary oppression.

Pressing the logic of Du Bois's formulation suggests a radical proposition: that African-Americans should celebrate their alienation, for *it* is the source of "second-sight in this American world." Although Du Bois implies in the 1903 version of the paradox the eventual resolution of the divided self in historical time, "to merge his double self into a better and truer self," much of what he writes later suggests that African-Americans accept, even embrace, the contradiction and paradox arising from dual identities and consciousness. Because they live in two worlds at once, African-Americans possess the power to see where others are blind. Alienation—raised to a conscious level, cultivated, and directed—has revolutionary potential. The insight of the oppressed is neither innate nor inherent; it must be worked for, struggled for. Once achieved, it becomes a tool for probing the deeper meanings and contradictions of experience and for creating change. For blacks, then, racial alienation can be the counterpart of class alienation, and it can serve the same revolutionary purposes.

It is not likely, of course, that Du Bois realized the fuller, more radical implications of his propositions in 1903, and certainly not in 1897. Over the following four decades, however, the proposition that double-consciousness could be both intractable and efficacious became more explicit in and central to Du Bois's thought and politics. It was an idea hammered out of intellectual and political struggles. On the one hand, he grappled with reconciling Marxian and Freudian explanations of the human condition while, on the other hand, he struggled to fashion an organizational strategy at the NAACP appropriate both to the hegemony of world capitalism and the tenacity of racial prejudice. For Du Bois, intelligence and politics, thought and experience, were necessarily interactive; his theories of race and anti-racist struggle—which many of his contemporaries and later historians have found so confusing and vacillating—evolved over a period of years out of the interaction between his intellectual and political labors. To understand him, therefore, one must endeavor to read his eloquent texts against the gritty backdrop of the organizational confrontations that simultaneously engaged him.

An analysis on these two levels approximates Du Bois's own, since he hardly distinguished between written texts and the text of experience. Indeed, his technique was almost naively reflexive, in that his own life became the text, the point of departure, for each of his major explorations of race, culture, and politics.

Much of Du Bois's value to us, certainly, is in his extraordinary responsiveness to the world around him. He lived such a long life, through periods of rapid change in the black experience, and was incredibly prolific throughout his life, especially during his quarter of a century editorship of the *Crisis*, where his responses were monthly. Thus, we literally observe Du Bois witnessing the fundamental transformation of African-American life from the mid-nineteenth to the mid-twentieth centuries, from a world lit by candlelight to the nuclear fire. It would have been strange, indeed, if he *had* remained "consistent."

Moreover, his multiple careers—historian, sociologist, poet, novelist, journalist, activist—were all crucial to his life project, providing multiple perspectives and multiple voices. Several of Du Bois's biographers have accepted, to some degree, the notion that his scholarship suffered because of his politics or that his scholarly demeanor undercut his political effectiveness; but Du Bois's life project was to develop a theory of society interactively with and through social and political practice ("work, culture, liberty") in order to achieve enlightenment *and* emancipation.

Du Bois's witness to the transformation in black life during the 1930s Depression is a useful period for exploring the maturing of his ideas about theory and practice that were merely implied in *Souls*. Here, one can appreciate the subtleties and limitations of his philosophy of racial uplift when tested by social crisis, the difficulties inherent to the African-American liberation struggle generally, and the systematic misreading and unresponsiveness of many of his critics.

This period was easily the most controversial in Du Bois's long life. Confronted with the Depression crisis, he argued for a fundamental shift in NAACP strategy: the fostering of independent black economic enterprises. Provocatively, deliberately, he labeled this scheme "voluntary segregation." After a heated debate over this issue in the pages of the 1934 *Crisis*, Du Bois resigned from the NAACP. Although most have recognized that other factors contributed to this rupture with the organization he had helped to found, scholars generally assert that the self-segregation issue was its fundamental cause, which, not coincidentally, was the interpretation that his antagonists at the NAACP sought to promote. For example, the Chicago branch urged the national office of the NAACP to accept Du Bois's resignation but to deliver a statement pointing to segregation as the cause of the conflict and not his economic program. Otherwise, Du Bois would "escape the burden of approving segregation," and the NAACP would be charged with "failing to rescue Negro workers and tenant farmers from their plight."

Du Bois's ideas brought down upon him a firestorm of criticism from his contemporaries and dismissive judgments from some of his biographers. He was accused of reviving the Booker T. Washington "separatist" philosophy which he had done so much to scotch. From Jamaica the exiled Marcus Garvey accused him of plagiarizing his self-help scheme, a criticism endorsed by a recent biographer of Garvey. Du Bois's biographers portray him as an old man, out of touch with reality, who had lost his way. Francis Broderick entitles his chapter that treats this subject, "Negro Chauvinism." There Du Bois is described as "retreating" to older formulas, "into the protective shell of his own race." Elliott Rudwick also calls Du Bois's plan a reactionary scheme and quotes the negative contemporary reaction approvingly.

The irony is that Du Bois saw this period as his most creative. After a half century of study and struggle along the color line, he had found the key to a theory of race relations and, thus, a program of racial uplift consistent with the paradoxes of the African-American experience. It is worth noting that in both the quasi-autobiographical *Dusk of Dawn*, published in 1940 (he was seventy-two), and the *Autobiography* of the late 1950s, shortly after which he joined the Communist Party, Du Bois remained content with much of the controversial program he had formulated in the 1930s.

The key fifth chapter of *Dusk of Dawn* is entitled "The Concept of Race," which Du Bois significantly describes as not so much a concept "as a group of contradictory forces, facts and tendencies." Thus, race no longer has the social-biological concreteness implied in the 1897 essay. Here, many of the themes of "The Conservation of the Races" and "Of Our Spiritual Strivings" appear again, but now reformulated in the context of Du Bois's more sophisticated understanding of human behavior and social action. The veil that once shrouded blacks from view, obscuring both their problems and virtues and their latent powers, has changed. It is now "some thick sheet of invisible but horribly tangible plate glass" sealing off a "dark cave," within which blacks are "entombed souls . . . hindered in their natural movement, expression, and development. . . ." The veil has become an imprisoning wall.

Blacks can be seen by the outside world now, but not heard. Consequently, all their gestures and expressions are incomprehensible, even absurd, to the white outsiders. After a while, the inmates begin to wonder if the outside world is real; they tend to become narrow, provincial, their interests and activities confined to the tomb; they become "inured to their experience." On the other hand, the wild and suicidal efforts of those who attempt to break through the glass (the revolutionaries, the deviants) only excite horror and terror in the outside world.

From this really quite horrible parable, Du Bois concludes that outsiders—however well-intentioned—cannot know the experience of those within and thus cannot speak for or lead them. Leadership can only come from among the entombed. Such leaders must be "race men," unselfish, loyal, and committed to unending sacrifice for the collective good. In chapter 7, "The Colored World Within," Du Bois restates the group economy idea, a project that cannot succeed without the dedicated and disciplined leadership of "race men."

In the final chapter of *Dusk of Dawn*, Du Bois describes the intellectual sources for the rethinking and reformulation of his social philosophy. During the period preceding his articulation of the self-segregation scheme and of his subsequent break with the NAACP, he had made the twin discoveries of Marx and Freud. From Marx he learned that there was a deeper structural basis for racial oppression; that it was not enough to fight for integration into a house that was inherently flawed. From Freud he learned to appreciate the irrationality of prejudice and its deep-seatedness. "I now begin to realize that in the fight against race prejudice, we are not facing simply the rational, conscious determination of white folk to oppress us; we are facing age-long complexes sunk now largely to unconscious habit and irrational urge, which demand on our part not only the patience to wait, but the power to entrench ourselves for a long siege against the strongholds of color caste.

What Du Bois claimed, then, was that his program was not defensive and reactionary, but forward looking and militant. The product of a long gestation period, his plan represented a blending from eclectic, yet seminal, modern intellectual forces: Marxism and Freudianism. Furthermore, it was not a retreat to nationalism, but a recognition of the international dimensions of the racial conflict, indeed, that African-Americans could be the vanguard of an international assault on class privilege. This dimension is something that neither Booker T. Washington nor Garvey could have envisioned.

In many ways Du Bois was naive and, certainly, misread the flow of future events—but then so did many other radicals during the Great Depression. Yet, I believe it is necessary to accurately represent his thinking processes and to acknowledge the integrity of those processes as he describes them. When we examine the content and timing of his writings in the *Crisis* together with his personal correspondence during this period, his reminiscences in *Dusk of Dawn* do ring true. This period was not one of despair and withdrawal but one of intense and excited intellectual creativity. In many ways, Du Bois was not retreating to older, discredited formulas but advancing toward new formulations that might address an as yet dimly foreseen crisis.

During the late twenties and early thirties, the Marxian theme of class struggle and the Freudian theory of a nonrational, unconscious basis for human behavior were woven into Du Bois's scheme to build a separate black economy. Throughout this period there remained a clear distinction between Du Bois's analysis of the problem, which was Marxist, and his solution, which was nationalist. "I am not turning to nationalism to escape Communism," he wrote in April 1933 to George Streator, his assistant at the *Crisis*.

> I could not have communism if I wanted it. There is no such choice before me. The only thing that I have to choose is annihilation by American capitalism peacemeal [sic] [or] racial organization in self-defense. Don't let communists or anybody else fool you into thinking that internationalism is at hand and that we have only to join it. Negro prejudice still lives.

The onset of the Depression was significant in confirming his fears about the fate of blacks in twentieth-century America and in conveying a sense of urgency to his project. It was not the catalyst for that project, but

rather a contributory factor, or the context for other factors. Du Bois claims
to have been a socialist since before the Great War, having voted with the
Party in New York City in 1912. He also had been exposed to socialist ideas
during his student days in Germany. Heretofore socialist, much less Marxist,
ideas had not loomed prominently in his analysis of the race problem.

Du Bois began to change after his 1926 visit to the Soviet Union,
where he declared that if the Russian society he saw was the result of the
Bolshevik Revolution, then he was a Bolshevik. Even this appeared to be
more a reflection of Du Bois's rhetorical style than a serious commitment to
Marxist-Leninist principles. Indeed, given his oft-repeated commitment to
nonviolence, Du Bois appeared more likely a Fabian than a Leninist.

The March 1928 issue of the *Crisis* did contain an article affirming the
mutual interests of black and white workers in reforming capitalism; it also
recognized that both black and white workers were blind to their common
economic interests and were likely to remain so. Two months later the
language was even stronger: it was "idiotic to hope that white laborers will
become broad enough or wise enough to make the cause of black labor their
own . . . in our day." By November 1929, Du Bois was dismissing political
democracy as an ineffective form of governance because (1) "the vast
majority of Americans are not intelligent," (2) they are economic slaves, and
(3) the country is "ruled by organized wealth."

These pronouncements seem to spring from Du Bois's basic populist
sympathies; apparently, they preceded his systematic reexamination of Marxian
thought. Indeed, he credits a speech at Howard University in 1930 as the
catalyst for recasting his economic ideas. Interestingly, the Howard speech also
has been cited as the opening gun of his campaign for the group economy/self-
segregation strategy. In that speech he argued that both Booker T.
Washington's program of industrial training and his own emphasis on
academic education had failed, both schemes overtaken by the fundamental
transformation of the American economy. But Du Bois realized that his speech
was weak on practical remedies, so "he began to study Marx in earnest."

By the end of that year, Du Bois—in an attack on President Herbert
Hoover's policies—declared the pursuit of private profit an unsound basis
upon which to organize an economy for the general good; "income [was] a
social product . . . not simply the result of individual effort . . . and must be
divided by human judgment." In this essay he also linked, in cryptic
fashion, the pursuit of profit and the oppression of blacks: "it pays today
from six to six hundred per cent to hate 'niggers' and keep them in their
places."

In the summer of 1932, the *Crisis* ran a symposium of black
newspaper editors' views on communism and the race problem, to which
Du Bois appended a recommended reading list of six books. In January

1933, he wrote Abram Harris, a black Marxist professor at Howard, requesting recommendations for additions to his own library on Marxism. "I have been re-reading Marx recently as everyone must these days." Two months later the *Crisis* published an article, "Karl Marx and the Negro," in which Du Bois declared Marx the greatest economic thinker of modern times and regretted that he had not lived to apply his "great mind . . . first hand" to the Negro problem.

What is interesting about this article, however, is that while it affirms Marx's greatness, it notes the limitation of his work with respect to the race issue—simply because Marx had not addressed that issue. This, then, is the unfinished business of Marxian analysis. Marx's analysis of the problem of capitalism was sound, but the solutions as they bore on the race problem remained to be formulated. Indeed, for Du Bois, "work, culture, liberty" continued to be the keys to unlocking the paradox of race and class. "I have no faith in anything which is so scientific that it will not be swayed by perfectly human motives, and among them, race prejudice." Cultural achievement would do more to break down race prejudice than anything else, he replied to a supporter, but cultural achievements of decisive scale required great economic progress.

Du Bois's intellectual embrace of Marxism did not yet involve a political embrace of American Communists, whom he regarded with utter contempt. Marx may not have known about the Negro problem, but the American Communist party of the 1930s was *willfully* ignorant. They were a group with "pitiable mental equipment," he wrote in April 1933. The only social equality their tactics would likely win for blacks was the equality of a jail cell.

Notwithstanding his admiration for the Russian experiment in socialism, he asked: "What part can [American Negroes] expect to have in a socialistic state and what can they do now to bring about this realization? And my answer to this has long been clear. There is no automatic power in socialism to override and suppress race prejudice. . . . One of the worst things that Negroes could do today would be to join the American Communist Party or any of its many branches."

Clearly, the source of Du Bois's contempt was the failure of the American Communists to recognize the intractability of racism among the white proletariat. At times, Du Bois argued that it was in the interests of white workers to discriminate against African-American workers. American capitalism had produced a kind of labor aristocracy whose prosperity was built on "a mud-sill of black labor." At other times he insisted that racism had origins more deep seated than material interests. "White labor has to hate scabs; but it hates black scabs not because they are scabs but because they are black. It mobs white scabs to force them into labor fellowship. It mobs black scabs to starve and kill them."

There was, then, a simultaneous recognition of the power of Marxian analysis of modern social ills—ills traceable to the fundamental structures of national and international capital—and of the psychological dimensions of this malady, wherein the oppressed were blinded to their true interests, wherein white workers oppressed black. The problem, then, was one of class *and* race. The solutions, likewise, had to be both internal and external to the black community.

"What is to be done?" Du Bois asked rhetorically. "There is to my mind," he wrote in a 1928 *Crisis* article,

> only one way out: Manufacturing and consumers co-operation among the major part of twelve million people on a wide and ever-increasing scale. There must be the slow, but carefully planned growth of manufacturing trusts, beginning with the raising of raw material on Negro farms; extending to its transportation on Negro trucks; its manufacture in Negro factories; its distribution to Negro co-operative stores, supported by intelligent and loyal Negro consumers.

Through such organization blacks would overcome race prejudice and monopoly capital and "insure the economic independence of the American Negro for all time."

As with socialism, Du Bois had been sympathetic to the idea of producer and consumer cooperatives for more than a decade. In the late twenties and early thirties, however, sympathy became commitment. Moreover, he now emphasized the power of the consumer rather than the producer. It was "a mistake to think that the economic cycle begins with production," he wrote in 1931, "rather it begins with consumption." Since America's black population exceeded that of many nations, its internal economic power as consumers should be organized. The consumer boycotts by blacks in New York City and Chicago during the early 1930s were for him proof of the latent power of consumer militancy.

Du Bois's socialism saved him from a bourgeois conception of cooperation. He drew his inspiration from cooperatives he had seen in Russia and read about in Europe, not from Marcus Garvey. Nor was this plan by any means a return to the petty capitalism of Booker T. Washington. You could not build a black economy on craftsmanship and mom-and-pop stores, he argued. The American economy had been fundamentally transformed. Individual craftsmen and shopkeepers were disappearing; the old trades were "now part of highly organized combinations, financed with large capital." Concentration, consolidation, monopoly capital were the order of the day.

Black labor was threatened with redundancy; it could expect help neither from big capital nor big labor. Furthermore, he wrote:

> If we simply mill contentedly after the streaming herd, with no clear idea of our own solutions of our problems, what can we expect but the contempt of reformers and slavery to a white proletariat? If we expect to enter present or future industry upon our own terms, we must have terms; we must have power: we must learn the secret of economic organization; we must submit to leadership, not of words but of ideas; we must lead the civilized part of these 12 millions of our race into an industrial phalanx that cannot be ignored, and which America and the world will come to regard as a strong asset under any system and not merely as a weak and despicable liability. . . .

Du Bois was equally insistent that his plan was not a return to Booker T. Washington's accomodationism. "I am convinced that the Negro has got to turn his attention primarily to his economic condition, to earning a living, and earning it in new ways," he wrote a supporter in March 1935. Yet, unlike Washington, he did not wish to make "Negro labor a part of the great industrial machine" and his plan intended "no essential change in the fight on racial segregation." He conceded that "it does mean that we have got to accept most of the segregation that we suffer today, and that there is no hope in our day or many years to come." This fact was inescapable, since *white* racial prejudice showed no sign of diminishing in the near future. "Under these circumstances, we have got to work together, and in racial groups, and if that is what my friends call Segregation, I am all for it because I have got to be."

Out of such necessity could come opportunities for effective racial leadership and profound social change. A movement for economic cooperation required the leadership of "Negroes of education and intelligence who regard their education not simply as an open sesame to a privileged position, but as means of service to a disfranchised and disinherited group of workers." Thus, the "talented tenth" of 1903 was reconstituted as the revolutionary vanguard for the 1930s, who would transform a disabling condition into a creative force. Booker T. Washington's philosophy had involved "the flight of class from mass" through material accumulation, Du Bois wrote in *Dusk of Dawn*, while his own program had involved a flight of class from mass through culture. It was now clear that class and mass must unite "for the world's salvation." For Du Bois, therefore, race consciousness undertook the role of class consciousness in Marxian theory: the latter was the basis for whites organizing for their liberation; the former could serve as the resource for black liberation.

There was a greater chance of this occurring among blacks because of their still limited class differentiation. "We who have had the least class differentiation in wealth, can follow in the new trend and indeed lead it." In this connection, I think it is important to recognize that Du Bois was not oblivious to existing or potential class interests splitting blacks; he simply felt that such conflicts had not matured to an extent that would prevent race unity.

In a letter to a French correspondent, Du Bois contrasted the effects of Anglo-Saxon racism with the color-blind, assimilationist policies of the French colonial administration, which drew the Senegalese elite away from the masses. "The net result is rather strange. The oppressed Negro in America and in English colonies is oppressed as a group and within that group is a potential educated leadership which stands with the group and fights for it. In black France, on the other hand, the dark masses have no leaders. Their logical leaders, like Diagne, Candace and others are more French than the French, and feel, quite naturally much nearer the French people than to black Africa or brown Martinique."

One of the first duties of the elite would be to reeducate the masses for the new social order, because cooperatives required "the habit and order of cooperation." The elite must establish such order and inculcate such habits:

> An economic battle has just begun. It can be studied and guided;
> it can teach consumers' co-operation, democracy, and socialism,
> and be made not simply a record and pattern for the Negro race,
> but a guide for the rise of the working classes throughout the
> world, just at the critical time when these classes are about to
> assume their just political domination, which is destined to
> become the redemption of mankind.

African-Americans were specially suited, therefore, to light the way for the rest of the world. Their oppression had inured them to hardship and sacrifice; exclusion from the larger world would render the social sanctions of "the colored world within" all the more potent. Blacks could achieve greater community discipline by virtue of their oppression. "We have an instinct of race and a bond of color, in place of a protective tariff for our infant industry. We have, as police power, social ostracism within to coerce a race thrown back upon itself by ostracism without; and behind us, if we will survive, is Must, not May."

Oppression bestowed more than discipline and endurance; it bestowed *sight*. The oppressed specially valued the American ideals of freedom and equality; thus, they could *see* where others could not. "Once in a while through all of us there flashes some clairvoyance, some clear idea, of what America really is. We who are dark can see America in a way that white Americans can not."

It is not difficult here to discern the continued parable of the cave. Looking through a glass darkly, neither white workers nor their black counterparts can see each other clearly. The outside leaders cannot lead the entombed. The only course open to those within the cave is to organize their inner resources—material and spiritual—to create a base from which the entire edifice can be reformed. Being black—thereby, capable of gaining strength, discipline, and solidarity from their oppression—the cave dwellers are blessed "with a second-sight" into the promise *and* the broken promises of America.

> Even as you visualize such ideas [he challenged Chicago students in 1926], you know in your hearts that these are not the things you really want [referring here to American materialism]. You realize this sooner than the average white American because, pushed aside as we have been in America, there has come to us not only a certain distaste for the tawdry and flamboyant but a vision of what the world could be if it were really a beautiful world. If we had the true spirit; if we had the Seeing Eye, the Cunning Hand, the Feeling Heart; if we had, to be sure, not perfect happiness, but plenty of good hard work, the inevitable suffering that always comes with life; sacrifice and waiting, all that—but, nevertheless, lived in a world where men know, where men create, where they *realize* themselves and where they enjoy life. It is that sort of world we want to create for ourselves and for all America.

Du Bois despaired of getting a hearing—much less action—on these lofty ideals and complex ideas from the NAACP leadership as it was constituted in the 1930s; and he was right. Even with the benefit of historical hindsight, Roy Wilkins—in his posthumously published autobiography, *Standing Fast*—still only saw a personal conflict between Du Bois and Executive Secretary Walter White. Even many of Du Bois's former allies saw merely a disgruntled sexagenarian. Thus, Du Bois turned for political support to the black youth—the college-bred "talented tenth," most of whom were less than half his age. Contrary to the image of an old man out of touch with reality, Du Bois actively cultivated allies in the NAACP's local branches during this period and sought to bring some of these onto the national board.

These efforts began at least as early as 1932 and met with some success, but not enough to shift the balance of power within the NAACP. Six months before his resignation, Du Bois wrote to Abram Harris, one of his young radical allies who fully agreed with him on the need to "purge" the NAACP leadership. Du Bois complained that they were still stymied by "the opportunism of [Walter] White and the reactionary economic philosophy of the Spingarns." So far, his effort to reorganize the Board of Directors had met only limited success. Despite the addition of Harris and the support of a few others, Du Bois's faction was still "a hopeless minority within a group of elderly reactionaries." He seriously doubted that they would be strong enough "to begin a fight for the root and branch re-organization of the N.A.A.C.P."

It was obvious to most knowledgeable contemporaries that Du Bois wanted to get rid of Walter White and White's alter ego Roy Wilkins. From his personal correspondence, it is clear that his friends Arthur and Joel Spingarn were targeted as well. The Spingarns were capitalists, he wrote George Streator in January 1934, and "the *Crisis*, so long as I conduct it, is going to be Socialist and Left Wing Socialist, and I am going to work out a philosophy on segregation that is going to take into account the realities of the situation in the South."

Therefore, the ideological struggle over segregation took place in the context of an ongoing struggle for control of the organization. The ideological differences may have provided the occasion for debate, but its energy came from the increasingly bitter infighting, and in this, neither Du Bois nor Harris were a match for Walter White. In May 1934, the Board approved a resolution barring the use of the *Crisis* to criticize the organization. Du Bois protested that he could not abide any such effort to muzzle him. He might just as well have said that the passage of this resolution signaled that he had lost his "root and branch" fight for the soul of the NAACP. In June 1934, he submitted his resignation, to be effective on July 1, 1934.

There was a last minute flurry of activity to find a compromise, but it was already clear to the principals what the outcome of the struggle had to be. When Du Bois—who was away from New York as a visiting professor at Atlanta University—had first heard of the Board's decision, he fired off a telegraphic message to Joel Spingarn: "My resignation is now inevitable."

The events leading to Du Bois's resignation are inextricably tied to and provide a context for evaluating the evolution of his social philosophy during the late twenties and early thirties. I think it is clear that his was not the reactionary scheme of a man of failing intellectual powers, nor was it simply a defensive response to the depression. Du Bois correctly foresaw the increased concentration of American economic power, although he overestimated the staying power of 1930s radicalism. He also failed to foresee the relatively rapid and significant incorporation of blacks into many sectors of the labor movement and the New Deal. Thus, he did not foresee, perhaps even discounted, the rapid rise of a black labor aristocracy, such as that described by E. Franklin Frazier in *Black Bourgeoisie*, whose interests and values, many would argue, diverged and continue to diverge from those of the black underclass. This development undercut the notion that class forces within the black community were not as important as racial forces pressing in from without.

However, he did sense that blacks would still be the last hired and first fired, and that large sectors of the potential black proletariat would never be proletarians at all, but remain outside the labor force—a permanent underclass. Because he recognized—even predicted—this development, he could not have thought that his separate economy idea could be the basis of any final solution to the race problem. These broader structural changes were issues the whole society—through the state—would have to address. The separate economy was merely a contingent, intermediate step to husband the strength of the black community for that larger struggle—the struggle to do away with *all* economic privilege and oppression. For Du Bois, the ultimate goal was always justice for all people. In his vision, blacks should use their unique resources to light the way for the rest of the world.

Furthermore, the organized power of black consumers was not as visionary as his critics claimed; that power would be demonstrated strongly in the Civil Rights Movement of the 1960s (and in recent years by Reverend Jesse Jackson's "Operation Push"). But, of course, that same Movement demonstrated the extraordinary organizational talent, dedication, and most of all, unselfish leadership necessary to mobilize that power effectively and to sustain it.

Such leadership is precisely what Du Bois assumed would be forthcoming from his talented tenth—a group he refers to in 1897 as "the first fruits of the new nation, the harbingers of that black tomorrow which is yet destined to soften the whiteness of the Teutonic today." And again in *Souls of Black Folk*, where he challenged yet again:

> Work, culture, liberty,—all these we need not singly but together, not successively but together, each growing and aiding each, and all striving toward that master ideal that swims before the Negro people, the ideal of human brotherhood, gained through the unifying ideal of Race; the ideal of fostering and developing the traits and talents of the Negro, not in opposition to or contempt for other races, but rather in large conformity to

the greater ideals of the American Republic, in order that some day on American soil two world-races may give each to each those characteristics both so sadly lack. We the darker one, come even now not altogether empty-handed: there are to-day no truer exponents of the pure human spirit of the Declaration of Independence than the American Negroes; there is no true American music but the wild sweet melodies of the Negro slave; the American fairy tales and folk-lore are Indian and African; and, all in all, we black men seem the sole oasis of simple faith and reverence in a dusty desert of dollars and smartness. . . . Merely a concrete test of the underlying principles of the great republic is the Negro Problem, and the spiritual striving of the freedman's sons is the travail of souls whose burden is almost beyond the measure of their strength, but who bear it in the name of an historic race, in the name of this the land of their father's fathers, and in the name of human opportunity.

Thus, in one of his earliest essays, Du Bois stakes out the main themes that mark much of his subsequent intellectual and political work. "Work, culture, liberty," are key, mutually supportive values essential not only to African-American liberation, but to all humankind's effort to live a morally satisfying and useful life. They express themes of political and personal commitment, of striving for self-knowledge and a sense of self, and of the essential material and moral conditions requisite to self-realization. Yet through this passage, too, comes the continuing themes of cultural paradox: first, one must recognize and value differences in order to achieve unities; and moreover, that oppression itself valorizes and empowers its cultural products—"the wild sweet melodies," the tales and folklore, the "simple faith and reverence." Therefore, it is not only the salvation, but the duty of the oppressed to realize themselves, their powers, in order to serve the larger purpose of saving humankind. It is a visionary charge, but then, being a visionary requires that one have vision. It is helpful, too, if one has "second-sight."

TOMMY L. LOTT

Du Bois on the Invention of Race

In his well-known address to the newly founded American Negro Academy, W.E.B. Du Bois entertained the question of the fate and destiny of African-Americans as a group, asking somewhat rhetorically, "Does my black blood place upon me any more obligation to assert my nationality than German, or Irish or Italian blood would?" His answer was that it is "the duty of the Americans of Negro descent, as a body, to maintain their race identity." The argument he advanced to support this claim has sometimes been understood to suggest that African-Americans as a group are obligated to maintain and perpetuate their culture in order to retain their authenticity. We should resist, however, becoming overly focused on this aspect of Du Bois's view, for it is fairly clear, on even the most cursory reading of his essay, that he was not particularly concerned with the African past as a standard for measuring the authenticity of African-American culture. Indeed, he proposed to resolve the dilemma of African-American double consciousness by appealing to a revisionist analysis of the concept of race that eschews a biological essentialist account of race identity.

One very good reason, frequently cited by commentators, for supposing that Du Bois was primarily concerned with the question of authenticity is his repeated criticism of African-Americans striving for "self-

From *The Philosophical Forum* 24, no. 1–3 (Fall–Spring 1992–93). © 1992 by The Philosophical Forum, Inc.

obliteration," seeking "absorption by the white Americans," or pursuing "a servile imitation of Anglo-Saxon culture." Although there certainly was a concern with authenticity expressed in Du Bois's remarks, I believe that it is somewhat misleading to take this to have been his primary motivation for raising these issues, for there is a very important reason why such issues were not in the foreground of his discussion of race, and why they do not figure into his argument regarding the obligation of African-Americans to maintain their race identity. Hence, I shall present a reading of Du Bois's essay, that, with regard to the question of race identity, deviates from several recent interpretations.

Du Bois's argument for the claim that African-Americans are obligated to retain their race identity is connected with his early view of the role of culture in the African-American quest for social equality. In particular, he maintained that the cultural integrity of African-Americans is crucial for their gaining acceptance as social equals. The view Du Bois stated in 1897 displays the late nineteenth-century historical context of African-American social thought; consequently, many features of the argument he presented can be found in the writings of his contemporaries. By contextualizing his argument I aim to show that he presented a notion of race that was in keeping with his own version of a race uplift theory of social change. According to my interpretation, his revisionist account represents a view of race identity that accorded with the prevailing African-American social philosophy at the turn of the century. I will begin with a brief discussion of his definition of race, followed by a sketch of some of the historical sources from which he may have drawn certain ideas to develop his argument for the duty of African-Americans to retain their race identity. I want to defend the plausibility of Du Bois's sociohistorical view of race identity against several, quite damaging, criticisms and thereby salvage the major thrust of his argument.

A REVISIONIST CONCEPT OF RACE

With the aim of presenting an account tailored to fit his theory of social change, Du Bois proposed the following definition of race,

> It is a vast family of human beings, generally of common blood and language, always of common history, traditions and impulses, who are both voluntarily and involuntarily striving together for the accomplishment of certain more or less vividly conceived ideals of life.

Unless we bear in mind why Du Bois was motivated to write about African-American identity, his definition of race will seem quite implausible, especially his stipulation that a racial group must *always* share a common history, traditions, and impulses, but need not always share a common blood or language. The reason Du Bois's proposal seems implausible is because he meant to implicitly contest the way the received view, which places a greater emphasis on common blood, has been socially constructed. Unfortunately, the insight that underlies his definition is diminished by the twofold nature of his account, an account which involves both a deconstruction of the received view as well as a reconstruction of his alternative conception.

Du Bois opened his essay with the statement that African-Americans are always interested in discussions regarding the origins and destinies of races because such discussions usually presuppose assumptions about the natural abilities, and the social and political status of African-Americans, assumptions that impede African-American social progress. He noted that the undesirable implications of some of these assumptions have fostered a tendency for African-Americans "to deprecate and minimize race distinctions." He took himself to be giving voice to their aspiration for social equality by advancing a conception of African-Americans that would allow a discussion of racial distinctions while accommodating the tendency of African-Americans, under the dominating influence of racism, to want to minimize references to physical differences in such discussions.

Du Bois was interested in formulating non-biological criteria for a definition of race mainly because he wanted to provide a more adequate ground for the group identity he considered a crucial component in the African-American's social agenda. He made this clear when, with the reference to the idea of race in general, he spoke of "its efficiency as the vastest and most ingenious invention for human progress." He suggested that, following the success model of other groups, African-Americans must *invent* a conception of themselves that will contribute to their social elevation as a group. His revisionist notion of race was therefore proposed at the outset of something African-Americans must self-consciously adopt for political purposes. We can notice that he did not fail to acknowledge the social construction of the concept of race when, in his citation of the eight distinct racial groups, he qualified his reference to them with the phrase "in the sense in which history tells us the word must be used." What shows us that he aimed to deconstruct the received view, however, is the way he juxtaposed his sociohistorical concept of race with what he referred to as "the present division of races," viz., the scientific conception of the three main biological groups; for he goes on to point out that biology cannot provide the criteria for race identity because, historically, there has been an "integration of physical differences." This fact leads him to conclude that what really distinguishes groups of people into races are their "spiritual and mental differences."

Some of Du Bois's readers have rejected his sociohistorical definition of race in favor of a definition based on physical differences. What Du Bois's detractors tend to overlook, however, is the fact that his definition does not deny the obvious physical differences that constitute race, nor does his discussion of race display any special commitment to the sociohistorical view he sets forth. A close reading will reveal that he only meant to deny the *viability* of a strictly biological account of race, and, furthermore, to assert that an empirical study of history will show this to be the case. Based on his own survey of anthropological findings, he tells us that when different groups of people came together to form cities,

> The larger and broader differences of color, hair and physical proportions were not by any means ignored, but myriads of minor differences disappeared, and the sociological and historical races of men began to approximate the present division of races as indicated by physical researches.

The aim of Du Bois's deconstruction of the concept of race was to create a means of employing the prevailing definition of race based on genetics, i.e., to allow him to continue speaking of "the black-blooded people of America," or the "people of Negro blood in the United States," while at the same time leaving room for him to question any undesirable implications of such definitions, i.e., to override definitions that imply that the physical differences which typically characterize the various races somehow justify social inequality.

THE AFRICAN-AMERICAN CULTURAL IMPERATIVE

But what bearing does Du Bois's revised notion of race have on his argument for the claim that African-Americans have a duty to retain their race identity? As Boxill has noted, one important reason Du Bois cites to support this imperative is that African-Americans have a distinct cultural mission as a racial group. On behalf of the Negro Academy, Du Bois asserted that, "We believe that the Negro people, as a race, have a contribution to make to civilization and humanity, which no other race can make." But what exactly is this unique contribution? I am not sure whether Du Bois had an answer to this question. He weakly stated that African-Americans are "a nation stored with wonderful possibilities of culture," which suggests that they do not yet have any such cultural contribution to make. He then goes on to speak of "a stalwart originality which shall unswervingly follow Negro ideals." And, although he makes passing references to "Pan-Negroism" and the "African fatherland," at no point does he advocate reclaiming any African cultural retentions. Instead, he prefers to tell us that "it is our duty to conserve our physical powers, our intellectual endowments, our spiritual ideals."

What then did Du Bois mean when he spoke of the duty of African-Americans to conserve their race identity in order to make a cultural contribution? His view of what constitutes African-American culture seem especially problematic when we consider some of his remarks regarding African-American identity. He states that,

> We are Americans, not only by birth and by citizenship, but by our political ideals, our language, our religion. Farther than that, our Americanism does not go. At that point, we are Negroes, members of a vast historic race that from the very dawn of creation has slept, but half awakening in the dark forests of its African fatherland.

If African-Americans share the same language, religion, and political ideals with other Americans there does not seem to be much left for them to uniquely contribute to American culture. Although, in some places, Du Bois spoke of the African-American's special mission in terms of a distinct cultural contribution he seems to have had more than simply culture in mind. I suspect that he really meant to speak of a *political* mission that culture in some way enables African-Americans to carry out. This is suggested, for instance, by his remarks regarding "that black to-morrow which is yet destined to soften the whiteness of the Teutonic to-day." What Du Bois may have meant here is simply that, through the establishment of a culturally pluralistic society, white cultures will no longer dominate. Instead, social equality will be fostered through a cultural exchange between the various races.

If we consider Du Bois's sociohistorical definition of race, along with his belief that African-Americans have a special mission, his rejection of biological essentialism and his failure to make use of the idea of African cultural retentions, begin to appear quite troublesome. For, as Appiah has keenly observed, his talk of Pan-Negroism requires that African-Americans and Africans share something in common other than oppression by whites. This lacuna in Du Bois's argument can be explained to some extent by considering the *tentative* nature of the duty of African-Americans to conserve their race identity. According to Du Bois, this duty lasts only "until this mission of the Negro people is accomplished." These remarks imply that the special mission of African-Americans has more to do with their struggle for social equality than with their making a cultural contribution; once social equality has been achieved, this duty no longer exists. We can see the explicitly *political* nature of this mission clearly expressed in the following remarks:

> (African-Americans) must be inspired with the Divine faith of our
> black mothers, that out of the blood and dust of battle will march
> a victorious host, a mighty nation, a peculiar people, to speak to
> the nations of earth a Divine truth that shall make them free.

Although the imperative to make a cultural contribution has more to do with politics than culture, there is nonetheless a link between them, for African-Americans must be inspired "out of the blood and dust of battle" to produce a unique culture that will contribute to world civilization. What makes African-American culture unique is its hybrid genesis within the context of racial oppression in America. The need for African cultural retentions is diminished given that the culture forged out of this experience will enable African-Americans to assume a role of political leadership among other black people. Du Bois's argument for the claim that African-Americans have a duty to conserve their race identity is backward-looking in the sense that it makes reference to the historical oppression of African-Americans, as a diaspora group, as a ground for this duty. His argument is forward-looking in the sense that it foresees an end to this oppression and, hence, an eventual release from the imperative.

NINETEENTH-CENTURY AFRICAN-AMERICAN SOCIAL THOUGHT

Some commentators have invoked biographical facts about Du Bois's own racial background to explain why he wanted to advance a sociohistorical account of race. While is it not unfair to see this as an important factor influencing his thinking about race, it is a plain misunderstanding to suppose that the reconstruction Du Bois proposed was wholly original. When we consider his argument within the context of African-American social thought at the turn of the century, certain quite noticeable details strongly indicate the influence of his contemporaries. He alludes to many concerns that had been expressed on both sides of the perennial separatist-integrationist debate by combining, under his own concept of cultural pluralism, certain tenets drawn from various doctrines of earlier emigrationist-assimilationist thinkers such as Blyden and Douglass. By far one of the most abiding and dominant influences on his thinking was clearly Booker T. Washington. We can notice the traces of some of Du Bois's nineteenth-century influences by paying careful attention to certain ideas that crop up in his essay.

According to Wilson J. Moses, Du Bois's argument in "The Conservation of Races" was directly influenced by Alexander Crummell, whose inaugural address to the Negro Academy expressed a similar preoccupation with the idea of "civilization" as a means of social elevation. Crummell, along with other nineteenth-century activists such as Henry Highland Garnet and Martin Delany, was prominent among the supporters of the African Civilization Society. The goals and values of nineteenth-century African-American nationalism were often situated in arguments regarding the development of "civilization" as a means of group elevation. With an eye to the place of African-Americans in a world civilization, Du Bois seems to reflect Blyden's earlier call of providence in his talk of an "advance guard" of African-Americans who must "take their just place in the van of Pan-Negroism." Appiah has suggested this reading, perhaps inadvertently, in characterizing Du Bois's remarks regarding the African-American message for humanity as deriving from God's purpose in creating races. The claim Du Bois makes here regarding the leadership role of African-Americans vis-a-vis other black people in Africa and the diaspora seems to capture the gist of Blyden's argument for emigration, although emigration was a proposal that Du Bois never embraced.

Despite the fact that his mention of "Pan-Negroism" presages the Pan-Africanism he would later adopt, Du Bois seems to have believed in 1897 that the uplift of Africa, and black people everywhere, could best be brought about by African-Americans pursuing cultural self-determination in America. Of course, the problem this poses for his sociohistorical account of race is that African-American and African cultures are significantly different. The idea of "Pan-Negroism" he derived from that account, i.e., "Negroes bound and welded together," failed to recognize the important cultural differences among the various groups of African and African diaspora people.

By contrast with Blyden's African nationalism, Frederick Douglass saw ex-slaves as Americans. He believed that, once African-Americans were educated and allowed to demonstrate their equality with whites, assimilation into the American mainstream would someday be possible. In some of his remarks, Du Bois avers to Douglass's view that slavery had severely damaged the dignity and sense of self-worth of African-Americans. He maintained that the first step toward social equality will be "the correction of the immorality, crime and laziness among the Negroes themselves, which still remains as a heritage from slavery."

Under the legal segregation that followed slavery Douglass's assimilationist view found a new expression in the philosophy of Booker T. Washington. Washington's strategy for changing the socioeconomic conditions of African-Americans was to appeal to the self-interest of whites. He gave priority to economic development as a key to the elevation of African-Americans as a group. Rather than demand social equality, Washington believed it would gradually come with the economic progress of the group. Notwithstanding their much-heralded disagreement over the role of political agitation, Du Bois seems to have accepted certain aspects of Washington's strategy. Along with Washington, for instance, Du Bois advocated social separation from whites "to avoid the friction of races." And Du Bois's assertion that "No people that laughs at itself, and ridicules itself, and wishes to God it was anything but itself ever wrote its name in history" seems to be a rewording of Washington's famous statement at the Atlanta Exposition that "No race that has anything to contribute to the markets of the world is long, in any degree, ostracized." Both claims are reminiscent of Douglass's earlier concern with the self-esteem of African-Americans as a group. Unlike Washington, however, Du Bois placed a greater emphasis on the cultural status of African-Americans. He argued against "a servile imitation of Anglo-Saxon culture" on the ground that African-Americans have a unique cultural contribution to make and that to accomplish this they must not assimilate. For Du Bois, social equality would be attained through the distinctive cultural achievements of African-Americans, who must retain their race identity in order to accomplish this.

When we consider Du Bois's idea of African-Americans gaining social equality through their cultural achievements we must not overlook some of the earlier proponents of this suggestion, viz., members of the various literary societies in the early part of the nineteenth century and the New Negro literary movement at the beginning of the 1890s. Maria W. Stewart followed David Walker in the tradition of advocating moral uprightness as the basis for elevating the race, a tradition which was perpetuated throughout the nineteenth century by various African-American voluntary associations. We can notice the sense of a mission, for instance, in Anna Julia Cooper's advocacy of an African-American literature "to give the character of beauty and power to the literary utterance of the race." In this vein then we should understand Du Bois's statement that "it is our duty to conserve our physical powers, our intellectual endowments, our spiritual ideals." His somewhat vague proposition here emanated from a history of ideas that assigned a specific role to culture in the elevation of African-Americans as a group.

Indeed, as a cornerstone of many turn-of-the-century theories of social change, the African-American cultural imperative created a strong expectation that educated African-Americans would employ their intellectual resources in the service of race uplift. On the assumption that culture and politics must coincide, Frances E. W. Harper and Pauline E. Hopkins presented arguments in their novels for the obligation of the black elite, viz., mulattoes, to refrain from marrying whites, or passing, and instead devote themselves to the betterment of African-Americans as a group. They aimed to influence some members of the group to remain loyal and to assume responsibility for elevating other members by arguing that there is a special duty requiring a sacrifice of social privilege. Du Bois seems to have heeded their teachings when he spoke against the loss of race identity in "the commingled blood of the nation," and when he raised the question "is self-obliteration the highest end to which Negro blood dare aspire?"

The duty to conserve African-American race identity so as to develop a distinct culture derives from an historical context in which the oppression of African-Americans as a group obtains. Under such conditions the function of culture is to resist oppression. Even if we accept the idea that African-Americans are, in some sense, collectively obligated to resist oppression we might still wonder whether they are, for this reason, obligated to conserve their race identity so as to develop a distinctive culture. With regard to the oppression experienced by African-Americans it seems that, for Du Bois, the right of resistance is tantamount to the right of cultural self-determination. Although African-Americans are, perhaps collectively, obligated to resist oppression in the sense that every African-American has a *right* not to acculturate into the American mainstream, this does not establish that African-Americans have a *duty* to conserve a distinctive culture.

RACE, ETHNICITY, AND BIOLOGY

When Du Bois defines race in terms of sociohistorical, rather than biological, or physical, criteria he seems to have blurred an important distinction between race and ethnicity, where the former is understood to refer to biological characteristics and the latter refers chiefly to cultural characteristics. Several commentators have taken him to task for lapsing into this confusion. Their criticisms, however, seem to presuppose that people can be divided into biologically distinct racial groups that develop in relative isolation. Du Bois's contention was that this ideal-type model of racial and ethnic groups lacks empirical validity, for sociohistorical factors have a greater significance for understanding the essentially *political* genesis, structure, and function of such groups.

Appiah, for instance, objects to Du Bois's sociohistorical definition on the ground that a group's history or culture *presupposes* a group identity and, therefore, cannot be a criterion of that group's identity. He attempts to refurbish Du Bois's talk of a common history by adding a geographical criterion such that a group's history is to be understood as (in part) the history of people from the same place. This move, however, seems needless on two counts. First, Du Bois makes clear that an important part of the history of African-Americans is their African past, and since he had little concern with cultural retentions, his point was largely a matter of geography. Secondly, as a criterion of group identity, geography does not add much, given that there are racially and culturally diverse people in various locations.

A similar objection has been raised by Boxill who points out that it is simply false to maintain that every black American shares a common culture. Instead, Boxill offers a physical definition of race that is reflected in the way the racist classifies people into races, whether they share a common culture or not:

> I propose that, insofar as black people are a race, they are people who either themselves look black—that is, have a certain kind of physical appearance—or are, at least in part, descended from such a group of people.

Boxill, however, is a bit too hasty in his dismissal of the obvious fact that the American system of classification, constructed on the basis of a racist ideology, breaks down when people of mixed blood do not neatly fit into the prescribed racial categories. He makes reference to the notion of "passing" to show that, with regard to people of mixed blood, a physical definition of race still offers the best account. But he overlooks the fact that this notion is fairly limited to the United States and perhaps to similar societies with a majority white population. Moreover, as I shall indicate shortly, many times the practice of racism, which informs Boxill's definition, seems to conveniently disregard the biological criteria he takes to be essential.

The best way to meet the objection that a definition of race based primarily on sociohistorical criteria confuses race with ethnicity is to accept it. In the United States the alleged confusion seems to have become a matter of institutionalized practice. College application forms, for instance, frequently display some such confusion when under the ethnic identity category they list *racial* designations such as "black" and "white" along with *ethnic* designations such as "Japanese" and "Hispanic." It becomes clear that such a system of racial and ethnic classification is constructed for political purposes when we take note of certain combined categories such as "Hispanic, not black." As primarily a linguistic designation, the term "Hispanic" can apply to groups of people who consider themselves white, black, or mixed-blood. Why then is there a need for a special category which designates a racial distinction that only singles out black people?

The idea that various notions of race have been constructed by racists for political purposes was well recognized in nineteenth-century African-American social thought. In his 1854 essay, "The Claims of the Negro Ethnologically Considered," Douglass accused the slaveholders of seeking a justification in science for the oppression of slaves. He pointed out that by engaging arguments that amount to "scientific moonshine that would connect men with monkeys," they wanted "to separate the Negro race from every intelligent nation and tribe in Africa." Douglass surmised that "they aimed to construct a theory in support of a foregone conclusion."

A similar accusation was published anonymously in 1859 in an article in the *Anglo-African Magazine*. The author begins with the claim that there is no pure unmixed Anglo-Saxon race, arguing that all whites with ethnic backgrounds (even with Egyptian blood) still claim to be Anglo-Saxon. The author then refers to the construction of the Anglo-Saxon race as "a legendary theory." The underlying racism of this theory, which relies on the Bible, is exposed by raising the question: if the curse of Canaan is used to prove that black blood is contaminated, what about the curse that marked out Anglo-Saxons for slavery? According to the author, Noah's curse did not point specifically to black people since Cush and Canaan were both sons of Ham. Ethnologists who use Biblical references to establish racial distinctions that imply black inferiority employ "a curious chain of evidence," for there is no African race, i.e., no group with pure African blood. The author reduces to absurdity the Biblical evidence for this belief, according to which:

> First, Abyssinians belong to a white race.
> Secondly, Ethiopians were the same as the Abyssinians.
> Lastly, the Negroes were Ethiopians.

The conclusion drawn from this *reduction* argument was that Negroes (Ethiopians) belong to the white race. The author's purpose in presenting this argument seems to have been to urge that all racial terms be treated as misnomers.

These nineteenth-century discussions of race indicate two of the most important factors underlying Du Bois's deconstruction of the biological concept of race, viz., racism and intermingling. Although the identity of every racial or ethnic group will involve both (a) physical or biological criteria and (b) cultural or sociohistorical criteria, whether, in any given society, (a) gains precedence over (b) seems to be a matter of politics, i.e., racism. But even in societies such as the United States where biological criteria have gained precedence, the fact of intermingling has rendered any attempt to establish rigid biological racial classifications problematic. When we consider groups such as Chicanos, Amerasians, or Cape Verdians it becomes clear that ethnic designations are needed to accommodate interminglings that have resulted in the creation of group identities that are based almost entirely on sociohistorical criteria.

THE DILEMMA OF BIOLOGICAL ESSENTIALISM

One major shortcoming of Du Bois's sociohistorical concept of race is that it fails to make clear how, in the face of racism, African-Americans are supposed to invent, or reconstruct, a concept of black identity that will contribute to the progress of the group. Racism is firmly grounded in scientific thinking regarding biologically determined racial types such that, for conceptual reasons, it seems undeniable that there are fundamentally yellow, black, and white people, despite any other ethnic, or cultural, designation that applies to them. As Appiah has noted, Du Bois's proposal to replace the biological concept of race with a sociohistorical one "is simply to bury the biological conception below the surface, not to transcend it." What is at issue, however, is whether the rigid dichotomy between race and ethnicity is tenable. Du Bois introduced sociohistorical criteria as a way to give an account of African-American group identity without presupposing this dichotomy. His insight was to draw from the history of racial intermingling in the United States both an objection to the biological essentialism of scientific classifications, as well as a ground on which to reconstruct African-American group identity in a social context dominated by a racist ideology.

With regard to the political aspect of Du Bois's reconstructionist project there is a dilemma posed by the ideological competition between Pan-African nationalists and Pan-Indian nationalists, both of whom have made appeals for unity to the same mixed-blood populations. Each nationalist group wants to lay claim to much of the same constituency as rightfully belonging to it, and each would justify this claim by reference to the relevant biological ancestry. Their respective injunctions regarding group loyalty make use of this essentialized conception of group membership for political purposes. In keeping with the biology inherent in their respective appeals for group loyalty, persons mixed with both African and

Indian ancestry are asked to identify with the group that best represents their physical appearance.

It is worth noting that the nationalist's motivation for establishing such rigid biological criteria for group membership is strictly political. Since black people and Indians are oppressed on the basis of race, rather than culture, the nationalists are rightfully inclined to seek to reconstruct the group identity of black people, or Indians, on strictly racial grounds. Du Bois, of course, recognized this and sought to achieve the same political ends as the nationalists, but without invoking the biological categories handed down from scientific racism. He wanted to accommodate the fact that intermingling had become an important feature of the history of African-Americans as a group. For Du Bois, then, group loyalty need not rely on a biological essentialism, given that most African-Americans are of mixed blood. As a criterion of group identity, he proposed to give culture a greater weight than physical characteristics.

The way biology is used to rationalize the American system of racial classification gives rise to an interesting puzzle regarding the dichotomy between race and ethnicity. Consider, for instance, the case in which two siblings are racially distinct, in some genetic sense, but have the same physical characteristics, as when a white male has offspring by both a black and a white female. We can speak of the offspring as being racially distinct on wholly genetic grounds, given that one child has two white parents and the other is of mixed parentage. The fact that this particular genetic difference should matter with regard to racial classification suggests a reason for the belief that race and ethnicity are not interchangeable concepts, viz., only the offspring of two white parents can be considered white.

This particular application of biological criteria becomes much more problematic, however, when the practice of tracing genetic background fails to neatly correlate with the practice of using physical characteristics as a basis for racial classification. We can see this problem by considering an example that involves a multiracial ethnic group that overlaps both black and white racial categories. Suppose that the female offspring of black/white mixed-blood parents has the same physical characteristics as the male offspring of non-black Hispanic parents, and further that they marry and have two children (a boy and a girl) who both, in turn, marry whites. Both are genetically black due to their mother's mixed blood, but since the girl no longer has a Spanish surname her children will be classified as white, while her brother's children will be classified as Hispanic. What this shows, I think, is not only that concepts of race and ethnicity are sometimes interchangeable, but also that, for sociological reasons, at some point genetics frequently drops out of consideration as a basis for racial classification.

We might wonder whether the emphasis Du Bois placed on sociohistorical criteria avoids the nationalist dilemma that arises on the biological essentialist account. Suppose that there are two persons with the same racial and cultural profile, i.e., each is of mixed heritage (with one black parent), each has the physical characteristics of a white person, and each has been acculturated into a white community. What if one decides to adopt a black identity despite her white cultural background? Can her newly acquired consciousness allow her to transcend her cultural background? Given the American system of racial classification, based on genetics, she is entitled to claim a black identity, something which seems to be ruled out on strictly sociohistorical grounds.

In many cases where members of multiracial ethnic groups seem to have pretty much adopted some version of Du Bois's sociohistorical criteria for their own group identity we can notice that the race-culture ambivalence engendered by the American system of racial classification is frequently resolved along cultural lines. For black Latinos, such as Puerto Ricans, Cubans, or Dominicans, language exerts an overriding influence on their group identity. Persons with black ancestry who have acculturated into these Latino groups would, in many instances, be more inclined to identify with people who share their cultural orientation than with people who share their physical characteristics, despite a great deal of pressure from the dominant society to abide by the prescribed racial classifications.

Du Bois has been taken to task for giving insufficient attention to the cultural differences among different groups of black people in various parts of the world. Indeed, his sociohistorical notion seems to break down when applied to culturally distinct groups of black people. But if in many cases culture gains precedence over race as a basis for group identity, he must have thought that there is something universal, or essential, in the cultures of all the various black ethnic groups, viz., a common history of oppression. Appiah has objected to Du Bois's sociohistorical essentialism by pointing out that it fails to uniquely apply to black people, for African-Americans share a history of oppression with many groups other than Africans or diaspora black people. This objection must be questioned, for I do not think it does much damage to Du Bois's suggestion that a commonly shared history of oppression provides a basis for African-American identity and for Pan-African unity.

What Du Bois was after with his reconstructed notion of race is best exemplified by considering its application to Jews. Membership in this group is determined mainly, but not exclusively, by a blood relationship (i.e., matrilineal descent) with other members of the group. Yet Jews are represented in all three of the biological races, most likely as a result of having intermingled. Jewish identity does not seem to be strictly a matter of culture, i.e., religion, or language, for during the Inquisition many people who were Jewish "by birth" were forced to convert to Catholicism (hence the term "Jewish Catholic"), and, presently, there are many individuals who have chosen not to learn Hebrew, or to practice a religion, yet in both cases they would still be considered Jews, and by and large they would themselves accept this designation. What then is essential to having a Jewish identity?

One very important factor which plays a major role in the construction of Jewish identity is the history of oppression commonly shared by Jews of all races and cultures. With regard to this oppression there is a sociohistorical continuity to the consciousness which unifies the group that is perpetuated by the persistence of antisemitism. Moreover, this consciousness seems to extend uniquely throughout the Jewish diaspora and, since the holocaust, has provided a rallying call for the maintenance of a homeland in Israel. What is important to notice in this regard is that contemporary Zionists in Israel have been accused of racism toward non-Jews, while antisemitism directed toward Jews seems to be virtually identical with other varieties of racism. What this shows, I think, is that there seems to be some sense in which racist practices can be attributed to a multiracial ethnic group, and equally, a sense in which such groups can be considered the victims of racism.

In considering how Du Bois's reconstructed notion of race can be applied to multiracial ethnic groups we must not assume that this is always by virtue of intermingling in the sense of some form of racial amalgamation. In both the United States and in Latin American societies where so-called "miscegenation" has occurred, the mixed-blood populations are largely the result of involuntary sexual contact between white masters and their slaves. In this historical context racism toward ex-slaves and their offspring has produced a value system such that "whitening" has become the racial ideal. Although this is, understandably, a dominant tendency among oppressed Third World people generally, we must not allow the influence of racism to blind us to a quite different sense in which racial identities have been constructed.

Consider, for instance, the fact that British colonialists sometimes referred to the natives of India and Australia as "blacks" and "niggers." Pan-African nationalism may very well be viewed as a response to colonialism, but can it therefore be restricted to groups of people of black African origin? There seems to be a clear sense in which people who are not of black African descent share a common oppression with black Africans and diaspora black people. In Australia there has developed a black consciousness movement among the aboriginals, who have appropriated a black identity heavily influenced by the sixties Civil Rights struggle in the United States. In England the term "black" is often used politically to include people of both West Indian and Asian descent. The reason for this development is that the Asian immigrant populations from Pakistan and India are politically aligned (in a way that is temporary and strained at times) with the West Indian immigrant population. The basis for the formation of this multiracial coalition under the rubric "black people" is the common history of oppression they share as ex-colonial immigrant settlers in Britain. The extension of the racial term "black" to non-African people in Australia, as well as to Asians in contemporary Britain, provides some indication that there is a sense in which a racial concept can be reconstructed to extend to a multiracial group that has not intermingled in the sense of having mixed blood.

Du Bois's proposal regarding group identity requires an adjustment in the biological essentialist criteria to account for intermingling in the sense of racial amalgamation, but what about multiracial group coalitions? By shifting the emphasis to sociohistorical consciousness he wanted to modify the biological requirement (influenced by scientific racism) to specify only a vague blood tie. Give the fact of racial amalgamation in the United States, he rightly maintained that African-American identity can only reside in sociohistorical consciousness. It is far from clear that he would have embraced all that this implies, viz., that sociohistorical consciousness figures into the social formation of racial and ethnic groups on the model of multiracial group coalitions as well.

RACISM AND COLOR STRATIFICATION

What if a peculiar sort of cultural exchange were to suddenly occur such that the sociohistorical consciousness that once resided in the biological group now known as "black people" also begins to manifest itself in the biological group now known as "white people"? Suppose further that, at some time in the future, the former group is exterminated (by genocide) or disappears (through amalgamation), and that the latter group inherits this consciousness. To what extent do we continue to apply the term "black people"? It seems that on Du Bois's account some such transference of consciousness would be allowed as long as there is, perhaps, a blood tie (say, "traceable") and the inheritors have a sociohistorical connection with their ancestors. If we treat Du Bois's stipulation regarding common blood as inessential it seems that his sociohistorical criteria provide a sufficient ground on which to establish the black identity of this biological white group.

While it may appear odd to speak of "white African-Americans," such an expression could conceivably be applied in some sense that parallels the present usage of the expression "black Anglo-Saxons," which does not seem odd. In each instance the respective expression would be applied by virtue of a transference of consciousness from one biological group to another, even when there is no blood tie between them. The reason that the expression "white African-American" may seem odd is because in the United States the concept of race applies strictly to blacks and whites in the sense that "traceable ancestry" really means that to be white is to have *no* non-white ancestry and to be black is to have *any* black ancestry. With few exceptions we can safely assume that there will be only a one-way transference of consciousness, i.e., black people will acculturate into the dominant white mainstream.

It would be a mistake, however, to rule out entirely the possibility of a group of white people appropriating something very much akin to the racial consciousness of African-Americans. In 1880 Gustave de Molinari documented his observation that the English press "allow no occasion to escape them of treating the Irish as an inferior race—a kind of white negroes." What is most interesting about this instance of bigotry by one white ethnic group directed toward another is that it was justified by appealing to the same scientific racism used to justify the oppression of black people, i.e., the idea that the Irish were a lower species closer to the apes. Moreover, presently in Northern Ireland, Irish Catholics are sometimes referred to by Protestants as "white niggers"—and, in turn, have appropriated and politically valorized this appellation. The link between African-Americans and, say, black South Africans is largely sociohistorical such that an important feature of African-American identity includes a commonly shared history of oppression, but only in this attenuated sense. Similarly, there is no reason to suppose that Irish Catholic identity could not conceivably include, as fellow colonial subjects, a commonly shared history of oppression, in this attenuated sense, with African-Americans and black South Africans.

The oddness of the concept of "white Negroes" or "white African-Americans" is a result of a special norm that places black people into a rock bottom category to which others can be assimilated for political purposes. The simianized portrayal of Irish Catholics figures into their oppression and degradation in a fashion similar to the function of such portrayals of African-Americans. What must be noted, however, is that black people are the paradigm for any such category. This indicates that racism is an ideology regarding the superiority of white people and the inferiority of nonwhite people. Du Bois made reference to the fact that this color spectrum is defined mainly by the black and white extremes. Although certain white ethnic groups, such as the Irish and the Jews, have experienced their own peculiar brand of racial oppression by other whites, they are not above engaging in racial discrimination against blacks.

The most telling criticism of Du Bois's attempt to reconstruct an African-American identity in terms of culture, rather than biology or physical characteristics is the fact that so much racism is based on color discrimination. Unlike most racial and ethnic groups, for black people physical characteristics are more fundamental than cultural characteristics with regard to racism. It is for this reason that black Jews experience discrimination by other Jews, or that there is a need to distinguish black Hispanics from all others. Racism based on color indicates that black people occupy an especially abhorrent category such that even hybrid groups that include mulattoes discriminate against them.

Although certain considerations regarding the intermingling of different racial and ethnic groups motivated Du Bois's revision of the notion of race his main concern was with the impact of racism on African-American group identity. He aimed to address the problem of color discrimination within the group by providing a concept of race that would bring African-Americans of different colors together. To the extent that color was an indication of class position among African-Americans he also dealt with the issue of group pride by rejecting the extremely divisive assimilationist racial ideal. He challenged the assimilationist doctrine of "whitening" by formulating the criteria of group identity in non-biological terms, a strategy designed to include African-Americans on both ends of the color spectrum. Group elevation does not require amalgamation and self-obliteration. Instead, social progress for African-Americans requires a conservation of physical characteristics (already multiracial) in order to foster cultural development. The strength of a group lies in its cultural integrity, which has to be situated in a dynamic historical process, rather than a biologically fixed category.

SHAMOON ZAMIR

A "Prosody of Those Dark Voices": The Transformation of Consciousness

In an address titled "The Need for New Ideas and New Aims," Alexander Crummell, founder of the American Negro Academy, urged African-Americans to forget the past in order to successfully enter modernity. According to Crummell, "memory . . . is a passive act of mind . . . the necessary and unavoidable entrance, storage and recurrence of facts and ideas to consciousness. Recollection . . . is the actual seeking of the facts, the endeavor of the mind to bring them back to consciousness. The natural recurrence of the idea or the fact of slavery is that which cannot be faulted. What I object to is the unnecessary recollection of it." Crummell's influence on the early thought of Du Bois has been well documented. The American Negro Academy's program to promote an interest in literature, science, and art among African-Americans as a way of developing a scholarly and refined elite was adopted with little modification by Du Bois in "The Talented Tenth." But Frank Kirkland, in a discussion of the problem of modernity and the past in the thought of African-American intellectuals, demonstrates that if Crummell's refusal of history and of active recollection leads anywhere, it leads to Booker T. Washington, not to Du Bois. Focusing his discussion of Du Bois on "Of the Sorrow Songs," the final chapter of *Souls*, Kirkland argues that Du Bois firmly ties the present and the future to the past and accepts the creative and critical function of recollection.

From *Dark Voices: W.E.B. Du Bois and American Thought, 1888–1903*. © 1995 by The University of Chicago Press.

For Du Bois, recollection pries loose from the continuum of past horrors fleeting revelations of enslaved Africans punctuating it with forms of expression that rendered their hopes and expectations of what counted as good and just reflectively transparent albeit constantly unfulfilled. It enables African-Americans to highlight fragments torn from the past and define them as motives for rending "the Veil"; it enables them to conceive themselves as breaking the repetition of unfulfilled expectations regarding what counts as good and just in their future-oriented present. Without it, they fall victim to the "irreverence toward Time" and to the "ignorance of the deeds of men," succumbing to a complacency of mind regarding a past that goes unredeemed and a future-oriented present that lends itself to being forgotten.

Crummell's refusal of recollection ties his programmatics to American exceptionalism, a problematic alignment that persists, so the conclusion to this study argues, in contemporary African-American critical thought. Several forms of this exceptionalism have already been encountered, from the social sciences to the work of Emerson and James. Max Horkheimer's critique of Pragmatism's refusal of the past is pertinent here because it offers a reminder that the failure of active remembering leads to the sacrifice of creative contemplation and truth:

> Pragmatism reflects a society that has no time to remember and mediate. . . . Like science, philosophy itself "becomes not a contemplative survey of existence nor an analysis of what is past and done with, but an outlook upon future possibilities with a reference to attaining the better and averting the worst." Probability or, better, calculability replaces truth, and the historical process that in society tends to make of truth an empty phrase receives its blessing, as it were, from pragmatism, which makes an empty phrase of it in philosophy.

This chapter examines not so much the way in which Du Bois recovers the facts of the past in his encounters with the acts of recollection already embodied in the great African-American spirituals as how these encounters lead Du Bois toward a transformation of consciousness. This transformation is described in part through a shifting ratio of the senses. Between the first and last chapters of *Souls* Du Bois moves from being seen by the "tall newcomer" to *hearing* the voices of the "black folk" as they sing the "sorrow songs." The sense of both distance and connection between the Harvard-trained black New Englander and the southern singers and their songs is captured with precision by the poet Jay Wright:

> All night, again, all night,
> you've been at your
> fledgling history,
> passing through the old songs,
> through the old laments.
> But here, in Harvard Square,
> the prosody of those dark voices
> is your connection.

But at the close of *Souls* Du Bois is not immersed in solitary study at Harvard; instead he is seen as a teacher at Atlanta University, listening to the music rising up through his window. In opening himself up to "those dark voices" that sing the spirituals, Du Bois finds himself and his political program for black leadership in the midst of another challenge. Confronted by the articulate knowledge of suffering embodied in the songs, Du Bois cannot sustain either the detached observational stance of the social scientist or the political narrative of a superior leadership pulling the primitive black masses into modernity. At the very moment that he is forced to acknowledge that the Talented Tenth may have something to learn from those they would lead, Du Bois is also pushed into involvement and response by the interactions of speech and hearing, interactions that undermine the sensuous detachment of the silent, observing scientist. The response is the writing of the book called *Souls of Black Folk*, imaged in its own closing moments as the labors of the "weary traveller" and as the text sent out into the world in the book's "Afterthought." Du Bois's foregrounding of listening, speech, and writing ties consciousness to the production of language and to the relationship of self to others (though here as elsewhere in *Souls* Du Bois never slips into romantic notions of collective identity). Consciousness cannot, therefore, be conceived of reductively as simply a content that can be "expressed" or "represented." The foregrounding of the production of language from within human contact also means that Du Bois's sense of consciousness and its activities is also more social and certainly more creative than the sense of it in either James's or Emerson's accounts. But at the same time it must also be stressed that while Du Bois places his own consciousness in relationship to the folk with accuracy and detail, the destabilizations of the self resulting from the social and historical placing in *Souls* do not lead to a position from which Du Bois can begin to imagine the possibility of political action in collective and populist terms.

Souls's final chapter can be read as an attempt to resolve the "contradiction of double aims" that traps the "black *savant*" and black artist alike. In "Of Our Spiritual Strivings" the black educator is caught in the double awareness that the knowledge needed to educate the black masses is a "twice-told tale" to most whites, and the knowledge needed to educate the whites is "Greek" to most blacks. Similarly, the black artist tries to work in a world where the whites despise the "soul-beauty" of black culture, but he cannot bring himself to abandon that culture in order to "articulate the message of another people." These dichotomies are dissolved into greater complexity in "Of the Sorrow Songs."

Du Bois's commentary on the spirituals focuses on the political and sociological meaning of the lyrics, not on the romantic and primitivist notion of some innate "soul-beauty." By adopting Herderian organic history, which makes folk culture central to national identity, as a frame for his commentary, Du Bois suggests that the spirituals and their political content must be made central to any national self-definition in America. The destabilization of white self-confidence also troubles the confidence of the black bourgeoisie because the insistence on the spirituals as an embodiment of historical knowledge also reverses the flow of knowledge and power between the Talented Tenth and the black masses. As in the first chapter of *Souls*, the crisis of the leadership elite is dramatized through the cave from Plato's *Republic*. The allegorical reworking is the culmination of a series of dramatizations of the crisis of leadership, dramatizations that dominate the last five chapters of *Souls*, and it is a reworking to which Du Bois returns years later in *Dusk of Dawn*.

This chapter examines Du Bois's treatment of this crisis, the ways in which he anchors his descriptions within a dramatization of his own relationship to the spirituals and the revisions of the Platonic allegory, and how the account of consciousness suggested above arises out of these materials. In the final section the account of consciousness and of the relationship of self and the African-American masses in *Souls* is compared to Du Bois's later autobiographical writings. The chapter begins with a brief look at Du Bois's commentary on the political content of the sorrow songs in the context of other nineteenth-century American accounts of folk culture and the spirituals.

The Sorrow Songs: Using an Unusable Past

In his essay "Negro Spirituals" (1867), Thomas Wentworth Higginson, the white commander of the First South Carolina Volunteers, the first

African-American regiment in the Civil War, wrote that by the singing of these songs the black soldiers

> could sing themselves, as had their fathers before them, out of the contemplation of their own estate, into the sublime scenery of the Apocalypse. I remember that this minor-keyed pathos used to seem to me almost too sad to dwell upon, while slavery seemed destined to last for generations; but now that their patience has had its perfect work, history cannot afford to lose this portion of its record. There is no parallel instance of an oppressed race thus sustained by the religious sentiment alone. These songs are but the vocal expression of the simplicity of their faith and the sublimity of their long resignation.

Throughout his essay Higginson offers a sympathetic account of African-American music, remarking on the beauty of the songs, suggesting the syncretism of African and non-African materials, and commenting on the social and historical content of the songs. But in the passage quoted above, while he acknowledges that the spirituals speak of suffering, Higginson nostalgically stresses their spiritual transcendence of material conditions, and at the same time—writing with the postwar confidence of the victor—relegates racist oppression to the past. The spirituals must now be preserved as museum artifacts precisely because their existence is in doubt; the history upon which they have fed has now come to an end.

Higginson's "Negro Spirituals" was, along with William F. Allen, Charles P. Ware, and Lucy McKim Garrison's *Slave Songs of the United States* (also 1867), the most notable early commentary on African-American music. Higginson's attitudes are worth noting because they are representative of the analytic and valuative frameworks of studies of folk culture within which—and also against which—Du Bois's own commentary on the spirituals takes shape.

The late nineteenth century saw the full development of a search for a usable past in American folklore studies. These studies sought in folk culture a set of values to place in opposition to the materialism and technological rationality the folklorists took to be the dominant spirit of their age. Though these studies were critical of contemporary social transformations, their organicist nostalgia also confirmed and validated contemporary progressive evolutionism. Du Bois was in touch with these developments not only through his reading of the work of Higginson and other early commentators on African-American music, but also via the work on the Scottish and English folk ballads undertaken by the Harvard communalists. Francis James

Child, Francis Barton Gummere, and George Lyman Kitteredge were all active during the years when Du Bois was a student at Harvard, and were working within a tradition of Herderian theorizations of national culture and literature that went back in America at least as far as Emerson and Whitman. The communalists held to a group theory of folk poetry, seeing it as the expression of a collective consciousness generated by a peasant or classless society that predated the atomization of the modern state, and as antithetical to the poetry of high art.

To some extent Du Bois was also invested in the reactionary (and potentially accommodationist) baggage of the organicist primitivism of late-nineteenth-century American studies of folk culture. He insists too often that "like all primitive folk, the slave stood near to Nature's heart," or that black Americans are "the sole oasis of simple faith and reverence in a dusty desert of dollars and smartness." Nor is Du Bois always able to sustain a cultural and linguistic definition of the *Volk*, as Herder did. He slips easily from the spiritual essentialism of his celebrations of the "*latent* genius" and "*innate* love of harmony and beauty" into at least a rhetoric of biological racial definition in his claim that "Negro *blood* has a message for the world" (all emphases added). But in the end Du Bois's commentary on the spirituals proves to be more politicized than the studies that precede it. Certainly, like Higginson, Du Bois accepts the songs as a record of the past. But unlike Higginson, he understands the songs not as a dead record but as a living recollection that continues to speak to the disgraces of a present that has by no means severed its links with the antebellum era.

The very opening of "Of the Sorrow Songs" announces a shift in cultural emphasis different from the rest of the book. All the chapters in *Souls* are prefaced by a quotation, usually from a well-known white poet identified by name, and some bars of music taken from the great and anonymous spirituals, with the source of the music always left unidentified (until Du Bois names the songs in the final chapter). In the last chapter, bars from "Wrestlin' Jacob, the day is a-breaking" are juxtaposed not to the words of one of the well-known poets but to lyrics taken from one of the spirituals. At the start of the chapter on the spirituals Du Bois writes:

> Little of beauty has America given the world save the rude grandeur God himself stamped on her bosom; the human spirit in this new world has expressed itself in vigor and ingenuity rather than in beauty. And so by fateful chance the Negro folk-song—the rhythmic cry of the slave—stands today not simply as the *sole* American music, but as the *most beautiful expression of human experience born this side of the seas*. It has been neglected, it

has been, and is, despised, and above all it has been persistently mistaken and misunderstood; but notwithstanding it still remains as the *singular spiritual heritage of the nation* and the greatest gift of the Negro people. (emphases added)

The implications of this exaggerated centralization are radical within the frameworks of Herderian organic history that Du Bois employs. For Herder, folk music is a basis for national self-definition. "Music," he argues, "is the first of the fine arts" among "the uncultivated nations," and in its rough and popular folk form it "displays the internal character of the peoples." When the above passage from *Souls* is read in this light, Du Bois appears to be doing more than offering his white reader a glimpse into the heart of black life behind the veil: he is suggesting that black experience, as it is embodied and voiced in the spirituals, must stand at the very center of any American national self-fashioning.

The shifting of black music to the center stage of national culture has two effects. First, by replacing high art's claims for representing the health of national culture with the counterclaims for the higher authenticity of black *folk* art, Du Bois is able to relativize the criteria by which racist evolutionary theories provided alibis for Anglo-Saxon superiority and for the assimilation or exclusion of minority groups:

The silently growing assumption of this age is that the probation of races is past, and that the backward races of to-day are of proven inefficiency and not worth the saving. Such an assumption is the arrogance of peoples irreverent toward Time and ignorant of the deeds of men. A thousand years ago such an assumption, easily possible, would have made it difficult for the Teuton to prove his right to life. Two thousand years ago such dogmatism, readily welcome, would have scouted the idea of blond races ever leading civilization. So woefully unorganized is sociological knowledge that the meaning of progress, the meaning of "swift" and "slow" in human doing, and the limits of human perfectibility, are veiled, unanswered sphinxes on the shores of science. Why should Aeschylus have sung two thousand years before Shakespeare was born? Why has civilization flourished in Europe, and flickered, flamed, and died in Africa? So long as the world stands meekly dumb before these questions, shall this nation proclaim its ignorance and unhallowed prejudices by denying freedom of opportunity to those who brought the Sorrow Songs to the Seats of the Mighty?

This passage comes near the end of the chapter on the spirituals, itself the last chapter of *Souls*. Du Bois is trying to draw out the broader implications of his discussion of the slave songs. He is himself unable to let go of the idea of civilization and to make the move to *society*, though he *has* reached the middle ground of a new and broader definition of culture. From this vantage point, and against the grain of his own dichotomization of primitive and civilized, he is at least able to grope his way to the idea that once the criterion for judging the "progress" or "backwardness" of a people is shifted from technological or imperial achievement to poetry, the hierarchy between "civilized" and "primitive" becomes unstable. The shift is from the spatio-temporal distancing of the knower and the known in conventional sociological and anthropological discourse toward what Johannes Fabian calls "coevalness" or "contemporality."

It is on this basis that Du Bois asks admittance for "those who brought the Sorrow Songs to the Seats of the Mighty." But if this, like the suppression of economic and political causality from the historical process in the passage, is another example of Du Bois's ethical idealism, the next paragraph of *Souls* asks abruptly, "Your country? How came it yours?" continuing, "Before the Pilgrims landed we were here." The asking of this question and Du Bois's reply, coming as they do in the midst of his summing-up of the meaning of the slave songs, suggest that this meaning is inseparable from the history of slavery and conquest upon which the nation is built. This is the second effect of Du Bois's centralization of black music within the national culture. The "message" of the songs, "veiled and half articulate" and buried "beneath conventional theology," turns out to be a revelation of their social and historical content:

> These songs are the articulate message of the slave to the world. They tell us in these eager days that life was joyous to the black slave, careless and happy. I can easily believe this of some, of many. But not all the past South, though it rose from the dead, can gainsay the heart-touching witness of these songs. They are the music of an unhappy people, of the children of disappointment; they tell of death and suffering and unvoiced longing toward a truer world, of misty wanderings and hidden ways.

Du Bois's sentiments here recall those of Frederick Douglass before him, who was "utterly astonished" upon his arrival in the free North "to find persons who could speak of the singing, among slaves, as evidence of their contentment and happiness." Douglass's discussion of the slave songs in his first autobiography in fact prefigures something of Du Bois's drift away from metaphysics and social science to a recognition of poetry as a different and powerful mode of understanding in *Souls*. Recalling the days when he had escaped to the North and was asked by the abolitionists to write his slave narrative, Douglass remembered that one leading abolitionist told him, "Give us the facts, we will take care of the philosophy." Douglass gave more than facts and something other than philosophizing in his first narrative when he asserted his conviction that "the mere hearing" of the slave songs "would do more to impress some minds with the horrible character of slavery, than the reading of whole volumes of philosophy on the subject could."

If the moving romanticism of Du Bois's writing on the sorrow songs, like his tempting language of secrecy and revelation, promises the white reader an encounter with the exotic, the subtlety with which Du Bois nudges the organicism into political history at key moments checks the predatorism of the cultural tourist and cuts short that same nostalgic flight that sentimentally primitivized the North American Indians in the midst of genocide. The progress of the sympathetic imagination in *Souls* is not without its hazards. It cannot rest on the leisurely self-confidence that seems to underlie James's expansive openness to the "laboring classes." It must be aware of its own complicity in the condition of the Other. What the white American reader finds behind the veil of the color line is, finally, a mirror. But if Du Bois destabilizes the position of the reader in the final chapter of *Souls*, his account of the songs leads to a simultaneous problematization of the assumption of privileged cultural access implicit in his own position as interpretive mediator between the songs and the reader. Within the organic history of the final chapter of *Souls*, Du Bois's dramatization of his own relationship to black culture is as important as his displacements of the white reader.

Voices from the Caverns and the Guardians of the Folk

To recall Jay Wright's poem on Du Bois, "the prosody of those dark voices" that sing the "old songs" *is* Du Bois's "connection" to his "fledgling history," but it is a connection that cannot be taken for granted. Du Bois's dramatization of his relationship to the songs is marked by a representational hesitancy that is symptomatic of the fact that his own understanding of the songs is itself partly grounded in sympathetic imagination (though different in kind from the white reader's). Du Bois's commentary is not based in an *exactly* shared history between his post-Emancipation northern self and the roots of the songs in a long history of southern violence and slavery, and therefore does not have the legitimation of absolute commonality. These differences, determined by factors of geography, class, and education, emerge only very allusively and elliptically in the final chapter of *Souls* because Du Bois appears to be caught between wanting, on the one hand, to disguise them in order to strengthen the political challenge to the white reader, and on the other hand, to acknowledge them within a nondogmatic art. A more immediate and concrete sense of the differences and the strategic hesitancies can be given by comparing Du Bois's accounts of his encounters with the "sorrow songs" in the chapter with his quite different accounts of these same encounters in his later autobiographical writings and, in one instance, also in an earlier part of *Souls*.

"Of the Sorrow Songs" opens with Du Bois's earliest recollection of hearing the spirituals and describes the powerful sense of recognition experienced by the young Du Bois:

> Ever since I was a child these songs have stirred me strangely. They came out of the South unknown to me, one by one, and yet at once I knew them as of me and of mine. Then in after years when I came to Nashville I saw the great temple builded of these songs towering over the pale city. To me Jubilee Hall seemed ever made of the songs themselves, and its bricks were red with the blood and dust of toil. Out of them rose for me morning, noon and night, bursts of wonderful melody, full of the voices of my brothers and sisters, full of the voices of the past.

Although there is here just sense enough of the distance and difference between North and South, as the shadow of strangeness and the "unknown" momentarily passes across the transparent meaning of the songs, the overwhelming sense of the passage is one of an intensely felt cultural identity experienced as an almost familial bond. When Du Bois returns to the memories of his earliest encounters with the spirituals at the end of his life, there is a much more inflected sense of cultural difference in his account. He remembers in his *Autobiography* (1968) that he "heard the Negro folksong first in Great Barrington, sung by the Hampton Singers. But that was *second-hand, sung by youth who never knew slavery*" (emphasis added). The songs were, then, an importation into the New England (and predominantly white) culture of Du Bois's hometown. And an importation weakened for Du Bois by divorce from its historic and geographic roots, a divorce that reflects the situation of Du Bois as a listener as much as that of the singers. Du Bois goes on to describe how he "heard the Negro songs by those who made them and in the land of their American birth" when he first went South as an undergraduate and taught school in rural Tennessee. There he attended his first revival meeting. As Du Bois details his sense of curiosity and excitement at the novelty of the situation, the sense is very much that of an ethnographic participant-observer reporting from the field. After the "quiet and subdued" church meetings in Berkshire, Du Bois finds himself in the midst of "a pythian madness, a demoniac possession" that reveals "a scene of human passion such as I had never conceived before." This same passage occurs in chapter 10 of *Souls* and provides a point of contrast within *Souls* for the descriptions that follow it in the book's final chapter. The feelings of the young Du Bois tend toward reproducing the exoticism that led the white middle-class reading public to seek out works that revealed how the other half lived at the turn of the century, but he registers the deeply disturbing effects of the passionate scene with a force that moves beyond exoticism.

Du Bois's recourse to images of the irrational aligns him with his mentor Crummell's dislike for black folk culture. For Crummell, African-American folk and proletarian culture had to be purged of its rudeness and heathen retentions. When most African-Americans were Baptists or Methodists, Crummell was an Episcopalian. The Episcopal church was associated with the black bourgeoisie and the upper classes.

> The church had dignified rituals and was far removed from the plantation culture that he identified with barbarism, depravity, and weakness. Episcopalianism, with its principles of "submission to authority, respect for rules, quietness and order," was congenial to Crummell's conservative temperament. The American Episcopal church brought him into contact with Anglicanism and nurtured his sense of participating in the literary and intellectual traditions of England. The Anglican music and architecture appealed to him, as did the Anglican liturgy. His religious sentiments were closely linked to aesthetic preferences that were uncommon among black Americans.

Du Bois's own self-fashioning in his first description in *Souls* of his earliest encounter with plantation culture is very much in the image of Crummell's Episcopalianism. But in Du Bois's account, what the young Du Bois sees as irrational is balanced by a mature evaluation of the cultural achievement of the spirituals. Out of this contrast Du Bois can generate gentle self-mockery. As he notes with restrained humor, "To be sure, we in Berkshire were not perhaps as stiff and formal as they in Suffolk of olden time; yet we were very quiet and subdued, and I know not what would have happened those clear Sabbath mornings had some one punctuated the sermon with a wild scream, or interrupted the long prayer with a loud Amen!"

Du Bois's recollections of an African song that had been handed down in his own family and his tracing of the genealogy of the song provide another useful point of comparison between *Souls* and later autobiographical writings. In the middle part of the final chapter of *Souls* he writes:

> My grandfather's grandmother was seized by an evil Dutch trader two centuries ago; and coming to the valleys of the Hudson and Housatonic, black, little, and lithe, she shivered and shrank in the harsh north winds, looked longingly at the hills, and often crooned a heathen melody to the child between her knees, thus:
>
> > Do bana coba, gene me, gene me!
> > Do bana coba, gene me, gene me!
> > Ben d' nuli, nuli, nuli, nuli, ben d' le.
>
> The child sang it to his children and they to their children's children, and so two hundred years it has travelled down to us and we sing it to our children, *knowing as little as our fathers what its words may mean, but knowing well the meaning of its music.*
> (emphasis added)

Again, the overriding sense here is of a transcendent bond. But at the same time the ambivalent wavering between not knowing the meaning of the words to the song (the lyrics appear to be from no known African language) and a fundamental understanding of the meaning of the music hints at the fact that although the historical continuity of black culture in America is hardly in doubt, it is nevertheless fractured enough to require a sympathetic leap.

Du Bois's later autobiographical writing presents a less transcendent vision. In *Dusk of Dawn* (1940) Du Bois writes that he is, in fact, not sure if his great-great-grandmother was born in Africa or in America and does not know where she learned the song. This acknowledgment comes at the close of a long section of the autobiography in which Du Bois traces his very mixed and very complicated family genealogy back to its French Huguenot, Dutch, African, and even Native American roots. The song sung by his great-great-grandmother becomes then his "only one direct cultural connection" with Africa. After quoting the passage on the African song from *Souls* at length, Du Bois adds that "living with my mother's people I absorbed their culture patterns and these were not African so much as Dutch and New England." The "African racial feeling was then purely a matter of . . . later learning and reaction," of Du Bois's "recoil from the assumptions of the whites" and his "experience in the South at Fisk," though "it was none the less real and a large determinant of my life and character."

The passages from the final chapter of *Souls* quoted above signal certain hesitancies, but these hesitancies are more than securely contained within Du Bois's impassioned acceptance of a common history of oppression. However, Du Bois's dramatization of his own relationship to the songs in *Souls* is more subtle than this. It manages finally to suggest the extent of both separation and identity and so resists the alibi of an essentialized idea of *communitas*. The scene that closes *Souls*, the climax of the final chapter, presents a tableau in which Du Bois's relationship to the songs is represented with greater self-reflexivity and complexity:

> If somewhere in this whirl and chaos of things there dwells Eternal Good, pitiful yet masterful, then anon in His good time America shall rend the Veil and the prisoned shall go free. Free, free as the sunshine trickling down the morning into these high windows of mine, free as yonder fresh young voices welling up from the caverns of brick and mortar below—swelling with song, instinct with life, tremulous treble and darkening bass. My children, my little children, are singing to the sunshine, and thus they sing:
>> Let us cheer the weary traveller,
>> Cheer the weary traveller,
>> Let us cheer the weary traveller,
>> Along the heavenly way
> And the traveller girds himself, and sets his face toward the Morning, and goes his way.

This curious scene is a careful revision of both Du Bois's own description of his hearing the spirituals at Nashville's Jubilee Hall that opens the chapter on the spirituals and of Plato's well-known allegory of the cave in his *Republic*, with Du Bois as Plato's enlightened man caught between the light of the sun and the darkness of the caverns. This double revision embodies a plural intentionality on Du Bois's part. Du Bois tries to dramatize simultaneously the independence and artistic integrity of the collective voice that sings through the songs and his own relationship to this voice as a bourgeois intellectual. Such a representational strategy comes as no surprise within the framework of organic history and, to some extent, Du Bois is inevitably trapped within this historical model's paradox of desired immersion and identity and the distance of interpretive authority. Nevertheless, to ignore Du Bois's own openness to displacement by the songs would be to misrepresent his writing.

Du Bois's treatment of the spirituals seems at first to be marked by a pronounced sense of cultural elitism or hierarchization that reinforces pastoral nostalgias. Nashville's Jubilee Hall, "towering over the pale city" at the opening of the chapter on the spirituals, has by the end become the academic tower of Atlanta University, where Du Bois taught from 1897 to 1910, and where he sits listening to the songs drifting up from below through the "high windows" of the university building. Where the young Du Bois, an undergraduate in his late teens, had been overwhelmed by his first hearing of the songs and an initial sense of community promised by "the voices of my *brothers and sisters*," the older professor sits alone in his office, a little more removed and reflective in his attention to the singing of "my *children*, my little children." This "older" Du Bois was, in fact, only in his mid-thirties at the time he wrote the last chapter of *Souls*, but the kindly (and grating) paternalism of the closing scene belies this fact and offers the reader a self-image that artificially stresses a greater sense of age and therefore a more pronounced sense of distanced contemplation.

There is, then, submerged beneath the sociological and aesthetic meditations on black music in the final chapter, an authorial self-fashioning and an autobiographical narrative of Du Bois's development from infancy (when the African song is first heard) to youthful immersion (in Tennessee) and to mature self-consciousness (at Atlanta University). This narrative is told as an ongoing dialectical engagement between Du Bois and the "sorrow songs" that unfolds primarily across the historically charged landscape of the South, from Nashville, Tennessee, to Atlanta, Georgia. Du Bois's commentary on the songs is itself a product of the older self and represents a discourse of a different, more self-conscious, nature than the songs themselves, the organicism of the latter being, within Du Bois's Herderian communalism, by definition unself-reflexive. Du Bois's particular interpretive access to the content at the heart of the songs is therefore guaranteed not simply by his fraternal or paternal bonds with the culture and history of the songs but also by those perspectives available to him as a trained academic, intellectual, and writer. The unveiling of the songs seems to be dependent upon their mediation by and incorporation into the different order of reflection and art represented by Du Bois's writing. This seems to shift the axis of articulation away from the songs themselves toward Du Bois's written synthesizing.

This self-fashioning on Du Bois's part pushes his dramatization of his relationship to the songs toward what James Clifford has described as the allegorical structure of "salvage, or redemptive, ethnography," where "the recorder and interpreter . . . is custodian of an essence, unimpeachable witness to an authenticity." As Clifford accurately notes, this structure "is appropriately located within a long Western tradition of pastoral." Within such an allegoric narrative, "the self, cut loose from viable collective ties, is an identity in search of wholeness, having internalized loss and embarked on an endless search for authenticity. Wholeness by definition becomes a thing of the past (rural, primitive, childlike) accessible only as a fiction, grasped from a stance of incomplete involvement." Clifford is describing what Frederic Jameson, in a discussion of historicism, has called "historical and cultural aestheticism," a stance in which "*historicity* as such is manifested by means of the contact between the historian's mind in the present and a given synchronic cultural complex from the past."

Nostalgic contemplation is never fully abandoned in Du Bois's commentary, and Clifford's ethnographic commentary does help describe the radical desire that is the content of Du Bois's or Higginson's critical nostalgia. Higginson's account of the spirituals offers a clearer example than *Souls* of what Clifford means by "salvage ethnography." Calling himself "a faithful student of the Scottish ballads," Higginson describes hearing and writing down the songs around the campfire as a gathering "on their own soil [of] these strange plants, which I had before seen as in museums alone": "Writing down in the darkness, as I best could,—perhaps with my hand in the safe covert of my pocket,—the words of the song, I have afterwards carried it to my tent, like some captured bird or insect, and then, after examination, put it by." But in Du Bois the sense of salvage ethnography does consistently give way. For one thing, Du Bois's account of the spirituals lays stress not on the recuperation of an essentialized wholeness from the past, but instead on an art that is responsive to historical change. Submerged in the commentary of the final chapter of *Souls* is a narrative of the gradual transformation of the slave songs. This narrative traces the development of the songs from their original African forms, first through their early American form in the music encountered by the young Du Bois in the rural South and by whites during the Civil War at Port Royal in "the Sea Islands of the Carolinas," then through the subsequent and greater hybridization of elements "both Negro and Caucasian," to the contemporary form of the songs heard in Atlanta at the end. It is true that for Du Bois the early forms of the songs are somehow more authentic than some of the later hybridizations. But his stress on the political content of the songs is also dependent on an acceptance of the transformation of the songs in response to a changing political history. In keeping with the *Bildungsbiographie* structure of *Souls*, the history of the songs runs alongside an autobiographical narrative in which the stages of personal development are in fact linked to specific encounters with the slave songs. To describe these moments of contact as "historical and cultural aestheticism" is to give only half the truth, because Du Bois is also responsive to the songs and can move from detachment to an openness to self-transformation.

The moment of response and change is most fully dramatized in Du Bois's revision of the opening scene of the "Sorrow Song" chapter (the encounter with the songs at Nashville) found at the chapter's end (with Du Bois hearing the songs at Atlanta). This revision unfolds within a rewriting of Plato's allegory of the cave and must be read through this other revision.

Plato's allegory is designed "to illustrate the degrees in which our nature may be enlightened or unenlightened." In a cave there are prisoners, chained and immobile since birth. Behind them there is a wall, and behind that a fire. Men carrying various objects pass between the wall and the fire. As these objects extent above the height of the wall, they cast shadows on the cave wall in front of the prisoners. The prisoners know nothing of reality other than these shadows, which they take to be reality. One prisoner becomes free and finds true enlightenment when he leaves the cave and walks out into the sunshine. The allegory is concerned with the dilemma facing this one individual, who is fully aware of a higher, transcendent reality but derided as a fool and rejected by the other unenlightened prisoners. Du Bois's location within the academic tower at the end of *Souls* appears at first simply to reproduce this dilemma. He is caught between, on the one hand, the vision of freedom promised by the transcendental "Eternal Good" and the "free . . . sunshine trickling down the morning into these high windows," and on the other hand the "prisoned" blacks and the "voices welling up . . . from the caverns of brick and mortar below." Du Bois's implied self-identification with Alexander Crummell, and the theories of education and progress that undergird that identification, suggests the obvious appropriateness of the allusion to the Platonic parable. Plato too is advocating the leadership of a cultured elite as a guarantee of "the welfare of the commonwealth." The allegory suggests that the guardians of the Republic must give up the contemplation of higher ideals and triumph over individualism by returning to the cave to help the prisoners. The thinker who leaves the cave *is* the enlightened one, who then takes the others toward enlightenment.

However, at *Atlanta* not only are the voices from below singing "to the sunshine" and urging on the "weary traveller" in his quest (where in Plato the prisoners have no conception of freedom), the voices from the caverns are themselves "instinct with life" and as "free" as the sunshine that represents higher enlightenment. If the University of Atlanta is supposed to represent the institutional embodiment of the program of educational reform outlined in "The Talented Tenth," then it is also important to note that Du Bois spends some time in "Of the Sorrow Songs" explaining that Fisk University, where he himself had studied, was founded on $150,000 raised by the Fisk Singers on their national and international tour begun in 1871. And if Plato's cave represents the senses and his outside an ideal enlightenment in an allegory that is concerned with justice and morality rather than optics, then it is also worth noting that it is the sensuous interaction of the singing voices and Du Bois's hearing that brings Du Bois to new understanding. There is here, in fact, also a reversal of the genealogy that marks the transmission across the generations of the African song handed down in Du Bois's family. Whereas that song was sung by the parents of each generation to their children, but with its meaning obscure to the "children" and their "fathers" alike, here the children sing to their father, who struggles to read the meaning of their songs. The evocation of the rending of the Veil at Christ's crucifixion most clearly indicates Du Bois's relation to the singers of the song. The Christian allegory is superimposed on the Platonic allegory. Du Bois occupies the same structural position in relation to the "prisoned" as the Roman centurion to Christ in St. Matthew's account of the crucifixion. He, like the centurion, experiences a moment of visionary perception.

Du Bois is not trapped between enlightenment and ignorance but poised between different forms of insight and understanding. "Beneath the conventional theology and unmeaning rhapsody" of the songs there is a hard and bitter knowledge of historical experience that challenges the transcendental cultural universalism championed in the progressive reformism of "The Talented Tenth." The slaves who created the spirituals and the voices that sing at the end of *Souls* have, unlike Plato's prisoners, suffered actual, not metaphorical, enslavement and oppression, and their music vocalizes a poetry of experiential truths, not unwitting falsehood. The poised tableau at the end of *Souls*, then, is not much an *allegorical* rewriting of Plato as a momentary breaking of the allegorical spell, because, in the midst of Du Bois's "historical and cultural aestheticism," it manages to acknowledge that the "prisoned" may be more than just symbols in support of an idealist political program. In opening himself up in sympathetic understanding to "the souls of black folk," Du Bois, like his projected white reader, finds a mirror behind the veil. The image at the close of *Souls* of the "weary traveller" who "girds himself" and "goes his way," cheered on by his "children," is not an image of a false collectivity parasitically recuperated into the promise of messianic leadership but a genuinely tragic and political vision that returns Du Bois for strength to the grounds of solitude.

The moment in which the voices of the prisoners singing to the sunshine urges the traveler to renew his journey recasts the moment in the first chapter of *Souls* in which "the shades of the prison-house closed round about us all: walls strait and stubborn to the whitest, but relentlessly narrow, tall and unscalable to sons of night who must plod darkly on in resignation, or beat unavailing palms against the stone, or steadily, half hopelessly, watch the streak of blue above." It is this earlier moment that introduces the famous passages on the "two-ness" of the African-American and on the "contradiction of double aims" experienced by the black middle class. In the final chapter the trope of the sunshine and the prisoners reintroduces the crisis of the "black *savant*" and "black artist," but, as the next section argues, also moves it toward different conclusions.

The Platonic revisions through which Du Bois dramatizes an ambivalence of cultural authority between the songs and himself as interpreter come as the conclusion to a series of chapters that are meditations on the role of religious leadership among African-Americans. After the survey in the first nine chapters of the political, economic, and educational issues that affect black American life, the last five chapters of *Souls* are concerned primarily with religious culture—particularly with the political and social function of the religious leader and with the jeremiad of the preacher-prophet as the dominant model of leadership rhetoric available to African-Americans. As in "Of the Sorrow Songs," Du Bois manages to establish both a historical and a contemporary understanding of African-American religious culture by combining anthropological and sociopolitical commentaries. However, acute assessments of the centrality of religion in African-American culture are juxtaposed to dramatizations of the fracture of faith. It is this fracture that underlies Du Bois's distinction between the political and historical content of the songs and the apparently "conventional theology" of their lyrics. The redemptive biblical typologies of religious prophecy are repeatedly qualified by personal experiences of loss and violence. Du Bois inverts the prophetic models of ascent and uplift. It is within the space cleared by these qualifications that Du Bois's model of his own insight and understanding can be properly described.

The terms in which Du Bois describes himself listening to the sorrow songs at the close of *Souls* refigure the description of Alexander Crummell's growth into enlightenment and leadership earlier in the book. In the twelfth chapter Du Bois argues that the education of Crummell at the hands of white abolitionists proved to be a process of mutual transformation. The white schoolboys discovered a realm "of thought and longing beneath one black skin, of which they had not dreamed before. And to the lonely boy came a new dawn of sympathy and inspiration." It is through the sympathy awakened by education that Crummell is able to overcome his hatred for the white world and to see for the first time "the sun-swept road that ran 'twixt heaven and earth," a vision of higher cultural ideals offered by the white world. But it is also because of this newly inspired sympathy that Crummell himself can hear "the bronzed hosts of a nation calling" and "the hateful clank of their chains" from "behind the forests," and can respond with a career of "protest" and "prophecy" as "a priest—a seer to lead the uncalled out of the house of bondage." Educational training and the revelation of higher goals necessarily entail a distancing from the repeated cycles of despair in the dark forest, and while sympathy promises a return to roots, it is a return in which both identity and difference must be acknowledged. Crummell answers the call of his fellow blacks, but as the priestly head of "the headless host."

The scene where Du Bois listens to the spirituals "welling up from the caverns of brick and mortar below" as the "free . . . sunshine," the enlightening embodiment of the "Eternal Good," trickles through the "high windows" refigures the dialectic of Crummell's sympathetic imagination moving between the "sun-swept road" and the "forest." Just as Crummell "girded himself to walk down the world," so too Du Bois as the "weary traveller" at the very end of the book "girds himself, and sets his face toward the Morning, and goes his way." Du Bois's placing of this allusive self-fashioning at the end of *Souls* seems at first to suggest that the autobiographical narrative of the book should be read as a teleological ascent. There is a way in which the book's double ontogenetic and phylogenetic narrative seems to suggest an optimistic reading as the most appropriate one for the book. The narrative seems, after all, to move from racist alienation to personal enlightenment, from continued social discrimination and exclusion to the fulfillment of educational ideals at the universities of Fisk and Atlanta as the "advanced guard" toils "slowly, heavily, doggedly" up the "mountain path to Canaan." This would align *Souls* with the redemptive biblical typologies and rhetoric of the "American Jeremiad" inherited by the slave narratives and with the uplift message of Booker T. Washington's autobiography, *Up from Slavery* (1901), a contemporary version of the slave narrative combined with the Horatio Alger myth. But, as Arnold Rampersad has suggested, *Souls* can also be read as an inverted slave narrative that reverses the plot of enlightenment and attained freedom. From this perspective, the narrative of *Souls* moves from Emancipation to the slave songs and their reassertion of continued oppression and violence, from a prelapsarian infancy to a repeated return to the condition of the divided self.

There is little in the actual chapter on Crummell to suggest that Du Bois is in any way critical or ambivalent about Crummell's political and cultural programs. However, he carefully places the unqualified eulogy to Crummell between the threnody for the loss of his infant son in chapter 11 and the fictionalized dramatization of the negation of his own adult ideals by racist violence and prejudice in chapter 13. The closing moments of "Of the Coming of John" (chapter 13), where John faces the sea as the lynch mob thunders toward him, refer the reader back to the closing moments of the chapter on Crummell, where, on the morning before his death and at the end of a life of solitary struggle and hardship, Crummell sits "gazing toward the sea." If the tragic end of "Of the Coming of John" cuts short the visionary projections of the eulogy for Crummell, these projected trajectories are already threatened by the Gothic omen of the death of the "first-born" in the previous chapter.

"Of the Passing of the First-Born" opens with biblical resonance: "Unto you a child is born." Du Bois sees "the strength of my own arm stretched onward through the ages through the newer strength" of the child's, and hears in "the baby voice" of his son "the voice of the Prophet that was to rise within the Veil." But the "hot winds" that roll into Atlanta from the "fetid Gulf" strangle this redemptive hope almost at birth. This sense of loss and personal grief is, however, mixed with a sense of relief. "All that day and all that night there sat an awful gladness in my heart,—nay, blame me not if I see the world thus darkly through the Veil,—and my soul whispers ever to me, saying, 'Not dead, not dead, but escaped; not bond, but free.' No bitter meanness now shall sicken his baby heart till it die a living death, no taunt shall madden his happy boyhood. Fool that I was to think or wish that this little soul should grow choked and deformed within the Veil!" This is perhaps Du Bois's most ironic and bitter condemnation of American racism. As Arnold Rampersad notes, "Of the Passing of the First-Born" is, in certain respects, "an almost classical elegy, in impassioned yet formal language. But it is one in which the central mourner, as a black, can find no consolation. Thus it is in truth anti-Christian, a bitter parody of the Christian elegy." John, the educated black hero who returns to the South to teach in the thirteenth chapter of *Souls*, is the embodiment of what Du Bois's infant son could have become. But John's death at the hands of a lynch mob also represents the life that the son has escaped through his untimely death. Du Bois only reinforces the anticonsolatory thrust of his mourning by placing its antireligious reversals after the chapter titled "On the Faith of the Fathers."

For the most part, Du Bois keeps personal life out of *Souls*. The autobiographical narrative is always woven along the edges of the cultural and political commentaries of the book. It reinforces or counterpoints, but is never the primary or sole site of exploration. Those denunciations of racism that draw upon autobiographical experience penetrate because their articulation is always so overly restrained. This is precisely why the impassioned grief of the elegy for the dead son is so unexpected and overwhelming. Suddenly, a personal loss that has little to do with the history or politics of racism occupies center stage, and stoic reticence gives way to melodramatic public mourning. Throughout *Souls* Du Bois has struggled to build a refuge of reason against both racism and the irrationality of "the vein of vague superstition" among African-Americans themselves. But the death of his son seems to unhouse the faith in rationality and providence alike, even if only for a moment. It is as if the seat of arbitrary violence and irrationality is discovered at the very heart of nature itself.

Comparison with Adams is again useful. Du Bois was thirty-one years old when his son died of dysentery. Adams was thirty-two when his sister died of a tetanus infection:

> The last lesson—the sum and term of education—began then. He had passed through thirty years of rather varied experience without having once felt the shell of custom broken. He had never seen Nature—only her surface—the sugar-coating that she shows to youth. Flung suddenly in his face, with the harsh brutality of chance, the terror of the blow stayed by him thenceforth for life. . . . He found his sister, a woman of forty, as gay and brilliant in the terrors of lockjaw as she had been in the careless fun of 1859, lying in bed in consequence of a miserable cab-accident that had bruised her foot. Hour by hour the muscles grew rigid, while the mind remained bright, until after ten days of fiendish torture she died in convulsions.

Adams's reaction to death is more immediately violent than Du Bois's. Du Bois's deep and paradoxical sense of loss and relief is contained within a highly formalized language that parodies Christian elegy by using the very language of messianic hopes and salvation. Adams's language reveals both the horror of the drop into chaos and the inability of language to hold that experience:

> Impressions like these are not reasoned or catalogued in the mind; they are felt as part of violent emotion; and the mind that feels them is different from the one which reasons; it is thought of a different power and of a different person. . . . For the first time, the stage-scenery of the senses collapsed; the human mind felt stripped naked, vibrating in a void of shapeless energies, with resistless mass, colliding, crushing, wasting, and destroying what these same energies had created and labored from eternity to perfect. . . . For pure blasphemy, it made pure atheism a comfort. God might be, as the Church said, a Substance, but He could not be a Person.

In the end, the literary imagination of *Souls* is not able to propose a model of political leadership that will answer the doubts of the book's deeply negative historical consciousness. The late nineteenth century and the early twentieth century are, for the African-American, "a time of intense ethical ferment, of religious heart-searching and intellectual unrest." Such a time of radical doubt "must give rise to double worlds and double ideals, and tempt the mind to pretence or to revolt, to hypocrisy or to radicalism," a division that Du Bois charts along the North-South axis. But if the polarization of dangerous "anarchy" and "hypocritical compromise" suggests a defense of the liberal center, Du Bois only reveals a middle ground occupied by assimilation or fatalistic acquiescence:

> Between the two extreme types of ethical attitude which I have thus sought to make clear wavers the mass of the millions of Negroes, North and South; and their religious life and activity partake of this social conflict within their ranks. Their churches are differentiating,—now into groups of cold, fashionable devotees, in no way distinguishable from similar white groups save in color of skin; now into large social and business institutions catering to the desire for information and amusement of their members, warily avoiding unpleasant questions both within and without the black world, and preaching in effect if not in word: *Dum vivimus, vivamus.*

Du Bois adds that "back of this still broods silently the deep religious feeling of the real Negro heart, the stirring, unguided might of powerful human souls who have lost the guiding star of the past and are seeking in the great night a new religious ideal." Crummell is the "guiding star" that promises the incarnation of this ideal, and it is an ideal that Du Bois fully endorses in "The Talented Tenth." But it is also an ideal whose horizon of possibility perpetually recedes in the face of the political and cultural history charted by *Souls*. At the end of *Souls* Du Bois himself appears not as a Moses guiding "his" people out of the wilderness but as "the weary traveller." In the romantic trope of the weary traveler Du Bois attempts to put alongside the vitalist and messianic ideals of activity another notion of action in which the value of the work of meditative and creative consciousness is recognized.

Thoughtful Deed: The Senses of Prophetic Imagination

In the brief "Afterthought" that concludes *Souls*, Du Bois asks the reader to "vouchsafe that this my book fall not still-born into the world-wilderness," and hopes that from it will "spring . . . vigor of *thought* and *thoughtful deed*" (emphases added). The possibility here that thinking may constitute meaningful action or that action needs to be informed by meditative intelligence challenges the equation of contemplation with passivity or detachment. In his analysis of the ways in which anthropology structures its knowledge of its object, Johannes Fabian uses this equation as a point of departure for his critique. "We need," argues Fabian, "to overcome the contemplative stance (in Marx's sense) and dismantle the edifices of spatiotemporal distancing that characterize the contemplative view." Fabian is right to suggest that such distancing tends, "first, to detemporalize the process of knowledge and, second, to promote ideological temporalization of relations between the Knower and the Known." Against this separation Fabian proposes that, as paradoxical as it may sound, "consciousness, individual and collective," be considered the "starting point" of any "materialist theory of knowledge." The definition of consciousness given is closely matched by Du Bois's dramatizations in "Of the Sorrow Songs." Fabian means "not disembodied consciousness . . . but 'consciousness with a body,' inextricably bound up with language":

> A fundamental role for language must be postulated, not because consciousness is conceived as a state internal to an individual organism which would then need to be "expressed" or "represented" through language (taking that term in the widest sense, including gestures, postures, attitudes, and so forth). Rather, the only way to think of consciousness without separating it from the organism or banning it to some kind of *forum internum* is to insist on its sensuous nature; and one way to conceive of that sensuous nature (above the level of motor activities) is to tie it to the production of meaningful sound. Inasmuch as the production of meaningful sound involves the labor of transforming, shaping matter, it may still be possible to distinguish form and content, but the relationship between the two will then be *constitutive* of consciousness. Only in a secondary, derived sense (one in which the conscious organism is presupposed rather than accounted for) can that relationship be called representational (significative, symbolic), or informative in the sense of being a tool or carrier of information.

In "Of the Sorrow Songs" the emphasis on hearing and response, on the interaction of self and others, on the coevalness of the Other, all support a model of consciousness that is closely aligned with the one Fabian describes. Furthermore, while Du Bois is not exactly offering a *theory* of knowledge in *Souls*, the distance between *Souls* and *The Philadelphia Negro* again suggests the validity of Fabian's distinctions between different conceptualizations of consciousness and different structures of knowledge. One need only compare the scene in which Du Bois listens to the spirituals at Atlanta in *Souls* with the panopticon gaze of the Victorian sociologist and moralist as he surveys the Seventh Ward in *The Philadelphia Negro* to grasp the distinctions:

> Starting at Seventh street and walking along Lombard, let us glance at the general character of the ward. Pausing a moment at the corner of Seventh and Lombard, we can at a glance view the worst Negro slums of the city. The houses are mostly brick, some wood, not very old, and in general uncared for rather than dilapidated. The blocks between Eighth, Pine, Sixth and South have for many decades been the center of the Negro population. Here the riots of the thirties took place, and here once was a depth of poverty and degradation almost unbelievable. Even to-day there are many evidences of degradation, although the signs of idleness, shiftlessness, dissoluteness and crime are more conspicuous than those of poverty. The alleys near, as Ratcliffe street, Middle alley, Brown's court, Barclay street, etc., are haunts of noted criminals, male and female, of gamblers and prostitutes, and at the same time of many poverty-stricken people, decent but not energetic. There is an abundance of political clubs, and nearly all the houses are practically lodging houses, with a miscellaneous and shifting population. The corners, night and day, are filled with Negro loafers—able-bodied young men and women, all cheerful, some with good-natured, open faces, some with traces of crime and excess, a few pinched with poverty. . . . Some are stevedores, porters, laborers and laundresses. On the face of it this slum is noisy and dissipated, but not brutal, although now and then highway robberies and murderous assaults in other parts of the city are traced to its denizens.

It could be argued that Fabian's linking of consciousness to the sensuous body could be taken as a description of James's account of consciousness too. But Fabian's linking of consciousness and the production of language offers the possibility of conceiving of consciousness as a *praxis*, an activity of creative transformation, which James's stress on consciousness as passive selection and crisis management toward equilibrium never gets to. Du Bois's transition (discussed a little later) from hearing the songs to leaving his academic tower as the "weary traveller" and offering the world his book in response in the "Afterthought" does move toward conceiving the work of consciousness as potentially creative and transformative.

While Fabian's account of sensuous consciousness helps describe the processes of transformation in the final chapter of *Souls*, his separation of contemplation and consciousness is less useful in that it tends toward a false dichotomy. If Fabian means by contemplation nothing more than positivist myths of detachment and objectivity, then his argument finds obvious alignments with the critiques of sociological positivism discussed in chapter 3. But in her critique of methodologism Gillian Rose insists that the theoretical and meditative functions of consciousness have their own value and should not be ignored by social science. Similarly, in H. T. Wilson's critical account of sociological paradigms that he calls "the American ideology," a defense of speculative thought leads to the conclusion that "contemplation unrelated to mastery, far from violating true openness to possibility and change, encompasses both as the real subject of its concerns." Rose's critique works out of Hegel, and Wilson's out of Marx. The two philosophers come together in the thought of Max Horkheimer, whose defense of contemplation against its refusal in American Pragmatism is pertinent here. For Horkheimer,

> pragmatism, like technocracy, has certainly contributed a great deal toward the fashionable disrepute of that "stationary contemplation" which was once the highest aspiration of man. Any idea of truth, even a dialectical whole of thought, as it occurs in a living mind, might be called "stationary contemplation," in so far as it is pursued for its own sake instead of as a means to "consistency, stability, and flowing intercourse." Both the attack on contemplation and the praise of the craftsman express the triumph of means over ends.

Horkheimer is quoting from James's *Some Problems of Philosophy* (1924), but the attitudes critiqued should be familiar from the discussion in chapter 1 of earlier texts by James. Also, Horkheimer's alignment of Pragmatism and technocracy reinforces the parallels drawn earlier in this study between James's ethical thought and what Wilson calls technocratic rationality and what Rose refers to as the positivist logic of validity.

Du Bois's departure from academia as the "weary traveller" and the production of his book at the end of *Souls* arise out of a simultaneity of contemplation and the work of sensuous consciousness. Du Bois is moved to action by opening his ears to the music *and* by his solitary meditation on the songs in his university office. The complexity of Du Bois's dramatizations of consciousness can be more fully grasped by adding to the comparisons with social-scientific and philosophical discourse an examination of the way in which Du Bois's account also suggests a revision of a model of prophetic imagination in American poverty.

Linking ethnographic writing to traditions of travel literature, Fabian argues that "the image of the 'philosophical traveler' whose roaming in space leads to the discovery of 'ages'" is a classic embodiment of the spatiotemporal distancing of Knower and Known. But Du Bois as the "weary traveller" is neither a salvage ethnographer nor a reincarnated priest-prophet in the image of Crummell or Moses. He is the companion of Blake's "Mental Traveller." In *The Mental Traveller* the "Babe" liberty is "begotten in woe" and "born in joy." But the child is "given to a Woman Old," society, "who nails him down upon a rock." As Foster Damon explains, Blake's poem "is the formula of the history of the idea of Liberty, showing how it is born, how it triumphs, how in its age its opposite is born, how it is cast out, how it then rejuvenates, until it becomes a babe again, and the cycle recurs." *Souls* too dramatizes the recurring struggles of the consciousness of freedom and of bondage. As in Blake, it is from a knowledge of this struggle that prophetic vision is created in *Souls*.

Prophecy is understood here not in a predictive or futuristic sense but as Northrop Frye describes it in his remarkable study of Blake: "an honest man is not quite the noblest work of God until the faith by which the just live develops into full imaginative vision. The fully imaginative man is therefore a visionary whose imaginative activity is prophecy and whose perception produces art. These two are the same thing, perception being an act. . . . It is the superior clarity and accuracy of the prophet's vision that makes him an artist, and that makes the great artist prophetic."

In American Transcendentalism, as in European Romanticism, poetic prophecy is preoccupied with the dialectics of passivity and activity. On the American side, the primary mode of transcending passivity is through a voluntaristic act of *seeing*. A brief examination of Emerson and Whitman, particularly of the triumph in their work of sight over the other senses and of a self defined by seeing, will provide a context in which the poetics of *Souls*'s structuring can be more clearly understood.

In *Nature* (1836), his first major work, Emerson seeks to reverse the Pauline relegation of prophetic vision to a future world in which the Fall is recovered. For St. Paul, "now we see in a mirror, darkly," but "when that which is perfect is come," then we shall see "face to face" (I Cor. 13:10, 12). Emerson, however, argues that "the foregoing generations beheld God and nature face to face; we through their eyes," and asks "Why should not we also enjoy an original relation to the universe?" The prophet of the New World restores his vision by becoming "a transparent eyeball" whose Platonic insight transcends society. By contrast with *Nature*, *Souls* opens not with a seeing subject but with a moment of being seen. Where Emerson seeks solitude in nature, the boy Du Bois is seeking the company of his white and black playmates when he is repulsed by the gaze of the "tall newcomer." The black body and not the "tranquil landscape" becomes the field of the "Not Me" in which the white subject unfolds its freedom. The moment in which the gaze penetrates is the moment in which the biblical veil descends and obscures vision in *Souls*. But if the penetrating gaze sets off a process of objectification and the division of consciousness, it also makes possible a "second sight." The look of Du Bois's new playmate is like that "certain Slant of light" that is both "An imperial affliction" and a source of tragic understanding in Emily Dickinson:

> Heavenly Hurt, it gives us—
> We can find no scar,
> But internal difference,
> Where the Meanings, are—

Not only does *Souls* open with being seen, it closes with Du Bois *listening* to the voices singing the spirituals, a more social act than seeing, and sending out into the world his *written* work. This presents a very different ratio of the senses than the one that dominates in Emerson, or even the more "amative" Whitman, and also a very different conceptualization of visionary action. Emerson's attempts to defend the mind as active in "The American Scholar" (1837) and Whitman's poetic self-fashioning in "Song of Myself" (1855) can help illustrate the differences between Du Bois's formulations and American Transcendentalism.

"The American Scholar" is a program for the cultivation of the life of the mind in the new nation. In it Emerson writes that "the so-called 'practical men' sneer at speculative men, as if, because they speculate or *see*, they could do nothing." Emerson takes this to be a false accusation:

> Action is with the scholar subordinate, but it is essential. Without it he is not yet man. Without it thought can never ripen into truth. . . . The preamble of thought, the transition through which it passes from the unconscious to the conscious, is action. Only so much do I know, as I have lived. Instantly we know whose words are loaded with life, and whose not.
>   This world,—this shadow of the soul, or *other* me,—lies wide around. Its attractions are the keys which unlock my thoughts and make me acquainted with myself. I run eagerly into this

tumult. I grasp the hands of those next me, and take my place in
the ring to suffer and to work, taught by an instinct that so shall
the dumb abyss be vocal with speech.

Despite this last image of collective toiling, Emerson's formulations of
the activity of visionary understanding and cultural leadership describe, for
the most part, a solitary and passive process. The sense of self-reliance and
mastery in the face of the "Not Me" is, after all, dependent upon the passivity
of seeing. In the passage from "The American Scholar" quoted above, the
transition from seeing to saying involves no process of *hearing*.
Notwithstanding the image of the ring of clasped hands, the scholar does not
work from a social location. What is vocalized is, in fact, not a social or
historical knowledge, but the passive emergence of preexisting Platonic
forms that are autonomous of consciousness. In Du Bois's revision of Plato,
however, the bright revelation of pure and transcendent forms in the light
outside the caves is eschewed in favor of the knowledge embodied in the
voices of those imprisoned inside the cave. As Denis Donoghue observes,

> the site of [Emerson's] poetry and his sageness is the history of
> voluntarism. The more we read *Nature*, the more clearly it
> appears that the whole essay is predicated upon the capacity of
> Will. Not knowledge but power is its aim; not truth but
> command. . . . So if we go back to the transparent eyeball passage
> and read it as a voluntaristic act rather than an instance of the
> Sublime, we find that the eyeball becomes transparent because a
> light higher than its own sensory light is made to shine through
> it. . . . We have access to [Emerson's work] only by recourse to
> the vocabulary of Will and to its social form, a pragmatics of the
> future.

The interactions of the senses and the social politics in Whitman's
"Song of Myself" are closer to those in Du Bois than to those in Emerson,
but they are still marked by a fundamental difference that is useful in
describing *Souls*. Whitman, like the author of *Souls*, is "attesting sympathy"
("Shall I make my list of things in the house and skip the house that supports
them?" he asks). He shouts "Hurrah for positive science!" but also tells the
scientist and the mathematician, "Your facts are useful, and yet they are not
my dwelling,/I but enter by them to an area of my dwelling." This dwelling
is what Du Bois, in turning away from social-scientific description in *Souls*,
calls the realm of "thought and feeling." In exploring this realm, the poet of
the "Song of Myself" touches and feels in his democratic openness in a way

Emerson never does (and with a corporeal candor that is also alien to the Victorian Du Bois): "I believe in the flesh and the appetites,/Seeing, hearing, feeling." And the poet's "voice goes after what [his] eyes cannot reach." In his social openness, Whitman is led to make vocal not just "the threads that connect the stars," but political outrage on behalf of the oppressed and socially excluded:

> Through me many long dumb voices,
> Voices of the interminable generations of prisoners and slaves,
> Voices of the diseas'd and despairing and of thieves and dwarfs,
> . . .
> Through me forbidden voices
> Voices of sexes and lusts, voices veil'd and I remove the veil,
> Voices indecent by me clarified and transfigured.

It is the poet's transfiguration of the voices that lifts the veil. This is closer to Du Bois, but the transfiguration dramatized in the last chapter of *Souls* is somewhat different.

As Larzer Ziff demonstrates, sight ultimately triumphs over the other senses even in Whitman, because the other senses are a threat to prophetic stability and self-confidence. With the appearance of the other senses, Whitman's prophetic power of digesting good and evil, ugliness and beauty, into the incorporative self on equal terms "becomes entangled in self-doubt."

> The doubtings, of course, are plotted. It is through a marvelous series of sights that he arrives at the middle point of *Song of Myself*, where he can stand up and, after naming so much else, name himself: "Walt Whitman, an American, one of the roughs, a kosmos." As he compiles those sights he brushes aside the opposition to his gathering strength that comes from sound and touch: "Trippers and askers surround me." But they are not the "Me myself," and when he affirms, "Apart from the pulling and hauling stands what I am," he does so by showing that he "looks."

Unlike Whitman, Du Bois does not attempt to recuperate a threatened self-confidence or a stable self and its powers of incorporation. In the final moments of "Of the Sorrow Songs" Du Bois is left listening. He does not master the songs but is sent out into the world by them. Tragedy and evil are not assimilated. It is true that, like Whitman, Du Bois transfigures the voices he hears. But he does not incorporate them into the imperial command of his own voice. Through his "Afterthought," he foregrounds the *writtenness* of his transfiguration and the separation between the spirituals and the "book" that is *Souls*. If the weary traveler is urged into a renewal of his exploratory journeying by the voices singing the spirituals, the creation of the book called *Souls of Black Folk* is a direct product of this responsive displacement.

The dislocation of Du Bois's representative bourgeois consciousness takes place of course not just in the final chapter of *Souls* but, in one way or another, throughout the book, and the sending of the book out into the world in the "Afterthought" suggests that the text is a cumulative synthesis of all that has gone before. Du Bois's fear that the book might fall "still born" into the world metaphorically gathers up the dialogues of fathers and sons, of parents and children, that dominate the last five chapters of *Souls*, from the faith of the fathers and the death of the newborn son to Crummell as father and John as defeated son, and finally to Du Bois as the father listening to the singing of his children. The plea to the reader that he or she "vouchsafe" the survival of the book is an invitation to sustain this gathering in a continued act of recollection and imaginative meditation in which the contemplation of what Horkheimer calls truth and the historical process is not sacrificed to an instrumentalist or exceptionalist future.

Missing the End: Toward Revolution

In *Dusk of Dawn*, the autobiography from 1940, the allegory of the cave and other moments from "Of Our Spiritual Strivings" are reworked toward more radical social transformations than are imagined in *Souls*. In a chapter titled "The Concept of Race," the lifelong struggle to define and explore the concept is described against the background of the early career (a biography already encountered in *Souls*) seen from the vantage point of Du Bois's trip to Liberia in the mid-1920s. At the end of the chapter Du Bois returns to the Platonic allegory and shifts the emphases of the earlier reworking in *Souls* in significant ways:

> It is difficult to let others see the full psychological meaning of caste segregation. It is as though one, looking out from a dark cave in a side of an impending mountain, sees the world passing and speaks to it; speaks courteously and persuasively, showing them how these entombed souls are hindered in their natural movement, expression, and development; and how their loosening from prison would be a matter not simply of courtesy, sympathy, and help to them, but aid to all the world. One talks on evenly and logically in this way, but notices that the passing

throng does not even turn its head, or if it does, glances curiously and walks on. It gradually penetrates the mind of the prisoners that the people passing do not hear; that some thick sheet of invisible but horribly tangible plate glass is between them and the world. They get excited; they talk louder; they gesticulate. Some of the passing world stop in curiosity; these gesticulations seem so pointless; they laugh and pass on. They still either do not hear at all, or hear but dimly, and even what they hear, they do not understand. Then the people within may become hysterical. They may scream and hurl themselves against the barriers, hardly realizing in their bewilderment that they are screaming in a vacuum unheard and that their antics may actually seem funny to those outside looking in. They may even, here and there, break through in blood and disfigurement, and find themselves faced by a horrified, implacable, and quite overwhelming mob of people frightened for their own very existence.

In *Souls* the reworking of the allegory focused on a set of doubts about the relationship of a member of the Talented Tenth to the black folk. Here the concern is with the relationship of the white world to the black world, with the figure of the black spokesman mediating between the two. The relationship of the two worlds is again presented through a differentiation of hearing and sight. The failure of hearing leads to a distortion of sight so that the "entombed" begin to appear in their frustration either as laughable or as a savage threat that can be contained only through mob violence. The source of enlightenment is not so much reversed as made reciprocal. Freedom lies outside the cave, but there is also a truth the white world needs to learn from the imprisoned.

The treatment of the black leader figure is more equivocal. The passage begins with attention focused on the "one" who has to speak on behalf of the prisoners to the outside world. (Here at least Plato's guardian seeks to bring knowledge out of the cave and not into it.) Later in the passage, attention shifts from the one to the many as the prisoners themselves become speaking subjects. Earlier in *Dusk of Dawn*, describing the impact of racist mob violence on his own stance of scientific objectivity and progress, Du Bois writes that "one could not be a calm, cool, and detached scientist while Negroes were lynched, murdered and starved." In the passage quoted above from the later "Concept of Race" chapter, it is when the spokesman's talking "evenly and logically" leads to nothing that the prisoners become collectively vocal. But if the reasoned arguments of the "one" fall on deaf ears, the efforts of the many can be seen only within the racist stereotypes of farce and savagery as long as their true meaning is silenced by the "plate glass" barrier between the two worlds.

With the failure of both individual and collective effort, Du Bois does not at first offer any alternatives. He circles back to a description of divided consciousness caught between two worlds, once again presented with intelligence within the limits of a radical conservatism. The "freeing and making articulate" of the "submerged caste" is imagined as the function of the spokesman's ethical address to the white world. The danger is that in the process of such advocacy the leader himself becomes an outsider to the group, and Du Bois recognizes that "outside leadership will continually misinterpret and compromise and complicate matters, even with the best of will." But to remain only within the group is to risk becoming "provincial and centered upon the problems of his particular group." In order to become "a group man, a 'race' man," the individual may have to sacrifice "the wider aspects of national life and human existence."

Much of this is familiar from the analysis of the "contradiction of double aims" from the first chapter of *Souls*. But the conclusion of *Dusk of Dawn* takes the autobiographical commentary in a direction quite different from the conclusion of the earlier book. The final chapter of *Dusk of Dawn* is called "Revolution." The chapter charts Du Bois's move "beyond my conception of ignorance and deliberate ill-will as causes of race prejudice" toward an understanding of other "hidden and partially concealed causes of race hate." These other causes are succinctly summarized as capitalism's planned perpetuation of material *and* spiritual and intellectual deprivation. The summary is itself placed between two visions of collective political action, one from the past, leading Du Bois toward a radical reformulation of his ideas, and the other a promise of future revolution. Consciousness and materialist understanding, self and collectivity, now begin to move toward a new synthesis:

> I think it was the Russian Revolution which first illuminated and made clear [the] change in my basic thought. It was not that I at any time conceived of Bolshevik Russia as ushering in any present millennium. I was painfully sensitive to all its failures, to all the difficulties which it faced; but the clear and basic thing which appeared to me in unquestioned brightness, was that in the year 1917 and then, after a struggle with the world and famine ten years later, one of the largest nations of the world made up its mind frankly to face a set of problems which no nation at that time was willing to face, and which many nations including our own are unwilling fully to face even to this day.

A "Prosody of Those Dark Voices": The Transformation of Consciousness 173

Those questions involved the problem of the poverty of the mass of men in an age when an abundance of goods and technical efficiency of work seemed able to provide a sufficiency for all men, so that the mass of men could be fed and clothed and sheltered, live in health and have their intellectual faculties trained. Russia was trying to accomplish this by eventually putting into the hands of those people who do the world's work the power to guide and rule the state for the best welfare of the masses. It made the assumption, long disputed, that out of the downtrodden mass of people, ability and character, sufficient to do this task effectively, could and would be found. I believed this dictum passionately. It was, in fact, the foundation stone of my fight for black folk; it explained me.

By the time *Dusk of Dawn* appeared in print Du Bois had already published his Marxist historiography, *Black Reconstruction in America, 1860–1880* (1935). In *Dusk of Dawn* twentieth-century liberalism's failure to "realize the fundamental change brought about by the world-wide organization of work and trade and commerce" is placed against the Marxist recognition that "economic foundations . . . are the determining factors in the development of civilization, in literature, religion, and the basic pattern of culture."

The base-superstructure argument is rudimentary in its statement. But the stress on political economy shifts the bewilderment of the Talented Tenth in the face of historical disaster in *Souls* toward greater understanding of the causes of the disaster. At the end of *Dusk of Dawn* Du Bois still endorses the Talented Tenth, but in a very modified manner. In the chapter titled "Revolution" Du Bois prints the "Basic American Negro Creed," a political manifesto for African-Americans he had drafted in 1936. The third item of the Creed states that the function of the Talented Tenth is to determine "by study and measurement the present field and demand for racial action and the method by which the masses may be guided along this path." But the social Darwinistic rhetoric and moralistic idealism of the original "Talented Tenth" essay has now given way to a sense of the function of the elite within a broader political process. Economics dominates the concerns of the Creed. Du Bois proposes the establishment of "a co-operative Negro industrial system in America . . . in the midst of and in conjunction with the surrounding national industrial organization and in intelligent accord with the reconstruction of the economic basis of the nation which must sooner or later be accomplished." The next two items of the Creed urge the "Negro workers" to join forces with the "labor movement," and Du Bois asserts his belief "in the ultimate triumph of some form of Socialism the world over; that is, common ownership and control of the means of production and equality of income."

Du Bois had appended the draft of his credo to a paper titled "The Negro and the New Deal" commissioned by the Associates in Negro Folk Education, working under the American Association for Adult Education, for a series edited by Alain Locke. The manuscript was rejected. *Dusk of Dawn* itself was completed just as the world was plunged into the Second World War. But the disaster of the war and its aftermath did not dull Du Bois's radical hopes. When in the late 1950s Du Bois turned to the writing of another autobiography, he rearranged the chronology of his life so that the *Autobiography* began not with his childhood but with an extended account of his travels in the Soviet Union and communist China. Between this account, which formed part I of the book, and the rest of the *Autobiography* there was an "Interlude" titled "Communism." In *Dusk of Dawn* Du Bois had imagined the possibilities of socialism within a capitalist system and declared "I . . . am not a communist." In the "Interlude" in the *Autobiography*, Du Bois stated bluntly that he now believed in communism, meaning by communism "a planned way of life in the production of wealth and work designed for building a state whose object is the highest welfare of its people and not merely the profit of a part." There follows a radical denunciation of the myths of the free market and the American political system:

> Once I thought these ends could be attained under capitalism, means of production privately owned, and used in accord with free individual initiative. . . . I now believe that private ownership of capital and free enterprise are leading the world to disaster. I do not believe that so-called "people's capitalism" has in the United States or anywhere replaced the ills of private capitalism and shown an answer to socialism. The corporation is but the legal mask behind which the individual owner of wealth hides. Democratic government in the United States has almost ceased to function. A fourth of the adults are disfranchised [*sic*], half the legal voters do not go to the polls. We are ruled by those who control wealth and who by that power buy or coerce public opinion.

The last part of the *Autobiography* frames the account of the middle years of Du Bois's life with an account of his trial, indictment, and acquittal at the start of the 1950s on the charge of being an "unregistered foreign agent" (under the Foreign Agents Registration Act of 1938) in connection with his leadership of the Peace Information Center. In 1961, at the age of ninety-three and only two years before his death, Du Bois joined the Communist Party of the United States and that same year took up residence in Ghana at the invitation of President Nkrumah.

To give Du Bois's own descriptions of his turn to socialism in his later autobiographies as a coda to a study of his early writings is not meant to suggest that the meaning of those early writings can be grasped only teleologically, as if a logic immanent in the early works were somehow fulfilled in the later ones. The brief review of the later socialism is meant, in fact, to lead to quite the opposite argument. To argue for a teleological logic by which the young Du Bois becomes the older Du Bois would be to reproduce the Hegelian reading of Marx's thought by which the young Hegelian Marx becomes the old Marxist Marx by means of the immanent potential of the idealist logic of his early Hegelian works. But as Joachim Hoeppner argues in a discussion of the relation of Hegel to Marx, "history must not be studied from the front backwards, searching for the heights of Marxist knowledge its ideal germs in the past. The evolution of philosophical thought must be traced on the basis of the real evolution of society." Hoeppner adds that as far as the relation of Hegel and Marx goes, "it is not a question of knowing what Marxist content a Marxist investigator might today be able to read into . . . passages [from Hegel], but rather of knowing what social content they had for Hegel himself." Quoting this passage, Louis Althusser argues that Hoeppner's position on Hegel "*is also unreservedly true for Marx himself* when his early works are being read from the standpoint of his mature works."

> Of course, we now know that the Young Marx *did* become Marx, but we should not want to live faster than he did, we should not want to live in his place, reject for him or discover for him. We shall not be waiting for him at the end of the course to throw around him as around a runner the mantle of repose, for at last it is over, he has arrived. Rousseau remarked that with children and adolescents the whole art of education consists of knowing how to *lose time*. The art of historical criticism also consists of knowing how to lose time so that young authors can grow up. This lost time is simply the time we give them to live. We *scan* the necessity of their lives in our understanding of its nodal points, its reversals and mutations.

In investigating the thought and writings of Du Bois at the turn of the century, this study has sought to understand that moment as what Althusser calls a "nodal point" and to respect the complexity of its "reversals and mutations." It has tried not to hurry Du Bois, nor to "reject" or "discover" for him. The meaning and value of the early achievements are not derived from their contribution to a totalizing account of the whole life. The later socialism and the earlier dramas of Hegelian negativity are juxtaposed; the latter are not given as the germ that is fulfilled in the former. Du Bois's own autobiographical writings offer his readers a conceptualization of his life not so much as a linear trajectory but as a palimpsest in visible and continuous process. For the middle part of the *Autobiography*, dealing with the years from his childhood to the late 1940s, Du Bois drew almost entirely on previously published works. The results are not as impressive as some of the earlier works. But the framing of this middle section of the autobiography between an account of the trip to the Soviet Union and China, as well as the declaration of communist sympathy, and an account of his trial in the 1950s does create a formal structure of awkward tonal overlayering in which the different moments of the life are curiously available in simultaneous contrast. The last sentence of *Dusk of Dawn* offers a more self-conscious sense of the life as a continual process in which the telos of both biography and historical process is deferred. "I like a good novel," writes Du Bois, "and in healthful length of days, there is infinite joy in seeing the World, the most interesting of continuing stories, unfold, even though one misses THE END." The final lines of Du Bois's *Autobiography*, written in the last decade of his long life, tie the imagination of future achievement firmly to a living sense of the past in such a way that the recollective and contemplative model of consciousness from *Souls* is joined to the imagination of revolution, not superseded by it:

> This is a wonderful America, which the founding fathers dreamed until their sons drowned it in the blood of slavery and devoured it in greed. Our children must rebuild it. Let then the Dreams of the Dead rebuke the Blind who think that what is will be forever and teach them that what was worth living for must live again and that which merited death must stay dead. Teach us, Forever Dead, there is no Dream but Deed, there is no Deed but Memory.

The sense of the last sentence is not only that the dream is an activity in its own right, but also that there can be no meaningful action unless it is also an act of remembering feeding the dream.

MICHAEL B. KATZ AND THOMAS J. SUGRUE

The Context of The Philadelphia Negro: *The City, the Settlement House Movement, and the Rise of the Social Sciences*

In June 1896, W.E.B. Du Bois, then twenty-eight years old and married three weeks, received a telegram from Charles C. Harrison, acting provost of the University of Pennsylvania: "Are ready to appoint you for one year at nine hundred dollars maximum payable monthly from date of service. If you wish appointment will write definitely." Harrison had piqued the interest of one of nineteenth-century America's most promising young intellectuals. Du Bois had risen rapidly from humble origins in Great Barrington, Massachusetts. Educated at Fisk and in Berlin, he became the first African American to be awarded a doctorate by Harvard. Eager to escape his first job at parochial Wilberforce University in Ohio, where he had been teaching classics for two years, Du Bois moved with his wife Nina into an apartment in the Philadelphia Settlement at Seventh and Lombard Streets, near the heart of one of the city's largest African American neighborhoods.

Arriving in Philadelphia in August of 1896, the Du Boises found themselves in a city that was the antithesis of Wilberforce. Late nineteenth-century Philadelphia was an industrial giant, the second largest city in the United States. Traveling from the train station to the Philadelphia Settlement House, Du Bois undoubtedly sensed the dynamism, the promise, and the deep-rooted problems of a city undergoing wrenching economic changes. For most of the nineteenth century, Philadelphia had been a

From *W.E.B. Du Bois, Race, and the City.* © 1998 by University of Pennsylvania Press.

premier shipping and trading center, an outlet for the rich agricultural land of New Jersey, Lancaster County (Pennsylvania), and points to the west. Ships plied the Delaware River, loaded with southern cotton bound for the city; filled with corn, cloth, and shoes as they headed down the coast to Newport, Charleston, and Savannah. The region's transportation hub, by the 1850s Philadelphia had also become the heart of the nation's burgeoning railroad industry. Rail lines connected Philadelphia to Pennsylvania's rich veins of anthracite coal, only ninety miles to the northwest. And they connected the city to the steel and iron manufacturers of Pittsburgh and Wheeling, several hundred miles to the west. As the headquarters of the massive Pennsylvania Railroad empire, Philadelphia nurtured a business elite whose influence spread across the nation.

By the 1890s Philadelphia had achieved prominence as a center of industrial innovation and specialization. A national center of textile and clothing manufacturing, the city was home to one of the country's largest agglomerations of lace makers, carpet weavers, and fabric manufacturers. But no one industry predominated. The city housed a remarkably diverse range of manufacturers, including machine tool and hardware production, publishing, and tanning. Heavier industries also employed thousands of Philadelphians: steelmaking and forging, shipbuilding, and railroad engine assembly. Countless other specialty firms clustered in the city: Philadelphia was an important center of the American cigar industry, a major producer of dental instruments and cutlery, home to the world-famous Stetson hat makers, and a major producer of fairground carousels. Dozens of food processing plants, breweries, and dairies catered to the needs of the city's burgeoning population of laborers.

When he wrote *The Philadelphia Negro* Du Bois had grounds for optimism as Philadelphia rebounded from the depression of 1893–96. He marveled at the rapid growth the city had enjoyed in the decades following the Civil War, writing that "new methods of conducting business and industry are now rife. . . . Manufacturing of all kinds has increased by leaps and bounds in the city, and to-day employs three times as many men as in 1860, paying three hundred millions annually in wages; hacks and expressmen have turned into vast inter-urban businesses: restaurants have become palatial hotels—the whole face of business is being gradually transformed." The industrial city of the 1890s was, for Du Bois and many Americans, a strange and exciting world, one of extraordinary, if unfulfilled, promise.

As Du Bois entered the city for the first time, passing from the train depot through Center City toward the Philadelphia Settlement, he saw before him the entire industrial metropolis in microcosm. The ostentation of the city's new wealth was visible in the elaborate facade of the nearly finished Second Empire-style City Hall. Along Market Street stretched the cast-iron facades of the city's grand department stores, Lit Brothers and Wanamaker's. Around Rittenhouse Square and along Spruce and Locust Streets stood elaborate four-story Italianate row houses and posh clubs. The stately Georgian-revival mansions of Delancey Place and Pine Street housed many bankers, executives, entrepreneurs, and lawyers who had prospered from the city's economic boom. To the west, near the University of Pennsylvania, a new class of corporate managers who sought the area's quasi-suburban amenities and could afford the short trolley ride to the offices of Center City built substantial Queen Anne homes. A walk through the innumerable blue-collar neighborhoods that ringed Center City revealed neat blocks of small, impeccably maintained "Philadelphia-style" row houses that gave the city the highest rate of single-family homeownership of the nation's ten largest cities.

Yet for the vast majority of black Philadelphians the promise of the post-war city remained unmet. "After the war and emancipation," lamented Du Bois, "great hopes were entertained by the Negroes for rapid advancement, and nowhere did they seem better founded than Philadelphia." But those hopes, particularly in the economy and in housing, were dashed. Nearly 50 percent of Philadelphians, but only 8.2 percent of black residents of the Seventh Ward, the largely black section of the city that was the basis of Du Bois's research, found industrial employment. Although highly dangerous and often insecure, industrial work provided wages and opportunities for advancement unparalleled in the domestic and service sector where most blacks found work. One of the ironies of turn-of-the-century Philadelphia was that blacks lived in the closest proximity to the city's best industrial jobs, yet remained almost entirely closed out of them. Other ethnic groups established residential neighborhoods that allowed easy access to industrial employment. White working-class Philadelphians tended to live close to the city's mills, machine shops, and manufactories, and the factories served as the hubs of dozens of thriving neighborhoods. In the shadow of the mills, workers used their hard-earned savings to purchase modest row homes. A majority of white Philadelphians were homeowners.

The privilege of homeownership did not come as readily to black working families in the city. Housing conditions graphically highlighted the contrast between blacks and whites. Nearly a third of black Philadelphians lived in the Seventh Ward, a district that extended from the Delaware to the Schuylkill River in a narrow band across Lombard, Pine, and South Streets. The more substantial houses, home to the city's black elite, lined the major streets, particularly Lombard west of Ninth Street and Rodman Street. But most of the ward's blacks crowded into decrepit brick row homes huddled along the narrow alleys, courtyards, and back streets that broke through the city's relentless grid. Numerous "blind alleys and dark holes" subdivided the neat grid of Philadelphia. Many alley dwellers lived in "trinities," tiny houses with "three rooms one above the other, small, poorly lighted, and poorly ventilated" that often shared a common outhouse. Because nearly one-third of black Philadelphians depended on subtenants and boarders, their houses were often densely packed. The narrow streets ran as open sewers and waste disposal areas for the residents of the nearby houses. "Penetrate into one of these houses and beyond into the back yard, if there is one," wrote a city inspector quoted by Du Bois, "and there will be found a pile of ashes, garbage and filth, the accumulation of the winter, perhaps of the whole year."

Du Bois, the Seventh Ward, and the Settlement Movement

In the midst of this maze of courts and alleys, tucked into a bleak and inauspicious courtyard called Saint Mary Street on the border of the Fifth and Seventh Wards, was the Philadelphia Settlement. The Settlement, which cosponsored Du Bois's research with the University of Pennsylvania, originated in 1857 as the Saint Mary Street Colored Mission Sabbath School, founded by wealthy merchant George Stewart. The school later added a nursery, kindergarten, and playground. In 1884, under the leadership of Quaker philanthropist Susan Wharton, it became the Saint Mary Street Library and began classes and vocational training in carpentry and cooking. On April 1, 1892, Susan Wharton and her cousins Hannah Fox and Helen Parrish transformed the library into the Philadelphia College Settlement, which served the entire neighborhood, not just blacks. Fox and Parrish, influenced by the English housing reformer Octavia Hill, made housing their special interest. Fox donated a house for the Settlement. The Saint Mary Street Library Association also pledged $1,000 per year for two years and secured the use of the Stuart Memorial Church with a hall and three classrooms linked to the Settlement by Starr Garden.

From its inception, the Philadelphia Settlement was part of the College Settlement Association, which had encouraged its creation and, starting with $600 in 1892, made annual contributions toward its maintenance. Susan Wharton sat on the executive committee of the College Settlement Association, which formed in the spring of 1890 to promote settlement work among college women and to find money for settlements. "A College Settlement," pointed out Vida Scudder, secretary of its electoral board, "has a two-fold value." Its "primary and highest ambition" remained to concentrate "its power on the definite effort to bring brightness and help to a limited neighborhood." Less obvious, but of great importance, the "education of our college women is one great mission of College Settlements." The settlement movement, which had spread from Toynbee Hall in England first to Chicago and then to New York in the United States, rested on the assumption that "in the awakened intelligence and consecration of the cultured class lies, after all, the most serious promise for the success of that great movement toward social reconstruction in the midst of which we live."

As Scudder described their mission, settlements stressed the role of knowledge and of class in social improvement. Knowledge came through two activities: personal experience and social investigation. By bringing well-to-do young women and men to live among the poor and undertaking research, settlements fused the advantages of class and education in the formation of the new leadership cadre they believed essential to social reform. Although settlement workers lived among the poor, they did not expect social change to flow from the bottom of the social structure upward. Not grass-roots democrats, they resembled nineteenth-century missionaries to the heathen more than community organizers of the 1960s. Working in the settlement milieu, Du Bois not unexpectedly also stressed the importance of knowledge and class—within the black community and among whites. He looked to enlightened white leadership to lead the work of racial reconstruction, and he concluded that Philadelphia's black elite had abdicated its role in racial leadership. He hoped his massive study of black Philadelphia would light a fire under both. The road from the settlement house to the "talented tenth" was neither very long nor indirect.

The first of the college settlements originated in a gathering of four Smith College alumnae in the autumn of 1887. Conversation had turned to "the new economics, the new awakening of practical philanthropy in England, Toynbee Hall and the principles for which it stood." The women agreed on the need for parallel action in America and set to work. Their model differed from the British in two important ways: it rested on a secular rather than a religious foundation, and the leaders were women, not men. "In the autumn of 1888 an appeal was sent out from Boston that met with a ready and generous response. A house was taken at 95 Rivington street, New York, and the first College Settlement for Women was opened in October, 1889." The next year a group of college women organized the College Settlements Association with "electors" from Wellesley, Smith, Vassar, Bryn Mawr, and "the non-collegiate element." In the next two years alumnae from the Annex (Radcliffe), Packer and Wells, Cornell, Swarthmore, Mount Holyoke, and Elmira joined in the work.

By 1893 the Association had helped found two new settlements in Philadelphia and Boston. Philadelphia proved challenging and instructive because "all of the circumstances were so different . . . that it was seen the work would be, to a large extent, without precedent." Unlike those in New York, the settlement was "on a side street in a shiftless neighborhood among a less provident class of people, many of them being colored." As such, the Philadelphia Settlement opened a new area for research and social action.

Because Du Bois's *Philadelphia Negro* dominates images of the city's Seventh Ward in the late nineteenth century, it is easy to forget that blacks constituted a minority of the residents of the Fifth and Seventh Ward neighborhoods the Philadelphia Settlement served. Within the Seventh Ward, wrote Mrs. Eliza Butler Kirkbride, sometime candidate for ward school director, were both "unnumbered municipal problems" and "all the forces that perpetuate, as well as those that tend to destroy, a city's life. Although, of course not in every sense representative, it would yet be hard to find a more complete type in miniature of the American city in our time."

In 1892, Hannah Fox, then secretary to the Settlement residents, described Saint Mary Street, home of the Settlement, as "two blocks in length; on one side of it is the shopping street of the poor people; on the other, lodging houses and small stores of the negro population, while the intersecting streets are populated by German Jews and the representatives of many peoples who form a mixed population with no prevailing elements." Crossing and recrossing these streets was a "net-work of alleys, the houses in which are small and occupied by negroes." Helena S. Dudley, who became head resident, embellished Fox's description of the neighborhood. The street was

> not attractive. The houses are small, many of them wooden and look as if they were rotting away; the street is only two blocks long, with several courts leading from it, giving access to an astonishing number of small houses. . . . The grimy irregularity of the houses gives relief to the glimpses of sky behind; a tiny shop, with lattice window, has surely strayed hither from the London of Dickens; the park next the Settlement brings a pathetic memory of distant country spaces, and anyone who cares for the drama actualized can watch all day, without wearying, the shifting groups of half-clad children, with their varying nationalities—the dark Hebrew women, or patient negroes, or stout Germans, who live out their story day after day before the eyes of the street. The population of St. Mary's Street itself is made up chiefly of the most shiftless element of the colored people, with a plentiful and ever-increasing sprinkling of Russian and German Jews. The Italian quarter is a few streets to the south, but some stray Italians are in this district.

Even an observer on the left wing of the settlement movement, like Helena Dudley, saw ethnic diversity through the lens of conventional stereotypes as she described neighborhood life. "The children were very friendly, and the door never opened without a horde of curly-headed Jews or little 'pickaninnies' pouring into the hall. . . . The race characteristics are shown in picturesque contrast from our windows. The Jews work very hard. Opposite us is a house where you can see a lamp burning all night. Near it are men's fingers bending over a machine. . . . On the other side of the house is a court where the negroes live. Here work does not go on, or but very little of it, either by day or night. . . . During the summer nights there is scarcely an hour of quiet between the noise of the late revelers and that of the early workmen."

At least one activity sponsored by the Settlement, a military drill for black boys, remained segregated at the time, and white boys had a club of their own. Only "one club for little girls, it being a sewing class," had been formed by 1892–93. Dudley also noticed differences in the reading preferences of Jews and blacks who borrowed books from the Settlement's library. "The Jewish boys and girls read a good deal; they enjoy books of adventures, of travel and of history, whereas the colored boys are enthusiastic for Alger's thrilling romances." Even in the late nineteenth century, black youngsters, trapped by poverty, barred from jobs, and bruised by racism, turned for vicarious rewards to fantasy.

Through the lens of late nineteenth-century racial stereotypes, Dudley saw a typically heterogeneous urban neighborhood. As in other northern industrial cities, extensive ethnic diversity characterized late nineteenth-century Philadelphia. Although poor blacks were likely to live in close proximity to other blacks, the dispersion of Philadelphia's black population throughout the city meant that almost all blacks lived in close proximity to whites. About half the city's black population lived in the Seventh Ward and the adjoining Fourth, Fifth, and Eighth. But none of these wards was majority black. As a result, poor blacks and whites came into contact to a degree unimaginable in the late twentieth-century city. They shared the same dank alleys and crude outdoor facilities. They interacted in countless small ways—cooperative and hostile. Black and white children together played and fought in the same streets.

What united the district's population, "whatever their nationality," were poverty and the "pressure of great numbers." Families often lived "in one, or, at most two, rooms, and sometimes take boarders. The rooms are mostly bare. A large bed, straw mattress, with but few bed clothes, a stove, a few broken chairs, and children—these are the regular articles of furniture for St. Mary Street." The Philadelphia Settlement became an oasis amid the poverty of Saint Mary Street. The eleven-room house was "very cozy and compact. Down stairs there is a square hall, dining room, parlor, and kitchen, opening into one another. The fittings of the house are very simple but very pretty, and the effect on entering the hall with its open staircase and coal grate and archway leading to the little parlor, in which is a pretty flower window, is most pleasing." A reader of the Philadelphia Settlement's reports would not learn of the vibrant organizational infrastructure of black Philadelphia—the many churches, mutual benefit societies, branches of the Odd Fellows, and clubs. Although a reader would not know it from its reports, the Philadelphia Settlement moved into a community with an indigenous civil society, not into an institutional desert.

Unlike his Settlement associates, Du Bois did not fail to enumerate and interpret the many institutions that preceded the Settlement—and remained after it had left. First in importance were the churches. The "social life of the Negro centres in his church—baptism, wedding and burial, gossip and courtship, friendship and intrigue—all lie in these walls," wrote Du Bois. Du Bois counted 55 "Negro churches with 12,845 members owning $907,729 worth of property with an annual income of at least $94,968." All the major denominations located churches in or near the Seventh Ward and engaged in missionary work and charity. The Episcopal church at Eighth and Bainbridge ran two missions, helped with the Fresh Air Fund, operated an ice mission and a vacation school for thirty-five children, and employed a parish visitor. As well, it was the site of University Extension lectures and good music, and had organized an insurance society and Home for the Homeless on Lombard Street. Aside from churches, the most important organizations among blacks included "secret societies, beneficial societies, insurance societies, cemeteries, building and loan associations, labor unions, homes of various sorts and political clubs." The largest and most powerful of these was the Odd Fellows with 19 lodges and 1,188 members in Philadelphia. Black Philadelphia also produced seven newspapers and journals. The *Tribune* was the "chief news sheet . . . filled generally with social notes of all kinds, and news of movements among Negroes over the country." Black Philadelphians had founded their own institutions, besides organizations: the Home for Aged and Infirm Colored Persons, Douglass Hospital and Training School, Woman's Exchange and Girls' Home, three cemeteries, Home for the Homeless, and special schools—the Institute for Colored Youth, House of Industry, Raspberry Street Schools and Jones' School for Girls, YMCA, and University Extension Center. To be sure, observed Du Bois, black Philadelphia lacked the organizational density and maturity of the white city. Nonetheless, he found its accomplishments remarkable. "All this world of co-operation and subordination into which the white child is in most cases born is, we must not forget, new to the slave's sons." Like today's theorists of civil society or social capital, Du Bois stressed the importance of these voluntary associations; "it is apparent that the largest hope for the ultimate rise of the Negro lies in this mastery of the art of social organized life." While the leaders of the Philadelphia Settlement might agree, their reports remained blind to the associational life that flourished around them.

A remarkable variety of living conditions characterized the Seventh Ward. On its eastern side, around the Settlement, was "a district composed largely of Italians and Russians, recently arrived in this country and living under unfavorable conditions." At the western border of the Seventh Ward, on the Schuylkill River, was "a district which has all that a semi-commercial river bank in a large city displays," while "larger and more valuable residences" clustered along its northern edge. Its "southern boundary" was "devoted to small retail shops, supplying a large population of small householders." Whether rich or poor, most families in the Seventh Ward—4,083 of 5,722 in the early 1890s—lived in separate houses. Only 1,002 families lived in houses with two families each and 639 with three or more. In the whole ward but seventeen dwellings housed six or more families.

In the nineteenth-century "walking city" rich and poor lived in close proximity. On the bustling streets of Philadelphia, it was nearly impossible for the well-to-do to avoid the less fortunate, for whites to avoid blacks. The Seventh Ward included the handsome four-story brick town houses on the 900 block of Clinton Street, where Susan Wharton and Charles C. Harrison lived, and the block of South Broad Street, home to Hannah Fox. Proud stone and brick row homes, many with ten or twelve rooms, which housed Philadelphia's elite, lined Spruce and Pine streets, the grandest in the fashionable Rittenhouse Square area west of Broad Street. Gracious marble steps and cornices, tall windows, and ornate ironwork signaled to passersby the wealth of the residents within.

This world of wealth was not foreign to Philadelphia's African Americans, even if it was unattainable to them. As Du Bois noted, "the mass of Negroes are in the economic world purveyors to the rich—working in private houses, in hotels, large stores, etc." In the Seventh Ward, Du Bois and his assistant Isabel Eaton found that over 61 percent of black men worked as domestics and over 88 percent of black women found work in the service sector. Employment as domestics, housekeepers, cooks, and janitors barely provided a subsistence-level living, for as Du Bois acerbically noted, "from long custom and from competition, their wages for this work are not high." A sizable segment of the black population lived with wealthy white families; in 1880, 19 percent of Philadelphia's black women and 8 percent of black men lived in white-headed households. In her canvass of domestic workers, Eaton found 109 butlers, 76 coachmen, 4 valets, and 4 lady's maids in the ward. Even more blacks lived literally in the shadow of the Seventh Ward's rich, in thousands of small houses only a few hundred yards away from the city's most prestigious addresses. Far more than the modern city, Philadelphia remained a jumble of ethnicity, race, and class, of small clusters scattered in complicated patterns rather than in large, homogeneous areas.

The Seventh Ward, in fact, was experiencing transition. Blacks constituted about 30 percent of its residents, immigrants between 20 and 25 percent. About half of the native born had foreign-born parents. Du Bois pointed to the excess of women to men as a source of social problems among the ward's blacks; unbalanced sex ratios also marked the ward's whites and were largest among the foreign born. (In 1900, for instance, among the foreign born with foreign-born parents, women outnumbered men 3,221 to 1,899; among blacks, the numbers were 5,436 and 5,026.) Here, perhaps, lay another source of the ward's unsavory reputation. Although in the 1890s the city of Philadelphia grew from 1,046,964 to 1,293,697, the population of the Seventh Ward dropped from 30,179 to 28,137. Whites were leaving as blacks moved in: the white population declined from 21,177 to 17,496, while the black population increased from 8,861 to 10,462. During the Du Boises' residence, this demographic shift challenged the diversity of the Philadelphia Settlement and forced it to decide how black an institution it would become.

The Du Boises arrived a year after the Settlement had moved into larger quarters at 617 Carver (later Rodman) Street. Hannah Fox had purchased the new house along with the four adjoining houses, which she intended to use as model tenements. The Settlement also occupied property on Lombard Street. "The demolition of the old rookeries at Seventh and Lombard, and the erection of the building to be used as the Kitchen and Coffee House with a fine tenement house adjoining it in Lombard Street has done away with a most unsightly and unsanitary corner," observed the head resident—with no mention of the fate of the tenants displaced. In fact, many of the area's displaced (predominantly black) residents moved just a few blocks to the west, changing the complexion of the Seventh Ward. The new property reflected the Settlement's expanded activities. It took delight in the creation of Theodore Starr Park, built on the site of houses demolished on Sixth Street, and it announced the publication of a monthly newsletter, the *College Settlement News*.

The Settlement cooperated closely with public agencies that served the poor. The board of education appointed one of its residents as a second teacher in the kindergarten branch of the James Forten School at Sixth and Lombard. Another resident, Dr. Frances C. VanGasken, served as medical inspector for the Board of Health; the Free Library of Philadelphia appointed a resident as assistant librarian for the library's College Settlement branch. The daily program of regular work in the winter of 1894 and 1895 included the kindergarten, a doctor's office, a savings bank, and the library. Other activities were scattered throughout the week: carpenter shop, free-hand drawing, reading club, mechanical drawing, English classes, Clover Club, women's sewing class, Little Helpers, Area Club, Whittier Club, Dudley Pioneer Corps, Holy Club, games, gymnastic club, Tynall Club, Davis Cadets, Daisy Chain, Citizenship Club, choir drill, and lectures. The Settlement also organized special activities for its residents, including classes in social science, and sent representatives to speak at conferences of the College Settlement Association and elsewhere in the city. In 1894–95, for instance, the Settlement's delegates spoke at a conference of the Child Saving Agencies of Philadelphia, at three conferences of the Women's Union in the Interest of Labor, and at the Civic Club.

The Settlement also cooperated with the Society for Organizing Charity (SOC) and shared its belief in the importance of reducing indiscriminate relief through the application of work tests. One resident even became a visitor for the Fifth Ward branch of the SOC. The superintendent of the SOC, noted the Settlement's head resident, Katherine B. Davis, did as much as he could with limited funds, "but with no efficient corps of visitors and little money it is impossible to expect him, single handed, to cope with the situation. If we can do no more we shall at least offer the services of one or two residents as visitors for the coming winter." Whatever the situation in other cities and despite historians' claims about hostility between them, in Philadelphia no tension seemed to strain relations between the Settlement and the "scientific charity" movement.

Although residence lay at the heart of the original settlement idea, many women found difficulty in remaining in residence for relatively long times. In 1892–93, for instance, the average resident in the Philadelphia Settlement stayed only five months. The privilege of settlement residence, moreover, was not free; the cost was five dollars per week for residents and one dollar per day for visitors. Head resident Katherine B. Davis wrote of the problems settlements experienced "from a constantly changing family of residents." A permanent head worker by herself was "not sufficient to secure and fix" an "accurate knowledge of the neighborhood and its needs" and short-term residents could not take advantage of "large and important opportunities for helpfulness in connection with other agencies." The problem lay in familial expectations for unmarried, unemployed daughters. With "some justice" a father supporting a daughter believed her home should be beneath his roof. "He may be willing to spare her for a winter, even a year, but there are few fathers who, unless she marries or necessity compels, think it right for his daughter to be permanently away from home." With "self-supporting women" the situation differed. A growing number of young women, "whatever the financial condition of their parents," wanted "to take care of themselves," and parents increasingly respected this "natural desire" of "trained and educated women." For the Settlement the answer was clear: find income for residents by placing them in neighborhood jobs, which was a plan the Philadelphia Settlement followed with some success. In 1894–95, Davis reported, eight of eleven residents had remained six months or more, the "best showing since the Settlement opened."

To leaders of the settlement movement, the importance of residence could not be overemphasized. Living in a settlement house fostered the empathy essential to bridging the gap between classes through residents' identification with the problems of the poor and constructive working relationships with the neighborhood. Newspapers, commented Helena Dudley, had accustomed readers to lurid descriptions of misery; "ardent educators" brought "squads" of students to "penetrate with shocking curiosity into the most harrowing and hidden secrets of the miserable life of the poor." Reading about the poor, even inspecting their housing, however, did not substitute for living among them. No alternative could take the place of the need to "identify oneself" with the awful conditions described by the press, "to be as a neighbor among neighbors; to hear day by day the stolid, terrible gossip of the street; to take, as one insensibly comes to take, the point of view on matters moral and physical of people sleeping seven in a room. It is no longer the 'problem of the masses' that confronts one, but the suffering of the individual man or woman of like passions with ourselves." There were, then, good reasons beyond the need of an underpaid researcher to find cheap housing for the Du Boises to live at the Settlement.

Residence added lived experience to bare statistical facts. It also proved the commitment of the researcher to the use of knowledge for social improvement. Only high social purpose justified the intrusion into individual lives represented by research. Writing the introductory comments to *Hull-House Maps and Papers*, which, along with Charles Booth's monumental *Life and Labours of the People of London*, was the model for Du Bois's research in Philadelphia, Agnes Sinclair Holbrook observed, "Insistent probing into the lives of the poor would come with bad grace even from government officials, were the statistics so inconsiderable as to afford no working basis for further improvement. . . . All spasmodic and sensational throbs of curious interest are ineffectual as well as unjustifiable. The painful nature of minute investigation, and the personal impertinence of many of the questions asked, would be unendurable and unpardonable were it not for the conviction that the public conscience when roused must demand better surroundings for the most inert and long-suffering citizens of the commonwealth." Still, although the Du Boises lived at the Settlement, its annual reports did not list them as residents. (Isabel Eaton, by contrast, was listed among the residents as CSA fellow.) Whether this was because of their race or relation to the work of the Settlement remains unknown.

The idea that brought Du Bois to Philadelphia had originated with Susan Wharton, who first proposed a study of the Seventh Ward's black population. Wharton at the time served as a member of the Executive Committee of the Philadelphia College Settlement. In 1895 she assembled an interracial conference at her home of "persons interested in the welfare of this race." She also wrote to her neighbor, acting provost of the University of Pennsylvania, Charles C. Harrison, a retired sugar magnate, asking "the cooperation of the University in a plan for the better understanding of the colored people, especially of their position in this city. . . . The College Settlement wishes to co-operate in the movement and will probably engage a woman who can reside in St. Mary Street." Late in the fall of 1896, Harrison presided at a "parlor meeting" in her house. With his support added to that of others at the meeting, who included "representative colored leaders," Wharton asked the university's young sociology professor, Samuel McCune Lindsay, then active in the CSA, to organize the study; Lindsay chose Du Bois.

Du Bois believed that Philadelphia's reform-minded elite had brought him to the city with a hidden agenda. In the midst of one of its "periodic spasms of reform," he remembered, reformers wanted to document the cause of political corruption in "one of the worst governed of America's badly governed cities." They looked to an investigation with the "imprimatur of the University" to give "scientific sanction" to the already known source of corruption. The "underlying cause was evident to most white Philadelphians: the corrupt, semi-criminal vote of the Negro Seventh Ward." Settlement residents had mounted their own attack on corruption by repeatedly campaigning for the election of a woman from the Seventh Ward as a ward school director, but the ward's black voters helped defeat their increasingly vigorous campaigns, which enlisted the Settlement's entire staff.

Blacks remained loyal to the Republican political machine, which helped them with jobs. Excluded from nearly all desirable white occupations, blacks found a small opening in public offices and public works. Their votes seemed a fair price. Settlement workers might offer them better government, but they could not supply jobs. To the contrary, reform would "throw many worthy Negroes out of employment." The "very reformers who want votes for specific reforms," observed Du Bois, who saw the situation clearly, "will not themselves work beside Negroes, or admit them to positions in their stores or offices, or lend them friendly aid when in trouble." Even more, reformers missed the pride blacks took in their councilmen and policemen, who filled their positions honorably, even if they first obtained them through "shady 'politics.'" Should blacks, Du Bois asked, "surrender these tangible evidences of the rise of their race to forward the good-hearted but hardly imperative demands of a crowd of women?"

Many forces other than insensitivity to the importance of jobs, the machine, or the black vote, contributed to the defeat of the women candidates for ward school director. They met antagonism from the ward's schoolteachers, apathy from the affluent, and hostility to their gender. Canvassing "the various classes of votes," women reformers found themselves "impressed by the marked contrast in the attitude of the richer, better, and more educated classes toward municipal politics, as distinguished from that of the so-called ignorant people in the small streets." On the grand streets—Spruce, Pine, Delancey, Trinity Place—they met striking ignorance of the electoral process and the issues, not to mention apathy. There they encountered "citizens whose bosom swelled with pride as they declared: 'I never vote.'" In the "small streets," however, "the voter appeared to know these facts as well as the canvasers." Indeed, in these streets, "in the midst of all the wretchedness, dirt, and ignorance, there was scarcely a single instance of indifference to questions of government." In part, neglect of the election reflected disinterest in the public schools. The wealthy sent their children to private, the Catholics to parochial schools. "The only class of which the religious and moral portion" showed interest in public schools were "the colored population, because they send their children to them, and are obliged to do so, or keep them at home, none of the private schools admitting them." Realizing the importance and sorry state of the public schools, a number of black leaders, including the eminent educator Fannie Coppin, had supported the women reformers' bid for election.

Du Bois and some subsequent historians awarded at least some reformers too little credit for understanding political realities, and they read motives too singly. As she reflected on the defeat, one campaign organizer observed that in every division of the ward the machine kept "two or three men who all the year around are keeping up relations with the voters, obtaining, for instance, through the ward bosses, for men out of work, places on the traction lines and on railroads, helping to get their children transferred from school to school, and organizing political clubs whose rent and expenses are paid by the office holders." Even more, these men knew "every voter, at least by sight." Although their homes backed onto the houses of voters in the small streets, alleys, and lanes, wealthy reformers hardly knew their poor and working-class neighbors. Not surprisingly, ordinary voters had preferred the machine politicians who "had taken the trouble" to know them "before they asked for their vote" rather than the women who had ignored them until the campaign. The moral was clear: "each of us should . . . take the division in which she lives, and make it a point before the next election to know all about it. . . . If there is trouble, sickness or death in the little row of houses which are at the back of almost every one of our dwellings, it ought to be understood that the Civic Club [a reform organization of women founded in 1894] representative is the best person in the division to go to." Women reformers also should join with the Charity Organization Society to "investigate cases in the division, and distribute its relief." While they should not stoop to corruption, argued this now veteran campaigner, Philadelphia's elite women reformers needed to emulate the machine if reform hoped to win office.

If settlement workers failed to advance reform through politics, they could still deploy another potent weapon: research. Philadelphia's settlement house leaders participated in an international network of reformers committed to the power of social investigation. Indeed, research constituted a crucial component of settlement work. The "great movement toward social reconstruction," believed the college women, required hard facts. Documenting conditions among the urban poor would awaken the conscience of the rich and powerful and provide data for social and political reform. "A Settlement," wrote Helena S. Dudley, the head resident at Philadelphia, "can do little to solve the questions which perplex our philanthropic specialists. It may be that the cause of the evils we seek to remedy is too deep for our palliatives. But whatever the cause of the poverty, whatever the remedy, we all agree that we must have knowledge of facts."

From its early years, the College Settlement Association raised fellowship money for women college graduates to undertake applied social research while living as settlement residents. In 1893–94, for instance, the CSA sponsored three fellowships. Ada S. Woolfold, Wellesley, investigated "The Obstacles to Sanitary Living Among the Poor" in New York and Boston; Katherine Pearson Woods, "non-collegiate," studied "Diseases and Accidents Incident to Occupations" in Boston and Philadelphia; and Isabel Eaton, Smith, documented "Receipts and Expenses of Wage Earners in the Garment Trades" in Chicago and New York.

Eaton would hold another fellowship to work with Du Bois and investigate domestic service in Philadelphia. A contributor to *Hull-House Maps and Papers*, she probably had been recommended for the job by Jane Addams. (In October 1895 Susan Wharton had written to Addams: "Do you know of anyone capable of being an investigator of the Negro problem? Such a person would live at the Phil. Settlement and receive $300 for about ten months work. The University of Penna. to have entire direction of the investigation.") Wharton also invited Addams to lecture at the Philadelphia Settlement. Convinced of the role of research in social reform, Wharton almost certainly saw Du Bois's role as replicating the *Hull-House Maps and Papers* in Philadelphia. Du Bois, for his part, paid high praise to Florence Kelley and Addams. "Save Jane Addams," he observed at the time of Kelley's death in 1932, "there is not another social worker in the United States who has had either her insight or her daring, so far as the American Negro is concerned."

Du Bois's remarks referred obliquely to the settlements' shabby record with blacks. "The majority of settlement houses," reports historian Elisabeth Lasch-Quinn in *Black Neighbors*, "either excluded blacks, conducted segregated activities, closed down completely, or followed their former white neighbors out of black neighborhoods." Even Hull House compiled a far less than exemplary record on race. In its early years the Philadelphia Settlement's record appeared better than most. It chose to open in a partially black neighborhood; although some clubs were segregated, most activities attempted to bring together blacks and white immigrants. And, of course, it initiated and cosponsored Du Bois's great study of black Philadelphia.

Nonetheless, in 1897–98 the Settlement decided to move. It had been cooperating with other agencies to persuade the city to extend Starr Park, and it occupied space on which the park would stand. At first, "it was thought that a change not of a few squares only, but of some miles, might be advisable." Public opinion, however, forced the Settlement to retract. "To the minds of our friends we became birds of passage." Thus, in January 1898, the executive committee decided to remain "down-town," within a mile of the existing location. "We believe we have struck root deeply enough to make transplanting unwise." The new move, although short in distance, would bring a welcome change in the Settlement's demography. "A location something less than a mile distant, and further to the southeast, will bring us into touch with a more varied population, Jewish, Italian, German and English-speaking population of foreign birth, as well as a considerable admixture of Americans." Never intended as a wholly black institution, the Settlement found its demography almost certainly had been altered by the movement of whites out of the Seventh Ward and the increasing migration of blacks. Faced with the prospect of the identification of the Settlement as a black institution, the executive committee voted to move to an area with a far smaller black population. At their new location at Third and Christian Streets, the social workers found that they were "nearer the centre of our old constituency; we have a more varied population, racially and industrially." By 1899, the Settlement's new head resident reported that "the whole number of cases . . . are fairly balanced in number." Achieving that "balance" meant a dramatic decline in the proportion of blacks to other groups served by the Settlement. In 1898, about 15 percent of all patients visited by the Settlement's nurses were black; in 1900, only about 4 percent were black.

Du Bois and the Origins of Sociology at the University of Pennsylvania

The Settlement was not the only institution responding to demographic shifts. Two decades earlier the other sponsor of Du Bois's research, the University of Pennsylvania, had left center city altogether for forty-eight and one-half acres in the city's then-suburban western edge. Its first dormitories, "arranged on the 'cottage' plan of contiguous houses," opened in 1896–97; in all, the University occupied twenty-two buildings. Taught by 258 "officers of instruction," 1,984 of the 2,834 students came from Pennsylvania. None of the faculty and an indeterminate, but tiny, number of students were black. (The first black student graduated from the College in 1883 and from the Wharton School in 1887.) Undergraduate instruction in sociology took place in the Wharton School, founded in 1881, which, at the time, remained "the Course in Finance and Economy" of the College; the Department of Philosophy, in effect the University's graduate school, remained home to graduate instruction in sociology.

With a strictly research appointment, Du Bois did no teaching. As "assistant in sociology," he had been appointed by the trustees "as investigator of the social conditions of the Colored race in this City, in connection with the work of the Wharton School." Almost certainly as a concession to Professor Samuel McCune Lindsay, who had hired Du Bois, his presence merited one brief mention in the University's *Catalogue* during the second year of his appointment. In 1897, Lindsay had complained to the secretary of the University, Jesse Y. Burk, about the omission of Du Bois from the *Catalogue*. Burk responded lamely that he had not reported Du Bois's appointment to the editor of the catalogue because it "was not considered one which placed him on the staff. . . . Indeed I should not have known where to place or what to call him for the purposes of a circular of information." Although his name appeared the next year as assistant in sociology, a 1930–31 history of the sociology department at Penn by one of its professors, James H. S. Brossard, made no mention of Du Bois's presence or work. The most significant research in the history of the department still remained invisible.

In the 1890s, however, the university did not try to camouflage its support of Du Bois's research. To the contrary, Provost Charles C. Harrison, who had helped raise the money for Du Bois's appointment, described the purposes of Du Bois's study and asked for public cooperation. His letter of introduction for Du Bois not only supplied Du Bois with credentials; it revealed that the University found Philadelphia's black population at once a mystery and a problem in need of solution. Clearly, he did not expect Du Bois to find internal sources of strength or a population that could improve itself without the intervention of philanthropic white Philadelphians.

> In connection with the College Settlement, the Trustees of the University of Pennsylvania have undertaken the study of the social condition of the Colored People of the Seventh Ward of Philadelphia. The University has entered upon this work as a part of its duty and wishes to make the investigation as thorough and exact as possible. We want to know precisely how this class of people lives; what occupations they follow; from what occupations they are excluded; how many of their children go to school; and to ascertain every fact which will throw light upon this social problem; and then having this information and these accurate statistics before us, to see to what extent and in what way, proper remedies may be applied. Dr. W.E.B. Du Bois is the investigator on behalf of the University, and I write to bespeak for him your cordial reception and earnest cooperation.

Although sociology was new to Penn and its staff small, Du Bois found himself in an intellectual environment congenial to his research. How much interchange with his colleagues Du Bois enjoyed remains unknown. Nonetheless, an empirical account of the black residents of the city's Seventh Ward fit nicely with the thrust of sociological interests at Penn. According to Brossard, in Penn's sociology department the emphasis had been placed "overwhelmingly . . . upon good teaching," and the "problem type of course" had "predominated. The material presented to the students is concrete and factual. There has been among the members of the group little indulgence in philosophizing and a general reticence to theorize prematurely. There has been no overzealous bidding for professional recognition." Brossard accurately captured the department's emphasis on teaching and its practical, problem-oriented direction, which, certainly, reflected its placement in the Wharton School. However, he misrepresented the professional aspirations and accomplishments of its early members, who pioneered in the building of academic disciplines, organizations, and journals.

Robert Ellis Thompson, who became the initial dean of the Wharton School in 1881, had first taught a course in "social science" at Penn in 1869–70, but the first course identified as sociology, "The Elements of Sociology," was taught in 1891–92 by Dr. Frederick W. Moore, temporarily appointed instructor in sociology as a leave replacement for Professor Roland Falkner, who had joined the faculty in 1888–89 and taught statistics. Falkner and Davis R. Dewey of the Massachusetts Institute of Technology were the first two American professors with the word "statistics" in their professorial title. A graduate of Philadelphia's Central High School and, at age nineteen, of the University of Pennsylvania, Falkner became the first to teach statistics full-time; he described his undergraduate course, "Statistics," required for Wharton seniors, as "A study of population in Europe and America," which included "Structure of the population, numbers, density, races and nationalities, sex, age, conjugal condition and occupation" as well as several other economic, demographic, and social topics that paralleled the organization of Du Bois's research schedules. As statistician for the U.S. Committee on Finance, Falkner "directed the most exhaustive investigation of prices and wages in the United States up to that time." Falkner left Penn in 1900 to become chief of the Division of Documents at the Library of Congress.

Eminent as Falkner became, Penn's most famous social scientist remained Simon N. Patten. Patten had been recruited by the chairman of the Department of Economics, Edmund James. Appointed in 1883 after two years of graduate study in Germany, James became a leading player in the creation of economics as a discipline and in shaping the Wharton School. In class, James substituted the German professorial lecture for recitations and drills, and in 1885 he introduced the University's first research seminar. James wanted to turn Wharton into a "School of Political and Social Science." Although he failed to realize his grand design, his "vision of the practical university," according to the school's historian, "would remain the foundation of the Wharton School program." James attracted many of the serious sons of Philadelphia's elite. Although most entered business, several, including Falkner, went on to careers in academics or reform, or in journalism and letters. James hoped to influence public affairs not, as had his predecessors, through journalism but through research and the practical application of scholarship. Thus, for example, he wrote a long analysis of modern municipalities, the gas supply, and the "Gas Question" in Philadelphia and in 1889 transformed the Philadelphia Social Science Association into the American Academy of Political and Social Science. He was also instrumental in founding the American Economic Association. Nonetheless, despite James's accomplishments, Charles C. Harrison, a wealthy member of the trustees, long had disliked him, and when Harrison became provost he promptly forced James's resignation. James moved to the University of Chicago.

Among James's most enduring accomplishments had been hiring Simon N. Patten, a friend also trained in Germany and, according to Sass, "perhaps the greatest mind in the history of the institution." "For almost a third of a century," writes Brossard in his history of sociology at Penn, Patten, who came to Penn in 1888, "was a sort of spiritual father to the Wharton School." Although often identified as a sociologist, Patten remained primarily an economist noted for the originality and importance of his ideas (seen, for instance, in *The Economic Basis of Protection, The Development of English Thought, The Social Basis of Religion*, and *The New Basis of Civilization*), his inspirational teaching, and his involvement with the practical work of reform. Patten, according to his junior colleague Samuel McCune Lindsay, played "a much greater part than can ever be known in initiating and actually guiding the university extension movement, the . . . labor movement, housing reform, prevention of tuberculosis, education and training of social workers and other allied and similar activities. He was a big factor in the *Survey* and the periodicals that preceded it. He took an immense interest in the feminist movement. His mind was always at work on problems of practical, elementary, and secondary education." Patten's teaching reflected his interests in the intersection of politics and economics, the practical application of scholarship, and training in research. In the college, Patten taught "Political Economy"; in the graduate program, "History of Political Economy," "Practical Applications of Economic Theory," "The Problems of Sociology," and "Investigation of Special Topics," another research course.

In the 1890s, Patten shared the sociology-related teaching with Falkner and Samuel McCune Lindsay, his former student in Wharton. After his graduation from Penn in 1889, Lindsay had continued his education in Germany at Halle, where he received his doctorate in 1892. He joined the faculty of Penn in 1894 as the first full-time professor of sociology and began a distinguished career noted more for its contributions to public service than for original scholarship. Among his appointments were as commissioner of education for Puerto Rico, 1902–4; first secretary, later chairman of the National Child Labor Committee; president of the American Academy of Political and Social Science; director, New York School of Philanthropy; president of the Academy of Political Science; and president of the American Association for Labor Legislation. In 1907, he left Penn to become professor of social legislation at Columbia. Even more than Patten, Lindsay directed his teaching toward the application of social science to social problems and reform. Lindsay's "Descriptive Sociology," required of Wharton sophomores, included not only theory, represented by Spencer's *Study of Sociology*, but more practical texts as well, notably Amos Warner's *American Charities*. His course "Social Pathology" was an "advanced" study of "Pauperism and Treatment of the Defective and Delinquent Classes," compulsory for juniors. Also compulsory for juniors was his course "Sociological Field Work." In the first part of the course, Lindsay took students to "mills, factories and business establishments" and, in the latter, to "charitable and correctional institutions." It was, perhaps, as part of this course, or his elective "Charity Organization," that Du Bois shepherded a group of undergraduates around the Seventh Ward. ("I did no instructing save once to pilot a pack of idiots through the Negro slums.") Lindsay's courses revealed his interest in social problems, involvement with social reform, and association with philanthropic agencies outside the university. They also pointed to his embrace of "scientific charity," with its emphasis on investigating and classifying the poor using moral criteria; on centralizing charity; and on gathering empirical data about poverty and its concomitants, such as poor housing, disease, and the conditions of employment. In these years, Du Bois shared these conventional views about poverty, which began to lose favor only later in the 1890s. Lindsay's graduate courses also stressed the interplay between theory and practice: "Sociological Field Work" (which included "Study by individual investigation of the pathological phenomena of the slums"); "History and Organization of Philadelphia Charities"; "Modern Socialism"; and "Sociological Theory."

The titles of Lindsay's courses changed slightly in subsequent years; the course in charity organization was dropped; but the mix of theory and practice, with a strong fieldwork component and a concentration on social issues remained. (Lindsay may have dropped the course on Philadelphia charities because he had finished his research on the subject, published in 1895 as a directory of the city's "educational institutions and societies.") The single published notice of Du Bois's presence at Penn in a University catalogue appeared as a "Note" following the description of Lindsay's fieldwork course for 1897–98.

Note: The special sociological investigation of the condition of the Negroes in the Seventh Ward of Philadelphia, begun in September 1896, under the direction of William E. Burkhardt Du Bois, Ph. D., will be concluded by January 1, 1898. The results will be published by Dr. Du Bois, who was appointed Assistant in Sociology for the year 1896–97 to conduct the investigation.

Among the faculty at Penn, Du Bois remembered only Lindsay with any warmth. Lindsay had chosen him for the task. "If Lindsay had been a smaller man and had been induced to follow the usual American pattern of treating Negroes, he would have asked me to assist him as his clerk in his study. Probably I would have accepted having nothing better in sight for work in sociology. But Lindsay regarded me as a scholar in my own right and probably proposed to make me an instructor." How Lindsay first learned of Du Bois remains unknown. Nonetheless, by the time of his arrival, Du Bois would be well known in Philadelphia's social science circles. In 1897 the *Annals of the American Academy of Political and Social Science*, edited by Falkner and published in Philadelphia, carried a highly favorable review of Du Bois's 1896 book, *The Suppression of the African Slave Trade*, by Bernard C. Steiner of Johns Hopkins, who called it "a thoroughly good piece of work. His research has been exhaustive and accurate and he has so incorporated the results of that research that the reader has a true book and not an ill-digested collection of facts." At the time of his appointment to Penn, his book on the slave trade was in press. Both Du Bois's "training and personal qualifications for the projected work," wrote Lindsay in his introduction to the first edition of *The Philadelphia Negro*, "proved to be far greater than our highest expectations, and his signal services in the educational uplift of his people, both before and since his term of service at the University of Pennsylvania, have won for him a public recognition that renders any introduction of Dr. Du Bois quite unnecessary."

Also in 1896 in the *Annals*, Du Bois published a devastating review of Frederick L. Hoffman, *Race Traits and Tendencies of the American Negro*. Du Bois's critique foreshadowed key methods and themes he would use in *The Philadelphia Negro*. Hoffman projected the eventual disappearance of the Negro through a higher death rate influenced by "'race traits and tendencies' rather than . . . conditions of life." Du Bois concentrated his attack on Hoffman's methods and sources. Despite his many tables, Hoffman had failed to omit the "fallacies of the statistical method," which was "nothing but the application of logic to counting, and no amount of counting will justify a departure from the severe rules of correct reasoning." Du Bois showed how Hoffman relied on incomparable sets of statistics; incorrectly extrapolated from the small urban black population to the much larger rural population of the South; ignored trends prior to the 1880–90 decade; and omitted comparisons to a number of foreign cities with rates of mortality and population growth less favorable than those prevailing among American blacks. Hoffman had misidentified the phenomenon requiring explanation. Not the threat of population extinction but the contradictions in the data required analysis, wrote Du Bois in a passage that foreshadowed the major themes of his new research project: the coexistence of contradictory trends among blacks; the social and moral differentiation of black communities; crime as one outcome of dashed aspirations; and the pervasive force of white racial prejudice.

> The proper interpretation of apparently contradictory social facts is a matter requiring careful study and deep insight. If, for instance, we find among American Negroes to-day, at the very same time, increasing intelligence and increasing crime, increasing wealth and disproportionate poverty, increasing religious and moral activity and high rate of illegitimacy in births, we can no more fasten upon the bad as typifying the general tendency than we can upon the good. . . . Such contradictory facts are not facts pertaining to the "race" but to its various classes, which development since emancipation has differentiated. As is natural with all races, material and mental development has, in the course of a single generation, progressed farther than the moral. . . . On the other hand, when the younger generation came on the stage with exaggerated but laudable hopes of "rising," and found that a dogged Anglo-Saxon prejudice had shut nearly every avenue of advancement in their faces, the energies of many undoubtedly found an outlet in crime.

One might write the recent history of African Americans, albeit in less moralistic language, with the same themes.

In his autobiography, Du Bois claimed he started his study with "no 'research methods'" and "asked little advice as to procedure." The situation, however, was a little more complicated. Lindsay sent drafts of Du Bois's proposed questionnaire to many individuals and institutions for comment. (One survives in the Du Bois archives at the University of Massachusetts and one in the Booker T. Washington papers in Washington, D.C.) His letter read:

> Enclosed please find the proof-sheets of the schedules which have been adopted for the Investigation into the Condition of the Negroes in Ward Seven of the City of Philadelphia. We desire to make this investigation as thorough as possible and to have the results in such shape as to be comparable with similar work undertaken in other cities. The work is being done by Mr. W.E.B. Du Bois, Ph. D. (Harvard) and Miss Isabel Easton, B.L. (Smith), under the direction of this department of the University, which will print all results worthy of publication.

Will you kindly examine the enclosed proofs and return them at once with any corrections or suggestions which in you judgment will add to the value of the investigation?

One surviving response from an unknown writer at Cornell suggested following an existing model, either the U.S. Census of 1890 or the Massachusetts state census of 1895. Some of the instructions on the schedules, claimed the writer, should be fuller. "Are all persons having any trace of African blood negroes and will you not find objection raised to your using the term negro? Why not . . . the census word 'colored' or the word their journals prefer afro-american?" The writer also suggested a "less objectionable method of framing" item 11, "Wanting or defective in mind, sight, hearing or speech; maimed or deformed?" "The similar question on 11th Census aroused a storm of public indignation." The final version of the schedule incorporated the writer's suggested revision: "Sound and healthy in mind, sight, hearing, speech, limbs and body?" Indeed, changes between the draft schedule and the final version suggest that Du Bois received many recommendations from reviewers.

Du Bois did not sample. He personally "visited and talked with 5,000 persons." Where possible, he recorded on schedules. "Other information stored in my memory or wrote out as memoranda. I went through the Philadelphia libraries for data, gained access in many instances to private libraries of colored folk and got individual information. I mapped the district, classifying it by conditions; I compiled two centuries of the Negro in Philadelphia and in the Seventh Ward." The result of this work on which Du Bois "labored morning, noon, and night" was "that fat volume" which "few persons ever read . . . but that they treat . . . with respect, and that consoles me."

Du Bois's method, common to Progressive Era social scientists and reformers, was based on the belief in the importance of gathering information as the first step toward improving society. But Du Bois defined the task of research with even greater precision. "The social problem is ever a relation between conditions and action," he wrote, shortly after completing the research for *The Philadelphia Negro*, "as conditions and actions vary and change from group to group from time to time and from place to place, so social problems change, develop, and grow." The key was to realize that the Negro problem, "like others, has had a long historical development, has changed with the growth and evolution of the nation; moreover it is not *one* problem, but rather a plexus of social problems, some new, some old, some simple, some complex." As complex and historically grounded as the Negro problem was, research on the topic remained, in Du Bois's view, "lamentably unsystematic and fragmentary." Moreover, "much of the work done on the Negro question is notoriously uncritical; uncritical in choosing the proper point of view from which to study those problems, and, finally, uncritical from the distinct bias in the minds of so many writers." At the historical moment that black historian Rayford Logan later called the "nadir" of race relations in American history, Du Bois's call for the thorough study of black America was not merely academic. Researchers, Du Bois argued, should not simply gather information, but amass and interpret data with the greatest care so that "we might *know* instead of *think* about the Negro problems." Research represented the first step in the dispelling of ignorance.

By conceiving of the Negro problem as a historical problem, contingent and ever changing, Du Bois planted the seeds of a powerful critique of racial essentialism. The wretched conditions that faced the Philadelphia Negro did not spring from innate racial deficiencies, as conventional wisdom held. The impoverishment of urban blacks did not reveal hereditary inferiority, nor did alarmingly high mortality rates prove that the race, left to fend for itself in a Darwinian world, was gradually disappearing. Blacks' limited opportunities in the workplace were a historically specific manifestation of prejudice and discrimination, not of their inherent limitations. Du Bois rooted his study in a fundamental critique of biological notions of race. He rejected both the lingering monogenetic views that prevailed in black religious circles and the statistical Anglo-Saxonism that moved to the fore of the human sciences in the 1890s.

Du Bois's racial thinking was, however, far advanced from his ethnographic strategy. Philadelphia's blacks had not welcomed Du Bois with open arms. Encountering a "natural dislike of being studied like a strange species," Du Bois repeatedly "met again and in different guise those curious cross-currents and inner social whirlings. They set me to groping. I concluded that I did not know so much as I might about my own people." In the end, "I had learned far more from Philadelphia Negroes than I had taught them concerning the Negro Problem."

The tensions that run through *The Philadelphia Negro* were in part the result of the clash between Du Bois's assumptions and the reality of black Philadelphia. Du Bois's research agenda started with the conventional wisdom of charity organization and late nineteenth-century social thought. Du Bois, like many observers, focused on the pathologies of the family and on criminality, moving uncertainly between explanations that emphasized individual moral and behavioral deficiencies and those that focused on the forces of racial inequality, prejudice, and discrimination. Likewise, Du Bois argued for the redemptive nature of work for its own sake. But his experience led him to challenge, albeit tentatively, some of the central verities of late nineteenth-century charity. Whereas many reformers held that charity sapped the work ethic of the poor, Du Bois gave lip service to the ideal of self-help but offered a far more radical analysis of the causes of poverty than did many of his sponsors. The "centre and kernel of the Negro problem," wrote Du Bois, "is the narrow opportunities afforded Negroes for earning a decent living." Systematically excluded from most of the city's well-paying industrial jobs, Philadelphia's blacks were concentrated disproportionately in the service sector. As Du Bois wrote, in one of his best documented and passionate passages, "No matter how well trained a Negro may be, or how fitted for work of any kind, he cannot in the ordinary course of competition hope to be much more than a menial servant." Offering moving examples of black professionals who could not find employment, of artisans excluded from their trades, of high school graduates relegated to jobs as scrubwomen, Du Bois bristled particularly at the summary exclusion of blacks from the ranks of "foremen, managers and clerks—the lieutenants of industry who direct its progress." Perhaps referring obliquely to his own second-tier status at the University of Pennsylvania, Du Bois bitingly asked "what university would appoint a promising young Negro as a tutor?"

Du Bois certainly learned some hard truths about American academic life. "It would have been a fine thing," he recalled in his autobiography, "if after this difficult, successful piece of work, the University of Pennsylvania had at least offered me a temporary instructorship in the college of the Wharton School." Certainly, Harvard "had never dreamed of such a thing." Du Bois was not looking for a permanent appointment, but "an academic accolade from a great American university would have given impetus to my life work which I was already determined to make in a Negro institution in the South." What "galled was that such an idea never even occurred to this institution whose head was a high official in the Sugar Trust." Still, in 1898 he remained publicly supportive of Penn. There was "no better way" that the American university could "repay the unusual munificence of its benefactors than by placing before the nation a body of scientific truth in the light of which they could solve some of their most vexing social problems." Therefore, the University of Pennsylvania deserved "credit." For "she has been the first to recognize her duty in this respect, and in so far as restricted means and opportunity allowed, has attempted to study the Negro problems in a single definite locality."

The *American Sociological Review* showed its racism by not reviewing *The Philadelphia Negro*. However, reviews appeared in several other journals and magazines. Some reflected their author's position or prejudice: the pride of blacks (from *AME Church Review*: "At last we have a volume of the highest scientific value on a sociological subject and written by a Negro"); the casual racism common among historians (from the *American Historical Review*: "what Dr. Du Bois does not give, more knowledge of the effects of the mixing of blood of very different races, and of the possibilities of absorption of inferior into superior groups of mankind. He speaks of the 'natural repugnance to close intermingling with unfortunate ex-slaves,' but we believe that the separation is due to differences of race more than of status."); the patronizing pro-southern views of the *Nation* ("the lesson taught by this investigation is one of patience and sympathy toward the South, whose difficulties have been far greater than those of the North").

Three themes run through most of the reviews: praise for Du Bois's research and analysis, recognition of the obstacles to black employment, and commentary on race prejudice. Reviewers welcomed the empirical study of blacks and praised Du Bois's thoroughness and fair-minded presentation of the "facts." The reviewer for *Yale Review* called *The Philadelphia Negro* "not merely a credit to its author and to the race of which he is a member; it is a credit to American scholarship, and a distinct and valuable addition to the world's stock of knowledge concerning an important and obscure theme. It is the sort of book of which we have too few, and of which it is impossible that one should have too many." The *Charities Review* called it a "careful, painstaking, and intelligent study. . . . the book can be relied on as giving a true picture of the condition of the Philadelphia Negro." *City and State* enthused, "While the book abounds in statistics and is devoted to facts, it is as interesting as a novel, thanks to the skill with which the author has worked up his material." The review in the *Sunday School Times* singled out the barriers to employment described by Du Bois. "Even in Philadelphia it is almost useless for negro men and women to fit themselves for any higher work than household service or waiting in a hotel. Case after case is cited in which educated negroes have been debarred from any employment for which their education fits them." Employment barriers formed the major theme of the longest and most acute review, written for the *Journal of Political Economy* by social scientist and settlement worker Katherine Bement Davis. "Dr. Du Bois," she writes, "recognizes the economic side of the problem as that which presents at the same time the greatest importance and the greatest difficulties." "The causes which limit the occupations of the negro," Davis observed, "are twofold—first the inefficiency which comes from lack of experience and training, and second, the prejudice of the whites."

The reviewer for the *Outlook* argued that Du Bois's fair-minded restraint lent great weight to his account of discrimination. "In no respect does Dr. Du Bois attempt to bend the facts so as to plead the case of his race. . . . For this restraint he is well repaid in the greater effectiveness it gives to his chapter on the discriminations still in force against the employment of negroes. It is this chapter that especially appeals to the conscience of the Nation." Even the *Nation* acknowledged the force of racism revealed by Du Bois. "Turning from legal restriction to social repression, we find that race hatred has prevailed down to a very recent period."

"Many readers of this report," predicted Lindsay in his introduction, "will look most eagerly for what is said on the subject of race-prejudice and the so-called 'color-line.' I feel sure that no one can read Chapter XVI without being impressed with the impartiality and self-control of the writer. Dr. Du Bois has treated the facts he obtained with the delicacy of an artist." Du Bois had revealed that "the better-educated classes among the Philadelphia Negroes feel very keenly the injustice of the class antagonism that comes from the indiscriminate classing of all Negroes together, and the imputing to all of the shortcoming of the ignorant, vicious, and criminal. This fact, and the proof that such is the habit among the bulk of the white population, comes out frequently in the following pages." Like other readers, Lindsay found Du Bois's restraint admirable. By amassing facts and masking his outrage, Du Bois escaped the charge of bias. Echoing the retreat from "advocacy to objectivity" in American social science, Lindsay observed that Du Bois had "wisely refrained for the most part from drawing conclusions or introducing anything that savors of personal judgment."

In January 1898, before *The Philadelphia Negro* appeared in print, Du Bois summarized his conclusions about "Negro Problems" in a lead article for the *Annals of the American Academy of Political and Social Science* and foreshadowed the "fair-mindedness" and restraint that would so impress reviewers. "Fair-mindedness," in practice, meant pointing out failings among the black population. "Negro problems," according to Du Bois, "can be divided into two distinct but correlated parts, depending on two facts: First— Negroes do not share the full national life because as a mass they have not reached a sufficiently high grade of culture. Secondly—They do not share the full national life because there has always existed in America a conviction—varying in intensity, but always widespread—that people of Negro blood should not be admitted into the group life of the nation no matter what their condition might be." Of all the important parts of the nation, "the Negro is by far the most ignorant. . . . The great deficiency of the Negro . . . is his small knowledge of the art of organized social life—the last expression of human culture. . . . This is shown in the grosser forms of sexual immorality, disease and crime, and also in the difficulty of race organization for common ends or in intellectual lines." Racial prejudice, the "second class of Negro problems," lay at the root of blacks' "poverty, ignorance, and social degradation." Racism "makes it more difficult for black men to earn a living or spend their earnings as they will; it gives them poorer school facilities and restricted contact with cultured classes; and it becomes, throughout the land, a cause and excuse for discontent, lawlessness, laziness, and injustice."

Given Du Bois's restraint and candor, Lindsay found all the more compelling—"a serious charge, and worthy of reflection"—Du Bois's conclusion about the consequences of a racism that failed to draw social and moral distinctions among the city's black population. "Thus the class of Negroes which the prejudices of the city have distinctly encouraged is that of the criminal, the lazy and the shiftless; for them the city teems with institutions and charities; for them there is succor and sympathy; for them Philadelphians are thinking and planning; but for the educated and industrious young colored man who wants work and not platitudes, wages and not alms, just rewards and not sermons—for such colored men Philadelphia apparently has no use," Du Bois had written.

For Lindsay, racism, as limned by Du Bois, not only unjustly tarnished the reputation of respectable blacks and denied them the opportunity to earn a decent living; it also blocked the operations of scientific charity. Institutionalized in Charity Organization Societies, scientific charity, according to Lindsay, rested on three principles: "*Co-operation* and mutual helpfulness among existing charities; *Investigation* as a basis for the elimination of fraud and for the securing of suitable and adequate relief; *Restoration* of the pauper to normal working-power—the only rational end in relief work." Scientific charity assumed a connection between respectability and reward. Upright behavior led if not to wealth, at least to independence. It interpreted the great impediments to independence as twofold: indiscriminate charity that perversely encouraged dependence and immoral behavior that bred poverty. Through the reorganization of charity, the manipulation of sanctions (basing relief on work and good behavior), and individual counseling, scientific charity proposed simultaneously to reduce the cost of relief (or, in our modern terms, welfare) and raise individuals from dependence. Scientific charity also emphasized the distinction between public and private charity. Public charity shouldered the "more or less perfunctory tasks . . . too heavy for private shoulders to bear" and dealt "with a hopeless element in the social wreckage which must be provided for in a humane way, and prevented, if possible, from accumulating too rapidly or contaminating the closely allied product just outside the almshouse door." Private charity, by contrast, formed the "more conspicuous form of charity" and its "thousand little variations" served as the "measure" of the "real charitable activity of a city." Although founded in 1878, the Philadelphia Society for Organizing Charity, the primary vehicle for rationalizing private charity, remained hobbled, less effective than its counterparts in other major cities, according to Lindsay. The SOC, for one thing, had failed to streamline the city's private charitable apparatus. As late as 1895, 300 organizations handed out relief in the city, and 250 "educational ones" did "charitable work." The city's 675 churches also supplied both relief and education. Even this list remained incomplete. The SOC's financial administration remained decentralized in ward committees, leading to "much duplication in the appeals for money"; petty jealousies among existing charities discouraged cooperation; and the SOC's practice of handing out relief in emergencies contradicted the fundamental rules of good charity organization society practice, which restricted the umbrella organization to coordination, investigation, and referral. Anything else excited the "jealousy and opposition of other relief-giving agencies" and, ultimately, reduced charitable giving. With these impediments, charity organization in Philadelphia faced a difficult enough struggle, but what if artificial impediments intervened between the mechanisms of scientific charity and its expected outcomes? All would be in vain. This, for Lindsay, was the consequence of the racism so convincingly portrayed by Du Bois. "If the Negroes themselves, that is their upper ranks, cannot command these privileges and secure them, or, if competent to possess them, they are denied the possession by the organized prejudices of the stronger race around them, and these prejudices cannot be broken down, then scientific philanthropy is helpless to point the way to their improvement, and the present haphazard efforts of unthinking charity would better cease altogether." Du Bois had shown how racism fueled the "social wreckage" that threatened the contamination of respectable Philadelphia.

In her review, Katherine Bement Davis showed less concern with unleashing scientific charity than with exposing the roots of black poverty, as described by Du Bois. Together, Lindsay's introduction and Davis's review point to the uneasy coexistence of scientific charity and progressivism—of nineteenth- and twentieth-century approaches to poverty—in *The Philadelphia Negro*. Davis highlighted Du Bois's finding of a higher rate of employment among blacks than among whites: 78 percent of Seventh Ward blacks compared to 55.1 percent of the whole population of Philadelphia were reported in "gainful occupations." This result, which "was to be anticipated," indicated "an absence of accumulated wealth, arising from poverty and low wages." In three articles written for the *New York Times* in 1901, Du Bois continued to emphasize the economic consequences of employment discrimination by comparing the situation of blacks in Boston, Philadelphia, and New York. Blacks, he pointed out, as "a race are not lazy. The canvass of the Federation of Churches in typical New York tenement districts has shown that while nearly 99 per cent of black men were wage earners, only 92 per cent of the Americans and 90 per cent of the Germans were at work." Low wages, confinement to menial jobs, and exclusion from opportunities for advancement—not the lack of jobs—confronted black men. Despite the haunting parallels between Du Bois's urban North and our own, nothing more sharply distinguishes the present from the past than the addition of chronic joblessness to the insults associated with race in America.

Du Bois's Philadelphia and Ours

At first glance, the continuity between Du Bois's Philadelphia and ours leaps from the pages of his great book. Then, as now, African Americans experienced disproportionate poverty, clustered in the worst jobs, lived in segregated neighborhoods, watched their children die young, and suffered the insults of racism. The roots of current black poverty, marginalization, and the multiple crises of the inner cities appear in embryo in Philadelphia at the end of the nineteenth century.

First glances, however, can deceive. To tell the story of African Americans in Philadelphia in terms of continuity over a century would be facile. The context of black experience has altered so fundamentally that comparisons mislead and threaten to obscure the sources and dimensions of current circumstances and to inhibit the development of constructive and realistic responses.

Think, for instance, of the public and private assistance available to African Americans in need in Du Bois's time and ours. In the 1890s black Philadelphians could call on no form of public assistance as a right. The city had abolished outdoor relief (what today we would call welfare); there was no comparable state or federal program. Whether out of work, single parents, or elderly, blacks had to turn to private charity, notably the Society for Organizing Charity, which doled out miserable amounts of assistance following minute investigations of applicants' need and merit. Settlement houses offered very little help with food, shelter, fuel, or clothing. Churches and private charities provided a little more; some hospitals admitted charity patients; when all else failed, the poorhouse beckoned. For all its weaknesses, the welfare state of the 1990s—Temporary Assistance for Needy Families, Supplemental Social Security, Social Security, Food Stamps, Unemployment Insurance, Medicare, Medicaid—offers an array and level of benefits unimaginable in the 1890s.

In the 1890s, Philadelphia's African Americans, a majority migrants from the South, composed only about 5 percent of the city's population. A century later, for the most part natives of Philadelphia, they constituted about 40 percent. Their numerical presence translated into political power undreamed of a century earlier: high political office in city, state, and federal governments and a large presence among appointed officials. Their ascendance in government, the professions, and business, abetted by affirmative action, reflected the growth of a black middle class, seen as well in a great increase in homeownership and a radical decline in the percentage in poverty.

The growth of a black middle class fueled increased residential differentiation, as more affluent African Americans moved to the city's Oak Lane, Mount Airy, or Overbrook sections or to the near suburbs, such as Cheltenham and Yeadon. Although segregation remained high, even among affluent blacks, their dispersion helped increase the concentration of poverty in inner city neighborhoods, whose social structure became less diverse over time. Indeed, studies of language underscored the growing isolation of poor African American communities in inner cities.

In the late nineteenth century, American blacks lived mainly in the South. As sharecroppers and tenant farmers at the height of Jim Crow, they suffered from extraordinary poverty, exploitation, lack of opportunity, a repressive political regime, the constant threat of violence, and the denial of basic human freedoms. Northern cities represented lands of hope. African Americans migrated northward at a time of expanding work opportunity. Even if menial, jobs existed along with schools for children and a less proscriptive racial order. Looking back, the situation of blacks in turn-of-the-century Philadelphia looks bleak; from the view of a tenant farm in rural Virginia, it almost certainly appeared a world better. Despite deprivation and discrimination, African Americans in late nineteenth-century Philadelphia, even Du Bois, could look to the future with some hope and optimism.

The great irony is that the material improvement during the late twentieth century, the extension of civil rights, and the accession to political office accompanied lowered expectations of progress and the decline of Philadelphia and other once-great cities as arenas for mobility and generators of jobs. New sources of disadvantage and marginalization added to or modified preexisting roots of inequity. Some resulted from global economic changes that undermined manufacturing and sucked jobs out of older cities; others emerged from public policies: New Deal agricultural policies that drove blacks from the land; transportation policies that balkanized cities with freeways; subsidized suburbanization that lured whites from cities; government-encouraged redlining that denied mortgage money to African Americans; urban renewal that destroyed homes and warehoused poor families in cheap, segregated towers.

Within inner cities, especially among the young, observers talk of worsening race relations and a mood of nihilism and hopelessness acted out through drugs and violence. Institutional collapse fuels cynicism and hopelessness among the young in the ghettos of Philadelphia and other cities: not only do the police fail to protect; their corruption poses a threat to safety.

The failure of schools disadvantages youngsters in the job market in the global city. Cuts in social benefits—in Philadelphia, for instance, the state's decimation of General Assistance and the city's reduction in funds for social services—have shredded the safety net, with more tears coming. Even the infrastructure that makes daily life tolerable crumbles, especially in poor neighborhoods: street surfaces, pockmarked by potholes, decay; garbage and abandoned houses disfigure the landscape; water mains burst; bridges rust away; and cuts in public transportation appear likely.

African American disadvantage in Philadelphia has persisted throughout the twentieth century. But changes in its sources, shape, and contexts have resulted in a configuration of experience without historical precedent. The blend of interracial cooperation, self-help, and elite engagement recommended by Du Bois in the 1890s, as he later realized, could not attack the structural sources of the inequities he documented. They read as even more anticlimactic and inadequate today. The issue is not whether the circumstances of Philadelphia's African Americans are better or worse today than a hundred years ago. The point is to use history not to offer a perverse nostalgia, a facile lament for persistent immiseration. Rather, it is to use history to explain the very different world that Du Bois would find in Philadelphia today. Without a clear-eyed understanding of the new world of Philadelphia's African Americans and its sources, we are unlikely to see a more hopeful conclusion to the next century than to the one that marks the distance between Du Bois's Philadelphia and ours.

HERMAN BEAVERS

Romancing the Body Politic:
Du Bois's Propaganda of the Dark World

ABSTRACT: Although best known for his work as a sociologist, historian, and editor, W.E.B. Du Bois also authored numerous works of fiction and poetry. Despite their dismissal by critics as not much more than failed experiments that test the boundary separating poetry and prose, this article suggests that Du Bois's acts of creative composition are driven by his desire to exert critical force as part of his contribution to the effort of studying "Negro problems." Du Bois's creative writing can be understood as recapitulations of his enterprise as a social scientist and as an attempt to dramatize the workings of the American body politic. As social scientist, Du Bois manifests a vision of what his training allowed him to assert through organized, scientific study. However, as creative writer, Du Bois mediates this project by positing the need for heroic action in issues of gender and sexuality and presents a way to think about African American representations of masculinity in the twentieth century.

It is perhaps more than a coincidence that Esau, the disinherited brother of Jacob, figures into a number of texts produced by African American male writers at the beginning of the twentieth century. As we can observe in works by Paul Laurence Dunbar, James Weldon Johnson, and W.E.B. Du Bois, Esau's decision to

From *The Annals of The American Academy of Political and Social Science* 568 (March 2000). © 2000 by Sage Publications.

trade his birthright figures into discussions that are meant to evoke the tenuousness, if not the futility, of black political life in America. Johnson's invocation of Esau comes at the end of *The Autobiography of an Ex-Colored Man*, where the nameless protagonist, having denounced his claim to membership in the black race, declares, "I cannot repress the thought that, after all, I have chosen the lesser part, that I have sold my birthright for a mess of pottage."

Dunbar's collection of stories, *The Strength of Gideon*, published in 1900, some 12 years prior to Johnson's novel, finds him turning to prose fiction in order to protest racial injustice of the sort to be found in the United States at the turn of the century. That injustice, Dunbar suggests, is most evident in the realm of electoral politics, particularly as it relates to the black community's relationship to the Republican Party. Dunbar's decision to depict the exigencies of political participation has ironic overtones in light of the disenfranchisement of Southern blacks. But as a Northerner writing about the world with which he is most familiar, Dunbar undertakes to depict in "A Mess of Pottage" (which could be where Johnson got the idea for how to end his novel), "Mr. Cornelius Johnson, Office Seeker," and "A Council of State" the ways that even in the North, blacks play at best a marginal role in electoral politics. In these stories, Dunbar does not hesitate to provide images of black folk undone by their self-importance and political naïveté.

Du Bois takes up the image of Esau early on in *Darkwater: Voices from the Veil*, where in The Credo he asserts,

> I believe in the Training of Children, black even as white; the leading out of little souls into the green pastures and beside the still waters, not for pelf or peace, but for life lit by some large vision of beauty and goodness and truth; lest we forget, and the sons of the fathers, like Esau, for mere meat barter their birthright in a mighty nation.

It is easy to note the lyricism of the passage, but consider as well the way Du Bois links education to communal memory, as if to suggest that the role of the educator is (as his reference to the Twenty-Third Psalm would indicate) that of both shepherd and repository of collective memory. As Du Bois insists, lack of education creates a community ripe for exploitation, prone to squander its political resources (their "birthright in a mighty nation") in exchange for spoils that have little value in the public sphere.

Looking more closely at Dunbar, one notes that the figure of Esau has much to do with his realization that the black community is often driven, like Esau, by a sense of immediacy, an investment in short-term strategies that are characterized by negotiation and barter for goods which threaten black political capital. In the biblical narrative, Esau "sells" his birthright to Jacob when his bodily needs outweigh his investment in the future. For Dunbar and Du Bois to invoke him intimates the ways that each was aware of the need for a unified and coherent political agenda for the black community, one which avoided becoming bogged down in the quagmire of electoral politics, opting instead for a more messianic vision.

This is much more manifest in Du Bois's work than in Dunbar's. Dunbar opts to rely instead on ironic portrayals of black political ineffectualness. In "A Mess of Pottage," he depicts a black community, referred to as "Little Africa," as the object of a political struggle between the Democratic and Republican Party candidates during a gubernatorial election. As the story opens, Dunbar characterizes the Democratic Party as a group resigned to its lack of influence in the black community. Besides distributing money in Little Africa to gain influence, an act Democrats believe will not work to their advantage, the black community is seen as being so solidly Republican that the latter party takes them for granted, noting, "We've got 'em just like that."

As it turns out, however, the Democratic candidate for governor decides that winning the election means going to the black community in person, "carrying the war into the enemy's country." As a man with "a convincing way of making others see as he [sees]," Mr. Lane concludes that black votes go to the Republican Party because "those people go one way because they are never invited to go another," at which point he resolves to meet with the leading Republican power broker in Little Africa, Deacon Isham Swift.

When Lane discovers that all the claims about Swift are true—that the old man is staunchly Republican and indignant at the suggestion of voting otherwise (which means that others will be persuaded to think likewise)—he turns to the Reverent Ebenezer Clay of Mount Moriah, who proves to be much more acquiescent to his entreaties. As he introduces Mr. Lane to give a speech before his congregation, Dunbar's Reverend Clay proudly declares, "Of co'se Brothah Lane knows we colo'ed folks're goin' to think our own way anyhow." Dunbar is clearly relying on irony to make his point; the black community does not exercise independence of thought; rather, they are a community whose political activity is a matter of rote behavior, not negotiation. And, as Dunbar's decision to give Swift's adversary the surname Clay suggests, too often the black community is a malleable substance to be shaped according to the majority's political desires.

After Lane's speech and after the congregation files out and heads home, there is an obvious split in sentiment that Dunbar reveals to be generational in nature:

> Twenty years ago such a thing could not have happened, but the ties which had bound the older generation irrevocably to one party were being loosed on the younger men. The old men said, "We know," the young ones said, "We have heard," and so there was hardly anything of the blind allegiance which had made even free thought seem treason to their fathers.

Note the manner in which Dunbar makes the distinction between knowledge and hearsay, the effect of which is that solidarity is by no means a given. Deacon Swift's response to this rift is to denounce the Reverend Clay's decision to lead Little Africa down such a "treacherous course." As he gives an emotional speech, in which he insists, once more, that the party of Lincoln has demonstrated its devotion to Little Africa, the Deacon's son, Tom, sits unmoved by his father's rhetoric. When election day arrives, he sells his vote to the Democrats for five dollars, a transaction which becomes known to the entire community.

What motivates his betrayal, Dunbar suggests, is that, without ties to slavery, he "is not made of the same stuff" as his father. Dunbar prompts us to believe that his father, because of his sixth-grade education, lacks tough-minded integrity and feeling. Believing that he knows more than his father about political matters, Tom represents the sort of failed memory produced by an adherence to a materialism which negotiates on the basis that material prosperity is not a means, but an end in itself. Further, Tom's political involvement, because it represents a kind of ethical bankruptcy, is not the product of political subjectivity; rather, his decision to accept money from the Democrats is also a substantive break from the past. But as the passage above proposes, there is a marked difference between a political consciousness born of experience and that produced by indirect contact with historical events, and so we need to understand Tom's actions as those of an ahistorical subject.

Deacon Swift, in a fit of fatherly rage, makes Tom return the five-dollar note to the Democrats. Interestingly, Dunbar's investment in irony is such that he neglects to inform the reader which candidate wins the election. The reason for this is not only that we should assume the Republicans maintain their hold on Little Africa but also that who wins is beside the point. What is more important, as evidenced by the story's final scene, is the need for Little Africa to increase its distance from electoral politics. During a Wednesday night prayer meeting, Deacon Swift gets up and, in an interesting twist, announces, "Des' a minute, brothahs . . . I want to mek a 'fession. I was too ha'd an too brash in my talk de othah night, and de Lawd visited my sins upon my haid. He struck me in de bosom o' my own fambly. My own son went wrong. Pray fu' me!" The call for prayer that closes Dunbar's short story surely points to the need for a closing of ranks and a reassessment of the past. But I also want to press a bit harder here and insist that it also speaks to the ways that to be political is likewise to risk patriarchal crisis.

Although it is no revelation to see Dunbar's story working out a vision of politics as a bastion of male participation and agency, I want to suggest here that Dunbar's story reveals the ways that even as democracy was conceived as a break from monarchy, American politics retains the notion that power, as an instrument of patriarchy, can be handed from one generation to the next. This explains the way that Isham Swift views Tom's transgressions as a subset of his own actions. The dynastic anxieties we see worked out in this story intimate Dunbar's skepticism regarding black participation in American politics, electoral or otherwise. Because it is difficult to amass the kind of resources necessary to resist the temptation of corrupt behavior, Dunbar's story ends with the spiritual rumination of prayer, which means that the story actually depicts a regression of political agency rather than an advance. In lieu of power in the secular world, Dunbar suggests, there must be integrity which can, at the very least, lead the son to adopt the worldview of the father.

Irony notwithstanding, Dunbar's story bears relation to Du Bois's novel, *Dark Princess* ([1928] 1995), largely because he argues in "A Mess of Pottage" for how little there is to be gained by black participation in the electoral politics. As he demonstrates in "Mr. Cornelius Johnson, Office Seeker" and "A Council of State," the patronage that blacks seek is meant as a way to configure their marginality in political matters, not their influence. Dunbar's decision to depict this situation ironically may be more a product of his ambivalence about the role of the black artist in society, but this nonetheless leaves him with no way to propose an alternative.

Moreover, we might even consider the ways that Dunbar's growing disillusionment as an artist influences his depiction of black political possibility. Evidence of this arises when we look at the deacon's name, Isham Swift; buried within the name is an anagram which forms the question, "Is Ham (or perhaps more rightly the 'sons of Ham') swift?" Dunbar's in-joke leads us to conclude that whites certainly do not believe this to be so, especially if "swift" is intended to mean political savvy. But, as Darwin Turner has asserted about Dunbar, part of the difficulty here is one, given Dunbar's growing marginality and isolation as an artist, that suggests the

possibility that it is Dunbar himself who poses the question. If this be the
case, then what "A Mess of Pottage" and the other political critiques of
Republican abuse in the collection argue is either that blacks lack the
adequate civilization to participate in the politics of modernity or that like
Esau, blacks lack the ability to defer immediate gratification, which suggests
that only a short time out of slavery, they have become the epitome of the
modern subject: enslaved to public forms of material consumption, with
these becoming the "pottage" traded for not once, but time and again.

If Jacob, as biblical trickster, bears any relation to African American
narrative, it is because he represents stealth, but a form of stealth, cunning,
and forethought that works well in the political arena. Further, he represents
the act of linking futurity with nationhood, for as "the Supplanter" of his
brother's status, his actions determine not only his own prosperity but that of
his ancestral line as well, which is synonymous with nationhood (in the form
of Israel). But this points to what is lacking in Dunbar's critique, namely, that
the question of black patronage in northern electoral politics is a product of
the anxieties that are easily located in the white majority. Dunbar, so
disillusioned about African Americans' lack of political power, mirrors his
own artistic confinement and thus fails to consider that there is, in fact,
power to be exercised in the black community. If there is a messianic impulse
in Dunbar's fiction, it is up to his readership to discern it. There is little
possibility of this, however, because recognition of the ironic in political
matters becomes an end in itself.

Dunbar's decision to depict black political impotence ironically has
much to do with a pragmatism that ultimately works against the interests of
the collective. His political commentaries in *The Strength of Gideon* all end
with solitary black men, struck dumb by the speed of their falls from political
grace. Because they are men who glory in hubris, they are doomed to suffer
their sin with the sense that comfort from the black community is an
inadequate replacement for political influence. It is here that we need to turn
to W.E.B. Du Bois, first, because he dares to imagine Africa as a site of both
cultural and political density rather than as the site of either backwardness or
generational collapse.

But we can also note in Du Bois's fiction that he chooses optimism over
despair, and so we find him working in *Dark Princess* to transform Esau into
the Prodigal Son. This is no easy maneuver, for in addition to the difficulty
of bringing New Testament symbolic machinery into play, Du Bois must also
eschew the irony that Dunbar uses to enjoin political critique in favor of
allegory and romance, which requires a different approach to language and
thematic framing. Further, it also means that if we are to decipher Du Bois's
novel as a commentary on the state of African American political activity of

the 1920s, then his decision to incorporate the parable of the Prodigal Son into his novel has a great deal to do with a desire to complicate matters surrounding the political subject, to problematize perhaps the propensity of the black community to fall into neatly arranged camps whose interests diminish the community's collective power.

DU BOIS THE ARTIST

Much has been said about Du Bois's forays into creative writing, which can be seen as early as "On the Coming of John" and "On the Passing of the First-Born" in *The Souls of Black Folk* (1965) where he utilizes the fictive and the autobiographical, respectively, to good effect. And irrespective of one's critical assessment of it, his creative output is an impressive corpus of poems, autobiography, novels, and sketches. In thinking about this article, however, I have tried to imagine Du Bois holistically, as the romantic who authors *Dark Princess*, the social scientist who calls for a systematic (statistical) approach to the study of black life in "The Study of the Negro Problems" (1898) (and later, of course, *The Philadelphia Negro* [1995]), and the historian who produces *The Suppression of the African Slave Trade* (1899) and *Black Reconstruction* (1969). Such an endeavor is difficult; Du Bois's creative writing is not quite good enough for us to consider him in a class with Langston Hughes, Jean Toomer, Nella Larsen, or Zora Neale Hurston. But it is not so poorly conceived or realized that we can dismiss it either.

What is at issue here is how to reconcile Du Bois's notion that "the Negro is primarily an artist," an assertion he makes in 1913 in "The Negro in Literature and Art," which he published in *The Annals* of the American Academy (alongside a piece by Booker T. Washington on industrial education) with his assertion in "The Study of the Negro Problems," published some 15 years earlier, where he declares, "Consequently, though we ordinarily speak of the Negro problem as though it were one unchanged question, students must recognize the obvious facts that this problem, like others, has had a long historical development, has changed with the growth and evolution of the nation; moreover, that it is not one problem, but rather a plexus of social problems, some new, some old, some simple, some complex." The question of reconciliation is perhaps best approached by noting Keith Byerman's observation that Du Bois was "a theorist and historian of black writing," and as such

> Du Bois tended to see himself as a man of letters, one who demonstrated significant literary skills regardless of the subject

matter. He was also specifically a writer of literature, with a
number of published poems, stories, parables, reviews, novels, as
well as many more writings that were never published.

For Du Bois, "art helps to name the ideal ends for which the political
struggle is carried on." Thus, art was always a matter of propaganda. He
begins "Criteria of Negro Art," which appeared in *The Crisis* in 1926, by
juxtaposing two viewpoints, one which symbolizes a skepticism toward the
value of artistic expression and the other which delights in the relationship
between aestheticism and pleasure. He goes on to dismiss both viewpoints
summarily. "Let me tell you," he writes, "that neither of these groups is right.
The thing we are talking about . . . is part of the great fight we are carrying
on and it represents a forward and an upward look—a pushing onward."

In looking at his novel *Dark Princess*, I want to suggest that Du Bois's
approach exemplifies his assertions in "Criteria of Negro Art," for the novel
represents the act of bringing together what would appear on the face of
things to be disparate enterprises. But as Byerman notes, Du Bois's
investment in art making is of a piece with the writing of history. "The
novelist, not less than the historian or social scientist, does not render a pure
creation of fancy; quite the contrary, he stays as close to the facts as possible.
The novelist, in other words, is a historian who feels the necessity to speak
even if he cannot prove everything he says." Byerman helps us to understand
that Du Bois's approach to novel writing is less grounded in generic practice
than it is messianic discourse.

To write novels, Du Bois suggests, is to write a version of the truth. As
such, the novel creates a world that has an analogue in the real world. Looking
at *Dark Princess*, we cannot say that Du Bois partakes, however, of the social
realism that will be the vogue of the 1930s with the advent of Richard Wright,
but he does see the novel as performing cultural work of the sort represented
by prophecy, in this instance providing the reader with a strategy of
interpretation through which one can construct a vision of the future. As
prophet, Du Bois frees himself of the social scientist's and historian's dilemma
of looking at what is or what was in order to imagine what can be.

POLITICS AND ALLEGORY:
DARK PRINCESS

Commentators on *Dark Princess* have all located the novel in the
realm of political allegory, and I see nothing in the novel to dissuade me
from such a conclusion. But what interests me, and what occupies the

remainder of this article, is Du Bois's attempt to transform Esau, the disinherited, into the Prodigal Son. What this means, at least in political terms, is that Du Bois imagines a world where change does not issue from controlling societal conditions from the top downward in order to produce positive outcomes for the whole, but from letting the positive aspects of a life lived "below" flow upward.

In ways more reminiscent of Johnson's handling of the figure of Esau, Du Bois actually links an image of prosperity and upward mobility to his characterization. Indeed, this goes a long way toward asserting that political consciousness is not the product of material comfort. Rather, the truly committed freedom fighter will eschew comfort. This revisionary posture toward the biblical narrative has much to do with the ways in which even as we find Du Bois utilizing scripture, the narrative arc of his fictional treatment is a product of secular energies, marking the distance Du Bois sees between spirituality and political agency.

As Arnold Rampersad has observed, *Dark Princess* did not "find favor with the general public." Matthew Towns, the novel's hero, moves "between poles of passion and self-denial." While I agree with this assessment, I would amplify Rampersad's remarks and insist that Matthew Towns's problem in the novel is largely a matter of embodiment. As Wilson Moses has observed, Du Bois, though no lover of Christianity, was enamored of the notion of heroic redemption through suffering. The novel's messianic configuration, the way the novel ends with the birth of Matthew's son, "the Messenger and Messiah of the Darker Worlds," as the sign of Matthew's ultimate redemption, intimates that not only is the political future of blacks in American at issue, but masculine subjectivity as well. Moving through *Dark Princess*, we find Towns struggling with the exigencies of language; his is a life fraught with the need to make himself understood, for his story to be viewed in light of its representativeness. The difficulty Du Bois sets for himself in creating a romantic figure like Towns is creating a figure who is the embodiment of a redemptive consciousness but who eschews the impulse to channel this into religiosity, opting instead to locate redemption as a secular phenomenon.

What makes this important is Du Bois's vision of the body politic. For if Matthew Towns seeks redemption, he must do so because the body politic requires it, not for personal ends. Thus, we need to pay close attention to the references the novel makes to the body and physical exertion because, located in an allegorical framework, these carry symbolic weight. For example, late in the novel, after Matthew has fallen out of favor in the world of electoral politics, he consummates his relationship with Princess Kautilya, his political and romantic counterpart, and gets a job digging the new subway. Though one of the men working for political boss Sammy Scott offers him a job as a foreman or a time-keeper, Matthew says, "I told him I wanted to dig." In what represents an instance where Du Bois's ideological fervor overwhelms his artistic restraint, Kautilya observes, "We start to dig, remaking the world," leading Matthew to launch into the following speech:

> We must dig it out with my shovel and your quick wit. Here in America black folk must help overthrow the rule of the rich by distributing wealth more evenly first among themselves and then in alliance with white labor, to establish democratic control of industry. During the process they must keep step and hold tight hands with the other struggling darker peoples.

In a realist novel, perhaps, we might expect a very different response, one that draws more heavily on the vernacular in order to manifest Matthew's desire to be a "man of the people" in a more believable fashion. But in Du Bois's version of political allegory, this is not a necessity. He can work in proximity to his own sense of appropriate speech, even as he articulates the beginnings of what will become much stronger socialist leanings in the decades to follow.

The problem, of course, is that Du Bois sees the emergence of a critical consciousness that can "establish control of democratic industry" as a by-product of physical labor. But more important, as an instance where wage labor assumes a transformative posture, labor must become part of something larger, more grand in scope. It must unloose itself from a machine of accumulation (capitalism) and harness itself to a different, newer machine, whose emphasis is sharing and redistribution in a form of democratic socialism. Having chosen to produce a novel so steeped in allegory, Du Bois overcomes his own Victorian impulses in order to bridge the gap between mind and body.

What this means for Du Bois is that allegory is nothing short of a tactical maneuver. But as such, it plays for much higher stakes than irony because allegory, as Angus Fletcher argues,

> appears to express conflict between rival authorities, as in times of political oppression we may get "Aesop-language" to avoid censorship of dissident thought. At the heart of any allegory will be found this conflict of authorities. One ideal will be pitted against another, its opposite: thus the familiar propagandistic function of the mode, thus the conservative satiric function, thus the didactic function.

Dark Princess delights, then, in a plethora of oppositions: country versus city, electoral politics versus ritual politics, materialism versus aestheticism, to name a few. But we need to remember that Du Bois conceives *Dark Princess* as an allegorical project that utilizes the social realist elements of its plot to counterpoint its romantic impulses. Thus, Du Bois wishes to depict the triumph of good over evil, but ultimately, he casts this within the context of a global industrial democracy and the "joining of black America with the rest of the nonwhite world."

But it is here that I find *Dark Princess* to be a troublesome work of fiction. To accomplish this, Du Bois must perform a maneuver that aligns the erotic with political agency. This is a necessity foreshadowed when Matthew decides to marry Sara Andrews, a decision which Du Bois describes thus:

> He had not noticed Sara much hitherto. He had not noticed any woman, since—since—But he knew Sara was intelligent and a hard worker. She looked simple, clean and capable. She seemed to him noticeably lonely and needing someone to lean on. She could make a home. He never had had just the sort of home he wanted. He wanted a home—something like his own den, but transfigured by capable hands—and devotion. Perhaps a wife would stop this longing—this inarticulate Thing in his soul.

Although Sara has a moment in the novel when she looks at Matthew with something akin to erotic desire, their union privileges the material over the erotic. After the wedding, Matthew tries to place his arm about Sara's shoulders, but she warns him, "Be careful of the veil." As a woman fair-skinned enough to pass for white, Sara is remarkable as a character in African American fiction in that she possesses a high level of political savvy and drive, traits Du Bois finds redeeming. But her impulse to protect the placement of the veil not only recalls the controlling metaphor found in *The Souls of Black Folk* but demonstrates the manner in which it becomes a signifier of erotic impoverishment.

Caught in this dilemma, Matthew's task is to find a way to link body and action, to free himself from purgatory—symbolized by his participation in electoral politics and his marriage—and find redemption. When Princess Kautilya returns to the novel, having disappeared for over 100 pages (during which time she has become a union organizer and laborer and thus shuns temporarily the advantages of high birth), Matthew runs away with her, spurning the opportunity to have a seat in Congress. Their brief union leads at novel's end to the birth of their son, the "Maharajah of Bwodpur."

The messianic ethos of *Dark Princess* needs to be considered in light of Du Bois's attempt to recuperate Matthew from a state of disinheritance, to make him a prodigal. He accomplishes this move by deferring Matthew's marriage to the princess, organizing the fourth section of the novel as a series of letters between them, where they discuss the relation of work to revolution. This needs to be understood in the context of Du Bois's vision of art as propaganda. But here we need to understand that the word "propaganda" is derived from the Latin word *propagare*, which means "propagate." The romance that ensues between Matthew Towns and Princess Kautilya is a clear example of having one's cake and eating it too. I say this because we find Matthew one minute extolling the virtues of work, quitting all ties to politics and taking up the aforementioned job as a ditchdigger, but by novel's end, he is wealthy, powerful, and the father of a male heir, which means that his sexual potency is, in the way of all wealthy patriarchs perhaps, political capital as well.

In thinking about the idea of a body politic, I am reminded of Moira Gatens's observation that "the modern body politic is based on an image of the masculine body." Trying to envision a body politic redeemed by the rise of the "darker worlds," Du Bois produces what is, in my view, an allegory that collapses into masculine narcissism. Which is to say that, even as Sara Andrews and Princess Kautilya represent women who are remarkable for their intellect and political consciousness, ultimately Du Bois cannot find a way to value them equally, to allow them to be the agents of political change, no matter how catalytic their presence may be. The princess, the mother of Matthew Towns's son, is caught in a political dilemma: her kingdom, the Indian province of Bwodphur, requires that she either enter an arranged marriage or produce a male heir; she is enjoined by her sex from ruling the kingdom alone. Thus, at novel's end she announces, "Bwodphur needs not a princess, but a King."

This suggests that Du Bois's investment in allegory and romance is mediated by notions of propaganda to be sure, but propaganda of the sort whose success rises and falls (pun intended) on the male member. Indeed, the notion of the "darker worlds" assuming membership in the hall of nations, has much to do, as Wilson Moses has suggested, with a Wagnerian design, reminding us of opera's propensity to excess. *Dark Princess* is at once a hearkening back to the operatic tradition and a call for a heroic art. Thus, we might place the novel, as Moses does, as the harbinger of "new tradition in black writing," but it is also important, I think, to site the novel, not only in terms of its racial politics, but also its gender politics.

However, Du Bois's adherence to romance and allegory represents his decision to privilege a rhetoric of the body and suggests that the discursive intersection of race and masculinity requires nothing less than the tactical maneuver allegory assumes in *Dark Princess*: to make masculinity's perpetual

crisis into a sacrificial cross. Indeed, *Dark Princess* gives us repeated instances
where Matthew Towns (and to a lesser degree, his consort, Princess Kautilya)
moves from one sacrifice to the next, each one progressively smaller in scale,
moving from his life in the public world inward, toward his private life.
Thus, the novel begins with Towns being forced to give up medical school
and later the opportunity to serve in Congress, and finally, in order to
prepare himself for a struggle as yet undefined, he gives up his relationship
to Kautilya altogether (only to be reunited with her at novel's end).

This is also played out when Matthew's part in the foiled attempt to
destroy a train carrying a group of Klan members (and, coincidentally, the
princess as well) is revealed. When he is sentenced to prison, Matthew
protects the princess from being implicated in the conspiracy, taking the
punishment upon himself. Although we are meant to see this sacrifice as a
noble gesture, what interests me here is the way this scene serves a
revisionary function, providing Du Bois with the opportunity to return to
the rhetorical territory of his 1890 Harvard graduation address, entitled
"Jefferson Davis as a Representative of Civilization." In Du Bois's rendering,
Davis is a romantic figure, worthy of emulation and admiration when one
considers his individual traits apart from civilization. "A soldier and a lover,
a statesman and a ruler; passionate, ambitious, and indomitable; bold reckless
guardian of a people's All—judged by the whole standard of Teutonic
civilization, there is something noble in the figure of Jefferson Davis." But as
a symbol of the ways that white supremacy plays a destructive role in the
world, Davis is a figure to be regarded with some measure of skepticism. The
civilization Davis and men like him augur in is one whose "foundation is the
idea of the Strong Man—Individualism coupled with the rule of might."

As a man of heroic temper, Matthew Towns could most certainly
function in such a way in Du Bois's novel, but the plot of *Dark Princess* turns
on the relationship between sacrifice and redemption. In that sense, we see
Du Bois reconstituting the romantic hero. The civilization in which Davis
functions, as Teutonic hero, is one where Du Bois observes "the overweening
sense of the I and the consequent forgetting of the Thou." In many ways, the
Harvard graduation address lays out, in ways that are mirrored in *Dark
Princess*, "the change made in the conception of civilization," namely, the act
of "adding to the idea of the Strong Man, that of the Submissive Man." As
the address insists, no one is better suited for this role than the Negro, who
represents "the peculiar embodiment of the idea of Personal Submission."

This brings us back to where we began: Esau as a figure of indulgence
being transformed into the Prodigal Son, who returns to find himself
restored to power and status. In the former story, what justifies Jacob's
triumph is that it represents an instance of the weak outmaneuvering the

strong. In the latter narrative, what we see is the magnanimity of patriarchal power on one hand, but also the spoils that are the lot of the submissive man on the other. The ultimate challenge for Matthew Towns is one of mastering, of bringing into conceptual proximity political consciousness and an awareness of the body that arises from physical exertion. That Kautilya has their child unbeknown to him suggests that he is unaware of the fate that awaits him; he must submit, without knowing it, to political destiny. The birth of his child accomplishes this, not only because it is the result of an erotic endeavor but also because Matthew's relationship to the princess ensures, ostensibly, that the child will be the "text" upon which a new social contract in inscribed. And so, Matthew and Kautilya's act of consummating their relationship needs to be understood for the revisionary rhetoric that it is, for what it suggests, as an allegorical gesture, is that the redemption of civilization results, not from a cultural hybridity resulting from contact with whites, but from the "darker peoples" discovering their mutual interests and acting upon them.

But Matthew's return to his mother's cabin in Virginia is also Du Bois's rhetorical nod back to "Of the Meaning of Progress," a chapter in *The Souls of Black Folk*. While that experience marked an epiphany for the younger Du Bois, it was characterized by transience. To be sure, Du Bois wishes to suggest that it was a formative experience, necessary for the man who would do social science research in Philadelphia's Seventh Ward, but it also marks a transition which he cannot recover: "My log schoolhouse was gone. In its place stood Progress; and Progress, I understand, is necessarily ugly." The chapter ends with Du Bois musing on the irrecoverable past while riding to Nashville in the Jim Crow car. The end of *Dark Princess*, with its beautiful consort and male heir and the reconciliation with the mother, a former slave, is Du Bois's opportunity to link the African American past to a world of "darker races" beyond, whose common language is that of patriarchal discourse.

As Claudia Tate observes in the introduction to the latest edition of *Dark Princess*, Du Bois "aligns his political agenda with the pleasure principle." In its pages, we find the articulate hero who, contrary to the mores of the 1920s, represents the effort to link erotic desire to the search for an all-encompassing form of political subjectivity. Unfortunately, the form it takes, optimistic as it may be, is a relationship animated by patriarchal conventions. While it is clear that Esau is redeemed, the transformation into the Prodigal Son does not speak to the issue of gender oppression. Redemption, such as it is, means that Matthew is saved from exigencies of racial prejudice.

But I want to suggest that our work in the future, as Professors Griffin and Collins have insisted in their articles, must seek to problematize some of Du Bois's formulations—and nonformulations—about gender. Although Du Bois's intellectual prowess with respect to the discourses of race and class was ahead of its time in the 1920s, his attitude regarding gender, while tending toward progressivism, was highly reflective of the historical moment. As we ponder the new millennium (and Du Bois's place in it), we hope new ways to calculate performances of masculinity will emerge; thus we might view black feminist discourse and its call for gender equality not as threat but as legacy, indeed, as birthright, an invitation to see power as a shared and treasured thing.

HENRY LOUIS GATES JR.

W.E.B. Du Bois and the
Encyclopedia Africana, 1909-63

ABSTRACT: In 1901, W.E.B. Du Bois, the African American intellectual and activist, conceived the idea of an encyclopedia Africana. He envisioned a scientific and comprehensive work on Africa and peoples of African descent that would refute the Enlightenment notion of blacks as devoid of civilization and the hallmarks of humanity. Du Bois stood in a tradition of earlier black works seeking to vindicate the race, but World War I and his move from academia to the NAACP postponed his efforts. In 1931, however, Du Bois participated in an encyclopedia project initiated by the Phelps-Stokes Fund. His writing during this period reveals his thinking about the nature and form a pan-African encyclopedia would take. Beset by rivalries and, primarily, lack of support from the established philanthropies, the project died. In 1960, shortly before his death, Du Bois was invited to Ghana to launch an encyclopedia. If any of these attempts had succeeded, the evolution of African and African American studies in the academy would have been significantly different.

There is a dangerous and misleading lag between scientific knowledge of the Negro and intelligent interpretation today, and popular conception handed down from the past. The Negro race today, in the minds of most persons, is set apart as a group of

From *The Annals of the American Academy of Political and Social Science* 568 (March 2000). © 2000 by Sage Publications.

unusual and different individuals; and this attitude can be met only by setting forth the facts of the situation and letting the world know that the essential humanity of the black race is today well attested by a body of facts agreed upon, in all essential particulars, by those whose opinions are worth listening to.

—W.E.B. Du Bois

(1945)

On 5 April 1909, W.E.B. Du Bois wrote to the great pan-Africanist Edward Wilmot Blyden and several other scholars about his desire to edit an encyclopedia Africana, a veritable black *Encyclopaedia Britannica*, which could symbolically reassemble the fragments of the African diaspora set in motion by the European slave trade and the turn-of-the-century "scramble for Africa." Through an encyclopedia, Du Bois sought to marshal a mountain of evidence to refute the centuries of aspersion cast upon the character of the African by a racist West eager to justify the economic exploitation of Africa and its Africans. Thirty years later, Du Bois would recall that his first effort to edit his encyclopedia ended because of his involvement in the creation of the NAACP and the time commitment necessitated by his editing of *The Crisis* magazine:

> Another project in which I had long been interested was an Encyclopaedia of the Negro. As early as 1909, I had planned an Encyclopaedia Africana and secured on my board of advisors Sir Flinders Petrie, Sir Harry Johnston, Giuseppe Sergi, Dr. J. Deniker, William James, and Franz Boas; and on my proposed board of editors I had practically all the leading Negroes of the United States who were then inclined toward research. My change to New York and the work of starting the *Crisis*, and finally the World War, put this quite out of my mind.

In addition to these scholars, Du Bois wrote to many others, soliciting their collaboration in preparing a multivolume reference work "covering the chief points in the history and condition of the Negro race." While Du Bois had asked Blyden for names of "eminent white scholars" to serve on an international advisory board, "The real work," he confessed, "I want done by Negroes." Although he stressed to his correspondents that his plan was "still in Embryo," his stationery declared that he wanted the first of five projected volumes to be published in 1913, the "Jubilee of Emancipation in America and the Tercentenary of the Landing of the Negro." The remaining four volumes would be published between 1913 and 1919, as he wrote to W.T.B. Williams on 20 May. When he wrote to President Charles Eliot at Harvard inviting him to join the board of advisors, he said that 60 other scholars had already accepted his invitation, including the English ethnographers Sir Harry Johnston and Sir Flinders Petrie, Giuseppe Sergi of Italy, Franz Boas at Columbia, and Clark University President Stanley Hall—all of whose names appeared on the project's letterhead. Additional members of the board were Kelly Miller, Archibald Grimke, John Hope, Benjamin Brawley, Bishop William Sanders Scarborough, Henry Ossawa Tanner, Sutton Griggs, Anna Jones, George Edmund Haynes, Richard T. Greener, J. E. Casely-Hayford, William James, Albert Bushnell Hart, and Hugo Munsterberg, the latter three Du Bois's professors at Harvard. President Eliot declined but not before advising Du Bois to include entries on the influence of Islam in African societies and admonishing him to proceed only if he had secured adequate funding. This would turn out to be sound advice.

As he indicated in *Dusk of Dawn*, Du Bois initially planned for the encyclopedia to be "a co-operative and exhaustive scientific study of Negro history and sociology," to be edited by two boards—a board of white advisors and a "Board of One Hundred Negro American, African and West Indian Scholars." To identify the latter, he solicited nominations from a wide range of correspondents. Du Bois asked W.T.B. Williams to send him the names of "all colored persons in your state who had had thorough university training or its equivalent, and who would, in your opinion, be capable of joining in this work." Latter that year, in July of 1909, when J.R.L. Diggs, president of Virginia Theological Seminary and College in Lynchburg, wrote to Du Bois to propose a 10-volume series of books on Reconstruction to be written by blacks—"The educated Negro owes the world a history of reconstruction"— Du Bois sought to incorporate Diggs's idea into his own project. Diggs's "set of histories of reconstruction from the Negro point of view is excellent, and will fit into my encyclopedia project perfectly. I shall take it up in the fall," Du Bois promised. Du Bois's own study of Reconstruction, entitled *Black Reconstruction*, would not appear until 1935. Despite a lively and wide-ranging correspondence, Du Bois's desire to publish volume one of his encyclopedia in 1913 would not be realized.

Although Du Bois's announcement of this project in 1909 appeared to arrive like a bolt out of the blue, Du Bois had several encyclopedic antecedents, ranging from 1808 through 1907. Indeed, though he never admitted it, it is highly probable that the publication of *The Jewish Encyclopedia* in 1907—and all of the praise it received—was the determining factor in Du Bois's thinking, leading him to attempt to mount a project equivalent in range and scope for the black world. Despite this more immediate influence, however, the encyclopedic impulse among both African Americans and enemies of anti-black racism was quite strong and proved to be quite insistent throughout the nineteenth century.

TO REDRESS THE
WORLD'S IGNORANCE

The word "encyclopedia," of Greek derivation (*enkyklopaideia*), initially denoted a circle or a complete system of learning. At least since the first decade of the nineteenth century, the publication of compendia of black intellectual attainment has aimed to redress the world's ignorance of or skepticism about individual and collective black accomplishment in the realm of the arts and letters. At least since Hume alleged in 1748 that Africans had invented "no arts, no sciences," the purported absence of the hallmarks of civilization among blacks in Africa and the New World had to be refuted because it was drawn upon to justify the Africans' enslavement. A slave to ignorance was a slave by nature. Ironically, Hume's allegations—shared by Kant, Jefferson, and Hegel—would serve to generate a surprisingly stubborn impulse to restore African culture to its proper place as one of the world's great cultures by documenting the accomplishments of individual writers, artists, orators, scientists, physicians, lawyers, and preachers of African descent in biographical dictionaries and encyclopedias.

Make no mistake about it; these were charges of the utmost seriousness and gravity. Faced with the awesome task of reconciling the discovery of peoples and cultures of color—in the "New World" as well as in the old world of Africa—with received ideas of the nature of the human species, European speculative philosophers selected, over several centuries, various measures of "civilization" by which to place each newly encountered culture in its relation to European civilization on the great chain of being. Of these successive signs and marks of human sophistication, the absence and presence of "the arts and sciences" by the Enlightenment had come to be the definitive measure. With Gutenberg's invention of the printing press, and that resurrection of classical Greek and Roman texts so fundamental to Renaissance skepticism, it is not surprising that the verbal and written arts assumed a priority among these "arts and sciences." "That which makes man a god to man," wrote Francis Bacon in 1620, "is the knowledge of the arts and sciences" and, more precisely, the mastery of the written arts. Claims of the absence of these commodities implied nothing less than the subhuman status of Africans, as status that had obviously and unalterably been ordained by nature throughout the African continent.

The seriousness of these charges against the African's very humanity demanded comprehensive rebuttals from the friends of the blacks, initially, and from the blacks themselves, ultimately. The complex response to these allegations engendered by the seemingly unassailable intellectual stature of Bacon, Hume, Jefferson, Kant, and Hegel assumed the form of the "encyclopaedic catalogue" listing black men and women, living previously in Europe and America, whose artistic achievements, varying widely from the mundane to the sublime, were offered as proof of the African's intellectual equality. The collecting and cataloguing of even the slightest literary, artistic, or scientific success of the black person might well be said to be the predominant characteristic of early historical scholarship about blacks, at least since Henri-Baptiste Grégoire published in 1808 his *De la littérature des nègres ou Recherches sur leurs faculties intellectuelles, leurs qualities morales et leur litterature: suivies de notices sur la vie et les auvrages des nègres qui se sont distingués dans les sciences, les lettres et les arts*, and extending well into the first half of the twentieth century.

Grégoire's curious and slim book, translated into English in 1810, attacked vigorously by Tussac (1880) in his hysterical *Cri des Colons*, and purchased in bulk for his court at Port-au-Prince in Haiti by command of King Christoph himself, proved to be a text of monumental import. The book was widely reviewed and discussed. Such was the success of Grégoire's curiously romantic text, rife with wishful thinking yet surprisingly well documented, that it firmly established the encyclopedia genre as the mode of discourse fundamental to any meaningful defense of the African's intellectual parity with the European's.

Indeed, a full list of Grégoire's intellectual descendants could serve rather well as a chart of the texts by which each successive generation of black scholars sought to define its central task of defending "the race"; and this task, as it had been for Grégoire, remained for the following 150 years the encyclopedic, and sometimes hyberbolic, refutation of racist doubts not only about the fundamental nature of the black person's mind but also about the relation that African cultural artifacts bore to those of European civilization. A partial list of these encyclopedias and biographical dictionaries include the following, pregnant titles, which preceded and followed Du Bois's initial 1909 effort:

1.   R. B. Lewis's *Light and Truth; Collected from the Bible and Ancient and Modern History; Containing the Universal History of the Colored and Indian Race, from the Creation of the World to the Present Time* (1836);

2.   Hosea Easton's *A Treatise on the Intellectual Character of the Colored People of the United States* (1837);

3.   Abigail Mott's *Biographical Sketches and Interesting Anecdotes of Persons of Colour* (1826);

4.   James W. C. Pennington's *A Text Book of the Origin and History of the Colored People* (1841);

5.   James Theodore Holly's *A Vindication of the Capacity of the Negro Race for Self-Government, and Civilized Progress* (1851);

6.   H. G. Adams's *God's Image in Ebony; Being a Series of Biographical Sketches, Facts, Anecdotes, etc., Demonstrative of the Mental Powers and Intellectual Capacities of the Negro Race* (1854);

7.   Joseph T. Wilson's rather ambitious *Emancipation: Its Course and Progress from 1481 B.C. to A.D. 1875* (1882);

8.   George W. Williams's *History of the Negro Race in America from 1619 to 1880* (1883);

9.   William J. Simmons's *Men of Mark: Eminent, Progressive and Rising* (1887);

10.   Rufus Perry's *The Cushite; or, The Children of Ham (the Negro Race) as Seen by the Ancient Historians and Poets* (1886);

11.   James Haley's *Afro-American Encyclopedia* (1895);

12.   W. H. Crogman and H. F. Kletzing's, *Progress of a Race* (1897);

13.   Booker T. Washington's *A New Negro for a New Century* (1900);

14.   D. W. Culp's *Twentieth Century Negro Literature: Or A Cyclopedia of Thought on the Vital Topics Relating to the American Negro by One Hundred of America's Greatest Negroes* (1902);

15.   Daniel Murray's *Historical and Biographical Encyclopedia of the Colored Race Throughout the World; Its Progress and Achievements from the Earliest Period Down to the Present Time (25,000 Biographies, 5,900 Musical Compositions by Colored Composers)* (1912);

16.   John W. Cromwell's *The Negro in American History; Men and Women Eminent in the Evolution of the American of African Descent* (1914);

17.   Kelly Miller and J. R. Gay's *Progress and Achievements of the Colored People* (1917);

18.   Edward C. Garrett's "Negro Encyclopedia" (c. 1940, unpublished); and

19.   Joel A. Rogers's two-volume *World's Great Men of Color* (1946).

Perhaps because these pioneering encyclopedists of Africana were so successful in preserving the written record of black intellection and artistic achievement, a generation of scholars could eventually turn from the mere collection of biographies and anecdotes to the far more complex matters of analysis and interpretation. The fascination with the African mask after the 1895 Exposition at Paris and the subsequent birth of cubism, anthropological studies of arguments for "cultural relativity" and "the primitive," and Dvorak's valorization of the spirituals are aspects of the growing fascination of Europe with Africa and Afro-America, overlapping precisely with the European conquest and division of the continent south of the Sahara at the end of the century. W.E.B. Du Bois's response to this intellectual curiosity was, perhaps predictably in retrospect, to organize and contain it within the most profound form imaginable to his supremely fertile mind, an encyclopedia Africana. But it was not to be.

IT WOULD MARK AN EPOCH

In 1931, Du Bois received word that the Phelps-Stokes Fund had launched a project it called "The Encyclopedia of the Negro." Neither Du Bois nor Carter G. Woodson had been invited to the initial organizational meeting, held at Howard University on 7 November 1931. After he protested, Du Bois was invited to the project's second meeting on 9 January 1932. A letter (dated 30 November 1931) to James H. Dillard, the founder of the Jeanes Fund for the training of black teachers and of the Southern University Race Commission, reveals Du Bois's ambivalence about attending:

My dear Mr. Dillard:

I am a little puzzled about the matter of the Negro encyclopedia proposed by the Phelps Stokes Fund and others. As you know, I was not invited to the first meeting, but since then, an invitation has come to the second meeting.

I do not want to be over-modest or over-sensitive, but I initiated the scientific study of the American Negro in the United States and contributed something to it. To be left out of the original invitation to consider a Negro encyclopedia came pretty near being a personal insult and a petty one at that. On the other hand, it is a great project. If properly carried out, it would mark an epoch, and I have no right to let any personal feelings between me and the best accomplishment of this work. On the

other hand, if I should come in to help in this project, I should
have to criticize what seems to now to be its tendency, and under
the circumstances, I rather doubt how I should be justified in
criticizing even the beginnings already made. On the other hand,
I cannot sit in on a proposition of this sort as a figurehead.

As, of course, you realize, I could not for a moment
contemplate a Negro encyclopedia dominated and controlled by
Thomas Jesse Jones and Mr. Woofter. I do not, of course, want
to exclude them or what they represent, but a Negro
encyclopedia that was not in the main edited and written by
Negroes would be as inconceivable as a Catholic encyclopedia
projected by Protestants.

Du Bois concludes his letter to Dillard by saying, "Evidently I was not
wanted by those who started it." Nevertheless, Dillard persuaded Du Bois to
attend the 9 January meeting.

At that meeting, Du Bois was elected editor-in-chief. Du Bois, in turn,
now sought to persuade Woodson to join the board. He wrote to him on 29
January 1932. His line of reasoning with a recalcitrant Woodson bears
repeating, if only because Woodson's animosity toward the project—and
toward Du Bois—would soon become quite public.

My dear Sir:

I was asked to act as a Committee by the Conference on
Negro Encyclopedia to induce you to join us. I had hoped to see
you personally but had to rush back to Washington. When I am
there again, I shall talk with you. Meantime, as time is passing, I
am venturing to write.

I do not doubt but what you have made up your mind on this
matter and that nothing I can say will change it. However,
perhaps I ought to bring to your attention the motives that
influenced me.

*I was omitted from the first call, as you were, and for similar
reasons.* My first impulse on receiving the invitation to attend the
second meeting was to refuse, as you did. Then I learned that this
invitation did not come from the Phelps Stokes Fund, but was
the unanimous wish of the conferees and that if I refused to heed
it, I would be affronting them, even more than Stokes, and Jones.
Then, in the second place, I had to remember as both of us from

time to time are compelled to, that the enemy has the money and they are going to use it. Our choice then is not how that money could be used best from our point of view, but how far without great sacrifice of principle, we can keep it from being misused. By the curious combination of accident and good will, we appointed at the last meeting a Board of Directors and Incorporators, which leave out the more impossible members of the Conference. A place on that Board was left for you. If you do not accept it, that will leave us so much the weaker.

I hope you will see your way open to join us.

Woodson responded on 11 February:

My dear Dr. Du Bois:

I should have answered your confidential letter before I left the city for a long stay. I have nothing to say, however, except that I am not interested. *I never accept the gifts of the Greeks.*

I should add that the Associated Publishers, drawing upon data collected for this purpose since 1922 by the Association for the Study of Negro Life and History, would bring out its *Encyclopedia Africana by the end of 1933.* We welcome competition, because it is the spice of life.

Respectfully yours,
C. G. Woodson (emphasis added)

Woodson's claims that he had invented the idea of an encyclopedia Africana would surface dramatically in 1936.

Woodson's announcement of a rival project notwithstanding, Du Bois went to work organizing *The Encyclopedia of the Negro,* which, like his 1909 plan for an encyclopedia Africana, was pan-African in scope. Between 1932 and 1946, Du Bois worked tirelessly both to fund his project and to organize its editorial structure. In a letter to Edwin R. Embree, president of the Rosenwald Fund, dated 24 April 1935, Du Bois attempted to persuade him to fund the project, but more important for our purpose, Du Bois makes the argument—in response to Embree's objection that perhaps the time was not quite right for such an encyclopedia—for publishing sooner rather than later, despite the incomplete nature of knowledge and research about the Negro:

It seems to me that you forget that an encyclopedia is not a history. A history may have to be postponed in the writing until more source material is known, but even in that case, it should not be postponed until the collection of material is complete, because that would take a very long time. In any case and in the meantime, there should be some authoritative source from which children and the general public could learn as much as there is to be known about the particular period in mind.

With an encyclopedia, however, the case is even more imperative. An encyclopedia is not only a record of history, but also a record of present conclusions and opinions and whatever an encyclopedia gains in factual accuracy by postponement of publication, it more than loses in lessening its grip on current opinion. For that reason encyclopedias are published and then at reasonable periods revised. But at any particular time there ought to be an authoritative collection of the opinion and historical judgements of that particular day. In no case is that more demanded than in the case of the Negro problem.

You recognized the demand when you published "Brown America." What you did needs to be done on a larger scale by a wider group of scholars and public men, so the universities, colleges, schools and general readers will have a body of knowledge to which they can turn with the conviction that however incomplete it may be and it must be incomplete, it nevertheless expresses fairly well the current opinion of the best authorities of the day. In this time of crisis and inquiry to postpone such an undertaking for half a generation or more would be not only unwise but calamitous. We need, of course, further source material, but nothing is likely to be gathered or discovered which is going to change the basic facts concerning the Negro in this country. And in the same way, the loss which the truth concerning the Negro has sustained in having no such authoritative statement, covering for instance the time of Reconstruction, or the day of Booker T. Washington, is irreparable.

No, the time to move on this grand idea was now, Du Bois insisted, and he implored all and sundry to finance it, from George Foster Peabody, the wealthy philanthropist and friend of Franklin Roosevelt's, and Dixon Ryan Fox, president of Union College, to the WPA and the Federal Writers Project.

While beating the bushes for funds, Du Bois also was seeking more and more distinguished contributors, writing to H. L. Mencken; Roscoe Pound, the Dean of the Harvard Law School; Margaret Mead, then assistant curator of ethnology at the American Museum of Natural History in New York; Otto Klineberg, professor of psychology at Columbia; Harold Laski, the leader of the British Labour Party; Broadus Mitchell, professor of political economy at Johns Hopkins; and E. Franklin Frazier among others to write articles for *The Encyclopedia of the Negro.*

Pound, Mead, Klineberg, Laski, and Mitchell wrote enthusiastic responses. Only H. L. Mencken and E. Franklin Frazier declined Du Bois's request. Mencken admitted that he was not an expert on the subject, then advised him that the work, "if possible . . . ought to be done principally by Negroes—indeed, it would be best if it could be done wholly by Negroes." Frazier, on the other hand, admonished Du Bois for including too many "politicians," "statesmen," "big-Negroes," and "whites of goodwill." Throw out the encyclopedia's outline, disband the board of advisors, he wrote, reconvene an entirely new board consisting of scholars, and perhaps he might reconsider. Despite extremely favorable responses from many of the world's greatest scholars of the Negro in Africa and throughout the New World, Du Bois was finding it difficult to secure the $225,000 that he needed to publish a four-volume 2 million-word encyclopedia, which now would be written by "25 to 100 research aides" and an international body of experts submitting longer interpretive articles.

As if that were not frustrating enough, Carter Woodson in 1936 decided to attack the project, making public the claim that he had invented the idea. On 30 May 1936, the *Baltimore Afro-American* carried a front-page attack by Woodson on the project, on Du Bois, and on literary historian Benjamin Brawley. In an article dated 3 May 1936, entitled "Calls Du Bois a Traitor If He Accepts the Post"—subtitled "He Told Ofays, We'd Write Own History"—Woodson protested Du Bois's decision to solicit work from white scholars:

> What the colored man needs is not to aid this misrepresentation of the race by those who view it from without, but to resort to scientific methods to study his race from within and thus enable him to unfold himself to the world.
>
> This is a task which only the colored man himself can do. The white man, even when he is honest and sincere, cannot at his best write the history of colored people and portray their present status, when he does not live and move among them.

Moreover, Woodson continued, at last revealing his real motivation, "This is an effort to supplant me and my work." Woodson, like Du Bois, had taken the Ph.D. in history at Harvard; Brawley received a master's degree in English there in 1908. Rivalry, like politics, can take peculiarly local forms.

Du Bois did not respond publicly, but he did so privately, in a letter to the sociologist Robert Park, dated 3 March 1937:

> I am sending herewith a hundred sheets and envelopes of the Encyclopedia letterheads; also I am sending some data about the Encyclopedia Africana. You will find Mr. Woodson's version of his Encyclopedia Africana on page 15 of the January, 1937, issue of the "Journal of Negro History." You will note that he refers to action on the Encyclopedia Africana in 1921, if you will consult, however, the reports in 1921 (*Journal of Negro History*, 1921 Volume VI, pp. 126-130), you will find there is no notice or mention of any such Encyclopedia in the proceedings of the annual meeting of 1920, nor is there any notice in the meeting of 1921 reported in Volume VII, 1922, pp. 121-126. I believe both of these meetings took place during the time you were president of the Association. My project never went far enough to give me any claim to exclusive occupation of the field. It was merely one of my large ideas which never got down to earth or finance. It is barely possible that I should have pushed further had it not been for the World War; but as a matter of fact I didn't. I never heard of Mr. Woodson's project until after the Phelps-Stokes Encyclopaedia movement was started. When he mentioned it I immediately tried to find out when the idea was first made public, be [he] got angry and refused to give any specific answer. In the case of my Encyclopaedia Africana, I conceived the idea in 1909, and in 1911 while attending the Races Congress in London I talked about it with Sir Harry Johnston, Dr. W. M. Flinders-Petrie, and others. Previous to that I had correspondence with Professor William James, President [Charles] Eliot, and all of the Negroes whose names appear on the letter-head.

Despite this stormy, bitter controversy, Du Bois continued planning the encyclopedia with the able assistance of Rayford Logan, who, like Du Bois and Woodson, had earned the Ph.D. in history at Harvard. Their plan of work and table of contents were quite detailed, as Du Bois indicated in a letter to Anson Phelps-Stokes, dated 19 May 1937; the letter also provides an indication of the encyclopedia's projected structure:

We have finished the following work on the Encyclopaedia: the preparation of a manuscript of about one hundred and twenty-five pages giving a list of possible subjects for an Encyclopaedia of the Negro with a short bibliographical note under each subject. These subjects have been carefully revised from my original list of last year in light of criticism sent in from various scholars, and have been arranged alphabetically.

In addition to that we have made a careful estimate of the space these articles would occupy by the following method: three of the longest articles on Africa, the Negro Race, and the African Slave Trade; five long articles on the Negro in the United States, Negro in the West Indies, Negro in South America, Race and Miscegenation. These articles will occupy 350 pages and 280,000 words. Then we have allowed space for 250 chief articles occupying a thousand pages with 800,000 words. We have next allowed for 700 biographies covering the world and including Negroes, persons of Negro descent, and white persons connected with their history. This will occupy 560,000 words. In addition to this we have allowed 550 pages and 440,000 words for minor articles and an index of 200 pages or 160,000 words. This makes a total of 2,800 pages and 2,240,000 words. This calculation has been based on the *Encyclopaedia of the Social Sciences* and we have allowed 400 words to a column.

By this time, May 1937, Du Bois was quite optimistic about possibilities for funding of the project. Du Bois's assistant editor, Rayford Logan, once told me a poignant story about the failure of this project to receive funding. By 1937, Du Bois had secured a pledge of $125,000 from the Phelps-Stokes Fund to proceed with his project—half of the amount needed to complete it. Du Bois had applied to the Carnegie Corporation after a similar proposal had been rejected by the General Education Board, for the remaining half of his budget, with the strong endorsement of Phelps-Stokes. The president of the General Education Board, a group of four or five private foundations that included the Rockefeller Foundation, also lent his support. So convinced was Du Bois that his project, 28 years after he first articulated it, would be funded, that he invited Logan to wait with him at his office at 200 West 135th Street for the phone call that he had been promised immediately following the Carnegie board meeting. A bottle of vintage champagne sat chilling on Du Bois's desk in a silver bucket, two cut-glass champagne flutes resting nearby.

The phone never rang. Persuaded that Du Bois was far too "radical" to serve as a model of disinterested scholarship, and lobbied by Du Bois's intellectual enemies, such as anthropologist Melville Herskovits, the Carnegie Corporation rejected the project. In addition, Du Bois had been forced to resign his post as editor of *The Crisis* magazine just three years before, so he had a considerable number of intellectual and political enemies.

David Levering Lewis offers a moving account of what transpired at the meeting of the General Education Board, and its subsequent consequences:

> Now came a third turning point in Du Bois's career—the fulfillment of a grand idea that had been with him since the turn of the century, the multi-volume *Encyclopedia of the Negro.* "Cruel" is the word for best describing the roller coaster involving Du Bois and the major foundations over the funding of his ambitious project of research and education. His old faith in the power of ideas, scientifically formulated, to make the world better had welled up again after a quarter-century of activism and propaganda. The encyclopedia project generated preliminary endorsements and promises of collaboration from much of the international scholarly community. After his 1935 funding application was rejected by the Rockefeller-dominated combine of four or five private foundations comprising the General Education Board, he greatly revised and elaborated the proposal for resubmission, the Phelps-Stokes Fund providing seed money. Growing national and even international support for Du Bois among the experts began to exert formidable pressures for foundation funding of the encyclopedia. Rather surprisingly, one of the General Education Board's principal officers, Jackson Davis, had become an *Encyclopedia* convert, introducing Du Bois to the right New York notables, stroking his own trustees, and lobbying the Carnegie Corporation for favorable action on the Carnegie portion of the Du Bois grant application. Melville Herskovits, a competitor for foundation funds, began to fret about Du Bois's bagging the $250,000 research budget. He need not have worried. Clearly, an encyclopedia encompassing the full range of race and race relations in America and directed by Du Bois was to say the least troubling to the custodians of social science orthodoxy.
>
> The seven-member executive committee of the GEB—Raymond B. Fosdick presiding and John D. Rockefeller III

participating—rejected the *Encyclopedia* at the beginning of May 1937. In his conference a few days later with Carnegie Corporation president Frederick Keppel, GEB's Jackson Davis paradoxically pleaded for favorable Carnegie consideration of the project. "Dr. Du Bois is the most influential Negro in the United States," Davis reminded Keppel. "This project would keep him busy for the rest of his life." Predictably, Carnegie declined. Within a remarkably short time, the study of the Negro (generously underwritten by the Carnegie Corporation) found a quite different direction under a Swedish scholar then unknown in the field of race relations, one whose understanding of American race problems was to be distinctly more psychological and less economic than was Du Bois's.

The precise moment of preemption is recorded in a remarkable September 1939 exchange between President Robert Maynard Hutchins of the University of Chicago and Director Edwin Embree of the Rosenwald Fund: "Ed, somebody tells me that Keppel has rented the forty-sixth floor of the Chrysler Building and turned it over to a Swede named Gunnar Myrdal to make an elaborate study of Negro education. What's it all about?" "Bob, not Negro education, but the whole realm of the Negro in American civilization [to] take the place of the proposed Negro Encyclopedia in which the Phelps Stokes Fund has been greatly interested." When the president of the Phelps-Stokes Fund wrote Du Bois in 1944 at the time of the publication of *An American Dilemma* that "there has been no one who has been quite so often quoted by Myrdal than yourself," Du Bois must have savored the irony.

Nevertheless, Du Bois stubbornly persisted, even publishing two putative "entries" from the *Encyclopedia* in *Phylon* magazine in 1940, one on Robert Russa Moton, the principal of Tuskegee Institute between 1915 and 1935, the other on Alexander Pushkin. He even was able to publish two editions in 1945 and 1946 of *Encyclopedia of the Negro: Preparatory Volume with Reference Lists and Reports*. But the project itself could never secure adequate financial backing.

Du Bois struggled in vain to secure funding over the next several years, but he managed to publish in 1945 a 208-page "Preparatory Volume with Reference Lists and Reports"; a second edition appeared in 1946.

This remarkable volume is extraordinarily valuable as a compendium of secondary sources about Africa and African American history, culture, and social institutions. But most valuable is Du Bois's statement about "The Need for an Encyclopedia of the Negro":

> There is a need for young pupils and for mature students of a statement of the present condition of our knowledge concerning the darker races and especially concerning Negroes, which would make available our present scientific knowledge and set aside the vast accumulation of tradition and prejudice which makes such knowledge difficult now for the layman to obtain: A *Vade mecum* for American schools, editors, libraries, for Europeans inquiring into the race status here, for South Americans and Africans.
>
> Our knowledge of the Negro today is not, of course, entirely complete; there are many gaps where further information and more careful study are needed; but this is the case in almost every branch of knowledge. Knowledge is never complete and in few subjects does a time arrive when an encyclopedia is demanded because no further information is expected. Indeed the need of an encyclopedia is greatest when a stage is reached where there is a distinct opportunity to bring together and set down a clear and orderly statement of the facts already known and agreed upon, for the sake of establishing a base for further advance and further study. Under such circumstances it would seem that an encyclopedia of the Negro is necessary.
>
> In the case of the proposed *Encyclopedia of the Negro* these difficulties are increased because the prejudices and memories surrounding the subject have been more intense. There are hurts and fears; there are current controversies, which make a strictly scientific point of view of questions affecting the Negro race, difficult. Notwithstanding this, the body of accumulated knowledge is today so wide and dependable that it becomes all the more necessary that current social thought and discussion should be placed, to as large an extent as possible, upon a basis of accepted scientific conclusion.

In 1948, still another challenge to Du Bois emerged, this time initiated—incredibly—by the General Education Board, the Dodd, Mead publishing company, and Dr. Frederick D. Patterson, the president of the Tuskegee Institute, who had agreed to be its editor-in-chief. It was to be called "The Negro: An Encyclopedia," it would consist of 1 million words, and it would sell for $12. Two years later, Charles Wesley—still another

Ph.D. in history from Harvard—wrote to Du Bois to say that the Association for the Study of Negro Life and History, in the wake of Carter G. Woodson's death, had decided to publish "an Encyclopedia Africana" and did Du Bois have any objections? Du Bois wished Wesley well, but warned him—just as President Eliot had warned Du Bois in 1909—that the project would be an expensive one. Clearly the concept—and proprietorship—of an encyclopedia of the black diaspora had a vexed history in the first half of the twentieth century. Neither of these projects went beyond the planning stage.

On 26 September 1960, Du Bois reported that he had been invited by Kwame Nkrumah to move to Ghana to edit *The Encyclopedia Africana*. After a harried decade during which he ran for the United States Senate, was arrested and tried for being a Communist sympathizer, and had his traveling privileges suspended, what a relief this invitation must have been. Du Bois and his second wife, Shirley Graham, moved to Ghana in 1961, becoming citizens there in 1963. He described his reasons for accepting the invitation in the *Baltimore Afro-American* on 21 October 1961 and then again in an essay entitled "Ghana Calls" published in *Freedomways* in the winter of 1962. What he neglected to mention, however, was his disappointment and disgust with so many prominent Negro leaders who had failed to support him during his harassment by the government. Du Bois's anger at this would affect his design for the encyclopedia in its third and final incarnation.

On 15 December 1962, Du Bois convened a conference to launch the encyclopedia at the University of Ghana. It would be his last public speech. In his remarks, Du Bois recapitulated the history of his idea since 1909, then argued that "it is logical that such a work had to wait for independent Africans to carry it out," and now was the ideal time to edit "an *Encyclopedia Africana* based in Africa and compiled by Africans." Du Bois then told his audience:

> It is true that scientific written records do not exist in most parts of this continent. But the time is *now* for beginning. The encyclopedia hopes to eliminate the artificial boundaries created on this continent by colonial masters. Designations such as "British Africa," "French Africa," "Black Africa," "Islamic Africa" too often serve to keep alive differences which in large part have been imposed on Africans by outsiders. The encyclopedia must have research units throughout West Africa, North Africa, East, Central and South Africa which will gather and record information for these geographical sections of the continent. The encyclopedia is concerned with Africa as a whole.

Ultimately, Du Bois argued, "It is African scholars themselves who will create the ultimate *Encyclopedia Africana*. . . . After all, this is where the work should be done—in Africa, sponsored by Africans, for Africa." The completion of this grand project, he concluded, "is of vital importance to Africa as a whole and to the world at large." Dramatically curtailed in scope and coverage from its first two manifestations in 1909 and 1932, this *Africana* would have only a continental focus, rather than the diasporic focus of the other two. This *Africana* would serve as a tool in the liberation and consolidation of an emerging continent.

Du Bois died on the eve of the great March on Washington; indeed, Roy Wilkins announced his death during the proceedings. His secretariat for the *Encyclopedia Africana* continued after his death, and published three volumes of biographies in the late 1970s and early 1980s. Officially, it is still dedicated to fulfilling his dream of an encyclopedia about Africa edited by Africans, and has recently announced a publication date of the year 2009— 48 years after Du Bois launched the project in Ghana.

Had any of these attempts to edit the three versions of his encyclopedia been successful, how dramatically different would have been the evolution of African and Afro-American studies in the academy. An encyclopedia establishes a foundation of common knowledge on which subsequent scholarly inquiry can stand. It removes the necessity of reinventing the proverbial wheel each time scholars embark upon a subject unknown to them but one that has already been thoroughly explored by other scholars. Just as important, an encyclopedia makes it possible to disseminate this baseline of knowledge broadly and widely to schools at even the earliest levels, just as the *Britannica* did for millions of households. How much further along would the fields of African and African American studies be at the end of the century had the great Du Bois been funded in 1909 or in 1932 or had he lived beyond 1963 to see his more narrow, Africa-focused version completed? Du Bois's initial 1909 idea for an encyclopedia of the African diaspora would not be published until January 1999, when *Encarta Africana* was released on CD-ROM, 90 years after Du Bois first articulated the idea. *Africana: The Encyclopedia of the African and African American Experience*, the book version, was published in November 1999. Both, appropriately, are dedicated in memory of W.E.B. Du Bois.

Chronology

1868 William Edward Burghardt Du Bois born February 26 in Great Barrington, Massachusetts.

1883–85 Correspondent for the *New York Age, New York Globe*, and other black newspapers.

1884 Graduates from Great Barrington High School in June; gives Valedictory speech on Wendell Phillips. Mother May dies in the autumn. Works for a year at odd jobs.

1885–1888 Attends Fisk University, entering as a sophomore. Works summers in schools in Nashville area. Awarded B.A. in 1888. Speaks at graduation on Bismark.

1888 Enters Harvard University as a junior.

1890 Receives B.A. (*cum laude*) in philosophy. Gives commencement speech on Jefferson Davis. Begins graduate study in history.

1891 Awarded M.A. in history from Harvard. Begins study for the doctorate.

1892 Receives grant (half gift, half loan) from Slater Fund enabling him to study in Europe. Attends University of Berlin. Travels for two years in Western Europe.

1894 Returns to U.S. in the summer, riding steerage. In August, accepts position as Chairman of Classics Department at Wilberforce University.

1895	Receives Ph.D. in history from Harvard. Commends Booker T. Washington for his September 18 Atlanta Exposition speech.
1896	Marries Nina Gomer (deceased 1950). Children: Burghardt, Yolande Du Bois Williams. *Suppression of the African Slave-Trade* published. Leaves Wilberforce and accepts fifteen-month appointment to do field work in Philadelphia's Seventh Ward.
1897	Accepts position at Atlanta University. Edits *Atlanta University Studies*. Publishes *The Conservation of Races* (Washington, D.C.: American Negro Academy) and "Strivings of The Negro People," *Atlantic Monthly* 80 (August 1897): 194–198.
1899	Sam Hose lynched. Publishes *The Philadelphia Negro: A Social Study* (Philadelphia: University of Pennsylvania) and "The Negro and Crime," *Independent* 51 (18 May 1899): pp. 1355–1357.
1900	In July, attends first Pan-African Congress in London. Elected secretary. Attends Paris Exposition.
1903	Publishes *The Souls of Black Folk: Essays and Sketches* (Chicago: McClurg, 1903; London: Constable, 1905).
1902	Booker T. Washington, in a letter, commends Du Bois on his work at Atlanta. Efforts are made to persuade Du Bois to leave Atlanta and move to Tuskegee.
1904	Publishes "The Atlanta Conferences," *Voice of the Negro* 1 (March 1904): 85–90 and "Credo," *Independent* 57 (6 October 1904): p. 787.
1905	Niagara Movement organized; first conference held in Fort Erie, Ontario.
1906	Founds periodical *The Moon* (lasts one year). Atlanta pogrom. Organizes second Niagara Conference in August at Harper's Ferry.
1907	Third Niagara Conference, in Boston. Publishes with Booker T. Washington *The Negro in the South, His Economic Progress in Relation to His Moral and Religious Development; Being the William Levi Bull Lectures for the Year 1907* (Philadelphia: Jacobs). Founds *Horizon*, published until 1910.
1908	Niagara movement in decline. Fourth Conference in Oberlin, Ohio.

1909   Last Niagara Conference, Sea Isle, New Jersey. National Negro Committee meets (what will become the National Association for the Advancement of Colored People). Publishes *John Brown* (Philadelphia: Jacobs).

1910   Accepts offer to become director of publications and research for NAACP. Arrives in New York during the summer. In November, edits first issue of *The Crisis*, official publication of the NAACP. Publishes "The Souls of White Folk," *Independent* 69 (18 August 1910): pp. 1355–1357.

1911   In July, attends Universal Races Conference in London. Publishes *The Quest of the Silver Fleece* (Chicago: McClurg), a novel dramatizing the economic conflict between southern planters and northern capitalists during Reconstruction.

1913   Publishes "Negro in Literature and Art," *Annals of the American Academy of Political and Social Science* 49 (September 1913): 233–237.

1915   Publishes *The Negro* (New York: Holt and London: Williams & Norgate), a history of African and black Americans. Booker T. Washington dies.

1916   First Amenia Conference held at home of Joel Spingarn.

1918   "Close Ranks" editorial in *The Crisis* advocating Negro participation in World War I. In December, Du Bois sails for Europe to investigate condition of black troops.

1919   Du Bois organizes Pan-African Congress in Paris. Nortorious "Red Summer" in America involving numerous attacks upon black people.

1920   Publishes *Darkwater: Voices from Within the Veil* (New York: Harcourt, Brace & Howe, 1920 and London: Constable) and founds and edits *Brownies Book* for children. Tension with Marcus Garvey begins.

1921   Pan-African Congress in London, Brussels, and Paris.

1923   Minister Plenipotentiary and Envoy Extraordinary to Liberia, conferred by President Calvin Coolidge. Awarded Spingarn Medal. Organizes Pan-African Congress in London, Paris, and Lisbon. Attacks Garvey in February issue of *The Crisis*.

1924   Publishes *The Gift of Black Folk: The Negroes in the Making of America* (Boston: Stratford), a book detailing contributions of blacks to civilization.

1926   Spends two months in Soviet Russia. Founds black repertory theater group in Harlem, known as Krigwa Players.

1927   Krigwa Players win theater award in New York City. Pan-African Congress meets in New York City.

1928   Publishes *Dark Princess: A Romance* (New York: Harcourt, Brace), a book concerning the international conditions of black people and the ramifications of racism.

1930   Awarded LL.D. from Howard University. Publishes *Africa: Its Geography, People and Products* (Girard, Kansas: Haldeman-Julius) and *Africa: Its Place in Modern History* (Girard, Kansas: Haldeman-Julius)

1931   Scottsboro case begins.

1934   Breaks with NAACP and leaves editorship of *The Crisis*. Returns to Atlanta University as Chairman of Sociology Department.

1935   Publishes *Black Reconstruction: An Essay Toward a History of the Part Which Black Folk Played in the Attempt to Reconstruct Democracy in America, 1860–1880* (New York: Harcourt, Brace).

1936   Travels to Germany during the summer, sponsored by the Oberlaender Trust. Returns to American January 1937.

1938   Awarded LL.D. from Atlanta University and Litt.D. from Fisk University.

1939   Publishes *Black Folk, Then and Now: An Essay in the History of Sociology of the Negro Race* (New York: Holt).

1940   Awarded L.H.D. from Wilberforce University. Publishes *Dusk of Dawn: An Essay Toward an Autobiography of a Race Concept* (New York: Harcourt, Brace). Founds and edits *Phylon*.

1941   After gathering the black presidents of land grant colleges together, outlines his plan of economic redevelopment and stresses the need to include studies on the Negro's condition in the college curriculum.

1943   Elected to National Institute of Arts and Letters.

1944	Retires from Atlanta. Rejoins the NAACP as Director of Special Research.
1945	Publishes *Color and Democracy: Colonies and Peace* (New York: Harcourt, Brace). Consultant to the Founding Convention of the United Nations. Attends and is honored at Pan-African Congress in London.
1947	Publishes *The World and Africa: An Inquiry into the Part Which Africa Has Played in World History* (New York: Viking). Edits *An Appeal to the World: A Statement on the Denial of Human Rights to Minorities in the Case of Citizens of Negro Descent in the United States of America and an Appeal to the United Nations for Redress* (New York: National Association for the Advancement of Colored People).
1948	Fired from NAACP and given pension. Begins association with the Council on African Affairs.
1949	Makes peace pilgrimage to New York, Paris and Moscow.
1950	Chairman of Peace Information Center. U.S. enters Korean War. Nina Gomer Du Bois dies. Du Bois runs for U.S. Senate on American Labor Party ticket.
1951	Marries Shirley Graham on February 14. Publishes "I Take My Stand," *Masses and Mainstream* 4 (April 1951): 10–16. Du Bois, along with other officials of the Peace Information Center, is indicted for being an unregistered "agent of a foreign principal." Trial begins on November 8 and ends five days later with case thrown out. Publishes *In Battle for Peace: The Story of My 83rd Birthday* (New York: Masses & Mainstream).
1952	Lives in Brooklyn, New York. On February 14, State Department refuses to issue him a passport to travel to peace conference in Rio de Janeiro.
1955	Refused passport to attend World Youth Festival in Warsaw, Poland.
1957	Refused permission to attend Ghana's independence ceremonies. State Department keeps Du Bois's passport. Publishes first volume of "Black Flame" trilogy, *The Ordeal of Mansart* (New York: Mainstream).
1958	Travels to USSR, China, France, England and Sweden.

Awarded Lenin International Peace Prize; honorary degrees from Charles University, Prague, and Humboldt University, Berlin.

1959   Awarded honorary degree from Moscow University. Publishes *Mansart Builds a School* (New York: Mainstream).

1961   Publishes *Worlds of Color* (New York: Mainstream). Applies for and accepts membership into the Communist Party of the United States. Travels to Ghana to work on *Encyclopedia Africana*.

1962   *Autobiography* published in Soviet Russia.

1963   Having given up his United States citizenship, dies on August 27 in Accra, Ghana on the eve of the March on Washington. Lauded by Roy Wilkins, Executive Secretary of the NAACP.

1966   Excoriated by soon-to-be President of the United States, Richard M. Nixon, because a group of liberal and idealistic young Americans had established clubs on the nation's campuses bearing his name.

1968   *The Autobiography of W.E.B. Du Bois* published in the United States.

1970   *W.E.B. Du Bois: The Crisis Writing*, edited by Philip S. Foner, is published (Greenwich, Connecticut: Fawcett).

1972   *The Emerging Thought of W.E.B. Du Bois: Essays and Editorials from "The Crisis,"* edited by Henry Lee Moon, is published (New York: Simon & Schuster).

1973   *The Education of Black People: Ten Critiques, 1906–1960*, edited by Herbert Aptheker, is published (Amherst: University of Massachusetts Press).

Contributors

HAROLD BLOOM is Sterling Professor of the Humanities at Yale University and Henry W. and Albert A. Berg Professor of English at the New York University Graduate School. He is the author of over 20 books, including *Shelley's Mythmaking* (1959), *The Visionary Company* (1961), *Blake's Apocalypse* (1963), *Yeats* (1970), *A Map of Misreading* (1975), *Kabbalah and Criticism* (1975), *Agon: Toward a Theory of Revisionism* (1982), *The American Religion* (1992), *The Western Canon* (1994), and *Omens of Millennium: The Gnosis of Angels, Dreams, and Resurrection* (1996). *The Anxiety of Influence* (1973) sets forth Professor Bloom's provocative theory of the literary relationships between the great writers and their predecessors. His most recent books include *Shakespeare: The Invention of the Human*, a 1998 National Book Award finalist, and *How to Read and Why*, which was published in 2000. In 1999, Professor Bloom received the prestigious American Academy of Arts and Letters Gold Medal for Criticism.

ANTHONY APPIAH teaches in the Department of Philosophy at Harvard University. He is the author of *Color Consciousness: The Political Morality of Race* (1996) and an editor of *Africana: The Encyclopedia of the African and African American Experience* (1999).

HERMAN BEAVERS is an associate professor of English and Director of the Afro-American Studies Program at the University of Pennsylvania. He is the author of *Wrestling Angels Into Song: The Fictions of Ernest J. Gaines and James Alan McPherson* (1995) and "Tilling the Soil to Find Ourselves: Labor, Memory and Identity in Ernest J. Gaines's *Of Love and Dust*" (1996).

ARLENE A. ELDER is a professor of English and Comparative Literature at the University of Cincinnati. She is the author of *The "Hindered Hand": Cultural Implications of Early African-American Fiction* (1978), "Paul Carter Harrison and Amos Tutuola: The Vitality of the African Continuum" (1988) and "'. . . Who Can Take the Multitude and Lock It in a Cage?': Noemia de Sousa, Micere Mugo, Ellen Kuzwayo: Three African Women's Voices of Resistance" (1989).

HENRY LOUIS GATES Jr. is W.E.B. Du Bois Professor of Humanities at Harvard University, where he is also Chair of Afro-American Studies and Director of the W.E.B. Du Bois Institute for Afro-American Research. He is the author of *Thirteen Ways of Looking at a Black Man* (1997) and *Wonders of the African World* (1999) as well as an editor of *Africana: The Encyclopedia of the African and African American Experience* (1999).

THOMAS C. HOLT teaches in the Department of History at the University of Chicago. He is the author of *African-American History* (1990) and *The Problem of Freedom: Race, Labor and Politics in Jamaica and Britain, 1832–1938* (1992).

MICHAEL B. KATZ teaches in the Department of History at the University of Pennsylvania. He is the author of *The Undeserving Poor: From the War on Poverty to the War on Welfare* (1989) and *Improving Poor People: The Welfare State, the "Underclass," and Urban Schools as History* (1995).

TOMMY L. LOTT teaches in the Department of Philosophy at San Jose State University, San Jose, California. He is the author of *The Invention of Race: Black Culture and the Politics of Representation* (1999) and editor of *Subjugation and Bondage: Critical Essays on Slavery and Philosophy* (1998).

WILSON J. MOSES has taught at the University of Iowa and the Pennsylvania State University. He is the author of "Literary Garveyism: the Novels of Reverend Sutton E. Griggs" (1979), *Liberian Dreams: Back-To-Africa Narratives from the 1850s* (1998), and *Black Messiahs and Uncle Toms: Social and Literary Manipulations of a Religious Myth* (1993).

ARNOLD RAMPERSAD is Woodrow Wilson Professor of Literature at Princeton University and Director of the Program in Afro-American Studies. He is an editor of *Slavery and the Literary Imagination* (1989) and the author of *The Art and Imagination of W.E.B. Du Bois* (1990).

THOMAS J. SUGRUE is an associate professor of History at the University of Pennsylvania. He is the author of *Urban Crisis: Race and Inequality in Postwar Detroit* (1996) and a contributing editor to *W.E.B. Du Bois, Race and the City: The Philadelphia Negro and Its Legacy* (1998).

DARWIN T. TURNER was University of Iowa Foundation Distinguished Professor of English and Director of Afro-American Studies. He is the author of "The Negro Novelist and the South" (1967) and "Langston Hughes as Playwright" (1968).

SHAMOON ZAMIR teaches American Literature and American Studies at Kings College, University of London. He is the author of *Dark Voices: W.E.B. Du Bois and American Thought, 1888–1903* (1995).

Bibliography

Anderson, Elijah and Tukufu Zuberi, eds. *The Study of African American Problems: W.E.B. Du Bois's Agenda, Then and Now.* Thousand Oaks, Calif.: Sage Publications (2000).

Andrews, William L., ed. *Critical Essays on W.E.B. Du Bois.* Boston: G.K. Hall (1985).

Appiah, Anthony. "The Uncompleted Argument: Du Bois and the Illusion of Race." *Critical Inquiry* 12, no. 1 (Autumn 1985): 21–37.

Aptheker, Herbert, ed. *The Correspondence of W.E.B. Du Bois.* Amherst: University of Massachusetts Press, 3 vols. (1973–78).

Bell, Bernard W., Emily Grosholz and James B. Steward, eds. *W.E.B. Du Bois on Race and Culture: Philosophy, Politics and Poetics.* New York and London: Routledge (1996).

Broderick, Francis L. *W.E.B. Du Bois: Negro Leader in a Time of Crisis.* Stanford, Calif.: Stanford University Press (1959).

Bronner, Simon J. *American Folklore Studies: An Intellectual History.* Lawrence: University Press of Kansas (1986).

Byerman, Keith Eldon. *Seizing the Word: History, Art and Self in the Work of W.E.B. Du Bois.* Athens: University of Georgia Press (1994).

Carby, Hazel V. *Race Men.* Cambridge, Mass.: Harvard University Press (1998).

Childs, John Brown. "Concepts of Culture in Afro-American Political Thought, 1890–1920." *Social Text* 4 (1981): 28–43.

Clarke, John Henrik. *Pan-Africanism and the Liberation of Southern Africa: A Tribute to W.E.B. Du Bois.* New York: African Heritage Studies Association (1978).

Clifford, James and George E. Marcus, eds. *Writing Culture: The Poetics and Politics of Ethnography.* Berkeley: University of California Press (1986).

DeMarco, Joseph P. *W.E.B. Du Bois: Voice of the Black Protest Movement.* Urbana: University of Illinois Press (1960).

Edelman, Marian Wright. *Families in Peril: An Agenda for Social Change.* Cambridge, Mass.: Harvard University Press (1987).

Foner, Philip S. *W.E.B. Du Bois Speaks: Speeches and Addresses.* New York: Pathfinder Press (1970).

Fredrickson, George M. *The Black Image in the White Mind: The Debate on Afro-American Character and Destiny, 1817–1914*. New York: Harper and Row (1971).

Gates, Henry Louis, Jr. *The Signifying Monkey: A Theory of African-American Literary Criticism*. New York: Oxford University Press (1988).

Gooding-Williams, Robert. "Philosophy of History and Social Critique in *The Souls of Black Folk.*" *Social Science Information* 26, no. 1 (1987): 99–114.

Green, Dan S. and Edwin D. Driver. *W.E.B. Du Bois on Sociology and the Black Community*. Chicago: University of Chicago Press (1987).

Harris, Thomas E. *Analysis of the Clash Over the Issues Between Booker T. Washington and W.E.B. Du Bois*. New York: Garland Publishers (1993).

Harrison, Faye V. "The Du Boisian Legacy in Anthropology." *Critique of Anthropology* 12, no. 3 (1993): 239–60.

Hartz, Louis. *The Liberal Tradition in America: An Interpretation of American Political Thought since the Revolution*. New York: Harcourt, Brace & World (1955).

Holt, Thomas C. "The Political Uses of Alienation: W.E.B. Du Bois on Politics, Race and Culture, 1903–1940." *American Quarterly* 42, no. 2 (1990): 301–23.

Katz, Michael B. and Thomas J. Sugrue, eds. *W.E.B. Du Bois, Race and the City: The Philadelphia Negro and Its Legacy*. Philadelphia: University of Pennsylvania Press (1998).

Kirkland, Frank M. "Modernity and Intellectual Life in Black." *Philosophical Forum* 24, nos. 1–3 (1992-93): 136–65.

Lange, Werner. "W.E.B. Du Bois and the First Scientific Study of Afro-America." *Phylon* 44, no. 2 (1983): 135–46.

Lemke, Sieglinde. *Primitivist Modernism: Black Culture and the Origins of Transatlantic Modernism*. New York: Oxford University Press (1998).

Lewis, David L. *W.E.B. Du Bois: Biography of a Race*. New York: H. Holt (1993).

Lewis, W. Arthur. *Racial Conflict and Economic Development*. Cambridge, Mass.: Harvard University Press (1985).

Logan, Rayford W., ed. *W.E.B. Du Bois: A Profile*. New York: Hill and Wang (1971).

———. *The Negro in American Life and Thought: The Nadir, 1877–1901*. New York: Dial Press (1954).

Lott, Tommy L. "Du Bois on the Invention of Race." *Philosophical Forum* 24, nos. 1-3 (1992–93): 116–87.

Low, Augustus and Virgil A. Clift, eds. *Encyclopedia of Black America*. New York: McGraw-Hill (1981).

Marable, Manning. *W.E.B. Du Bois: Black Radical Democrat*. Boston: Twayne (1981).

Meier, August. *Negro Thought in America, 1880–1915: Radical Ideologies in the Age of Booker T. Washington*. Ann Arbor: University of Michigan Press (1988).

Moore, Jack B. W.E.B. *Du Bois*. Boston: Twayne Publishers (1981).

Moss, Alfred A., Jr. *The American Negro Academy: Voice of the Talented Tenth*. Baton Rouge: Louisiana State University Press (1981).

Muller, Nancy Ladd. "Du Boisian Pragmatism and 'The Problem of the Twentieth Century.'" *Critique of Anthropology* 12, no. 3 (1992): 319–37.

Paschal, Andrew G., ed. *A W.E.B. Du Bois Reader*. New York: Collier Books (1993).

Patterson, Orlando. *Slavery and Social Death: A Comparative Study*. Cambridge, Mass.: Harvard University Press (1982).

Paynter, Robert. "W.E.B. Du Bois and the material World of African-Americans in Great Barrington, Massachusetts." *Critique of Anthropology* 12, no. 3 (1992): 277–92.

Pilgrim, David. *W.E.B. Du Bois: In Memoriam: A Centennial Celebration of His Collegiate Education*. Bristol, Indiana: Wyndham Hall Press (1990).

Posnock, Ross. *Color and Culture: Black Writers and the Making of the Modern Intellectual*. Cambridge, Mass.: Harvard University Press (1998).

Reed, Adolph L., Jr. *W.E.B. Du Bois and American Political Thought: Fabianism and the Color Line*. New York: Oxford University Press (1997).

Rudwick, Elliott M. *W.E.B. Du Bois: A Study in Minority Group Leadership*. Philadelphia: University of Pennsylvania Press (1960).

———. *W.E.B. Du Bois: Propagandist of the Negro Protest*. Philadelphia: University of Pennsylvania Press (1968).

Smith, John David. *An Old Creed for the New South: Proslavery Ideology and Historiography, 1865–1918*. 1985. Athens: University of Georgia Press (1991).

Shamoon, Zamir. *Dark Voices: W.E.B. Du Bois and American Thought, 1888–1903*. Chicago: University of Chicago Press (1995).

Sollors, Werner. *Beyond Ethnicity: Consent and Descent in American Culture*. New York: Oxford University Press (1986).

Stepto, Robert. *From Behind the Veil: A Study of Afro-American Narrative*. Urbana: University of Illinois Press (1979).

Stull, Bradford T. *Amid the Fall, Dreaming of Eden: Du Bois, King, Malcolm X and Emancipatory Composition*. Carbondale: Southern Illinois University Press (1999).

Sundquist, Eric. *To Wake the Nations: Race in the Making of American Literature*. Cambridge, Mass.: Harvard University Press (1979).

Tallack, Douglas. *Twentieth-Century America: The Intellectual and Cultural Context*. London: Longman (1991).

Wintz, Cary D., ed. *African-American Political Thought: 1890–1930: Washington, Du Bois, Garvey, and Randolph*. Armonk, N.Y.: M.E. Sharpe (1996).

Acknowledgments

"The Political Uses of Alienation: W.E.B. Du Bois on Politics, Race, and Culture, 1903–1940" by Thomas C. Holt. From *American Quarterly* 42, no. 2 (July 1990): 301–20. © 1990 by American Studies Association. Reprinted by permission of John Hopkins University Press.

"Du Bois on the Invention of Race" by Tommy L. Lott. From *The Philosophical Forum* 24, no. 1–3 (Fall–Spring 1992–93): 166–82. © 1992 by The Philosophical Forum, Inc. Reprinted with permission.

"A 'Prosody of Those Dark Voices': The Transformation of Consciousness" by Shamoon Zamir. From *Dark Voices: W.E.B. Du Bois and American Thought*, 1888–1903. © 1995 by The University of Chicago Press. Reprinted with permission.

"The Context of *The Philadelphia Negro*: The City, the Settlement House Movement, and the Rise of the Social Sciences" by Michael B. Katz and Thomas J. Sugrue. From *W.E.B. Du Bois, Race, and the City*, ed. Michael B. Katz and Thomas J. Sugrue. © 1998 by University of Pennsylvania Press. Reprinted with permission.

"Romancing the Body Politic: Du Bois's Propaganda of the Dark World" by Herman Beavers. From *The Annals of the American Academy of Political and Social Science* 568 (March 2000): 250–63. © 2000 by Sage Publications, Inc. Reprinted with permission.

"W.E.B. Du Bois and the Encyclopedia Africana, 1909–63" by Henry Louis Gates Jr. From *The Annals of the American Academy of Political and Social Science* 568 (March 2000): 203–17. © 2000 by Sage Publications, Inc. Reprinted with permission.

Index